The Origins of David Hume's Economics

T0304187

David Hume devoted only a small part of his total output to questions of direct economic significance yet he is highly esteemed as an economics writer. His main philosophical work, the *Treatise of Human Nature,* failed to live up to Hume's expectations in terms of literary success. Hume reviewed the literary qualities of the *Treatise* and decided that it was written under a creative spurt of youthful enthusiasm. He wanted his ideas recognized and discussed and in the early 1740s turns his attention to essay writing. His early success in this genre encouraged him to explore further his ideas on the development of commercial society both politically and economically. The outcome was a series of essays that brought his philosophical ideas into line with a readership interested in exploring ideas about their own developing society.

The book covers Hume's biographical development; his self appraisal as a 'man of letters'; his philosophical writings with emphasis on their direct and indirect economic content; his self-aware criticism of his approach to the *Treatise* and the development of his rhetorical understanding of the needs/interests of his readers/potential readers; his rhetorical turn and Ciceronian adjustments to his writing within the genre of the essay, including his two *Enquiries*; his political essays and his nine essays conventionally classified as economic. The work aims to show how the *Treatise* and its vicissitudes gave rise to his economics.

The work takes a broad approach to Hume and his writings on economic topics from the *Treatise,* through the *Enquires* and on to his political and economic essay. The work also explores Hume's textual method and charts the move from abstruse philosophy to a Ciceronian engagement with social conditions and problems as developed in the *Political Discourses.* In addition, Hume's extensive use of analogies is also brought into clearer focus than is found in other texts. Overall, the book will be of great use to both postgraduates and undergraduates alike.

Dr Willie Henderson's works approach the analysis of economic ideas via context and content with emphasis put on the constructed nature of past economics writing. His background is interdisciplinary and he brings a diverse range of techniques and experience to his scholarly writing.

Routledge studies in the history of economics

The Origins of David Hume's Economics

Willie Henderson

Routledge
Taylor & Francis Group

LONDON AND NEW YORK

First published 2010
by Routledge
2 Park Square, Milton Park, Abingdon, Oxon, OX14 4RN

Simultaneously published in the USA and Canada
by Routledge
711 Third Avenue, New York, NY 10017

*Routledge is an imprint of the Taylor & Francis Group,
an informa business*

© 2010 William Henderson

Typeset in Sabon by Glyph International Ltd.
First issued in paperback in 2013

British Library Cataloguing in Publication Data
A catalogue record for this book is available from the British Library

Library of Congress Cataloging in Publication Data
Henderson, Willie, 1947–
The origins of David Hume's economics / by Willie Henderson.
  p. cm.
Includes bibliographical references.
1. Economics–History. 2. Hume, David, 1711–1776. I. Title.
HB75.H423 2010
330.15'3–dc22

ISBN13: 978-0-415-74831-5 (hbk)
ISBN13: 978-0-415-77863-3 (hbk)
ISBN13: 978-0-2038-4844-9 (ebk)

To Elzbieta

Contents

Acknowledgements

This work was produced during the time I held the post of Director of the Royal D. Alworth, Jr. Institute for International Studies at the University of Minnesota Duluth.

I am particularly grateful to the Chancellor of the University of Minnesota Duluth, Dr Kathryn Martin, for the invitation to work as Director. The conditions under which I worked as Director and the resources and conditions made available to me in the running of Alworth Institute made for a wonderful experience.

I also thank Dr Linda Krug who was Dean of the College of Liberal Arts during much of my tenure and who supported the Alworth and my research interests on several occasions. Thanks also go to Greg Fox and Dr Vince Magnesson for an active interest in the initiatives at the Alworth. As a result, and with the support of the Program Associate Dr Cindy Christian, I was able not only to expand the programme and raise its public profile, but I was also able to continue to engage in research and writing. This book is the outcome of four years work and its publication marks the end of my period spent in north-eastern Minnesota.

Comments have generously provided on *some* aspects of this book by David Beard, Peter Davis, José Castro Caldas, Luís Francisco Carvalho, David Gore, Sebastian Mitchell, Warren Samuels, Linda Thomas and Jack Russell Weinstein. Elzbieta Stadtmüller provided emotional support and read through the whole manuscript and offered comments.

Thanks go to Oxford University Press for permission to quote from David Fate Norton and Mary J. Norton (eds) (2000) *David Hume A Treatise of Human Nature* and from Tom L. Beauchamp (ed) (1999) *David Hume An Enquiry concerning Human Understanding* and Tom L. Beauchamp (ed.) (2006) *David Hume An Enquiry Concerning the Principles of Morals.* Thanks go to the Liberty Fund for permission to quote from Eugene F. Miller (ed.) (1985) *David Hume Essays Moral, Political and Literary.*

Preface

This book is an attempt to trace the development of Hume's economics writing from its origins in the *Treatise* to its final expression in the series of essays published in his *Political Discourses*. The development of Hume's essays is the result of his disappointment with the reception of the *Treatise*. Hume had, as will be shown, very high hopes for the 'science of human nature'. He thought that by putting moral philosophy on a scientific foundation of observation and experience it could equal or even outperform natural philosophy. The relative failure of the *Treatise* was of major concern to him. In an effort to find an audience he wrote the *Abstract*, a book review or 'puff' (the term, which has entered the literature, is originally that of Keynes and Sraffa, who identified that anonymous pamphlet as Hume's work). The *Abstract* is the result of a reappraisal of Hume's textual method as developed in the *Treatise* and based on the idea of tracing out a 'long chain of reasoning'. Hume reaches an understanding that such long chains demand too much of the reader. He alters his approach in the *Abstract* and in his entire subsequent writing save in Book three of the *Treatise*.

Subsequently he reflects further on the relationship between 'abstruse philosophy' and society and ordinary understanding. This leads him to take a further step towards amending his rhetoric. In merging 'abstruse' with easy philosophy, Hume takes a Ciceronian stand. It is in this rhetorical turn and the experimentation which followed that Hume's economics writing gains its persuasive appeal. The *Treatise* and his disappointment with its reception, though not with its basic principles, and the subsequent rhetorical adjustments constitute in this book, the origins of Hume's political and economic writing.

Hume is a towering figure in the Scottish Enlightenment. Scholarship on Hume in general and on his economics writings is vast and profound. There are several works of very high quality that treat Hume's writing to a literary analysis (Danford, Box, etc.). There has also been recently attention given to Hume's economics in its wider cultural context (Wennerlind and Schabas, 2008). It might seem unnecessary to produce another work on Hume. The intention here is somewhat different for the other works. I wanted to produce a book that would help those coming new to Hume to gain some insight into the depth and breadth of his work, while focusing on the consistency of his approach to political and economic ideas. I wanted to bring together an understanding of his writing as writing with an understanding of his economics as economics writing. Hume makes an excellent subject for study with respect to the crossover point of economics and literature. Hume wanted to achieve literary fame. It was his constant ambition to see his works published, acknowledged and discussed. Hume's success as an economics writer owes a great deal to his communicative as well as his analytical skills. I have tried in this work to take an approach that demonstrates the significance of his writing abilities for the shaping of his essays while linking his analytical approach to both the *Treatise* and the *Enquiries*. In this sense there is considerable attention paid to describing Hume's output as well as analysing it. This means that, as the approach is chronological rather than synthetic, that a certain amount of repetition is unavoidable.

This book is, I hope, a work of scholarship though it is not a work of advanced scholarship. I have come late to Hume and without the advantage of long-accumulated experience of reading Hume and reading the secondary literature on Hume. I have, however, the benefit of a sustained interested in how economic discourse has developed over time not, however, directly with respect to the development of the technical apparatus of economic analysis, rather with respect to the communicative efforts of economic thinkers. This has helped shape the book's structure and internal logic.

The publication of the *Treatise* brought only failure in his eyes. It was noticed by a few, including by Adam Smith's successor at Glasgow, Thomas Reid, and criticized or dismissed. Even the *Enquiries* failed to generate the kind of audience and influence for which Hume longed. It was only with the publication of his essays, the result of his rhetorical turn, that Hume first made his literary reputation. In what follows here, a path through Hume will be chartered, using literary techniques and other analyses, to reveal aspects of Hume's thought, particularly his economic thinking from the *Treatise* through to the essays, with particular reference to the economics essays. In this way, this work aims to introduce Hume to those students and interested academics who wish to know something, of an introductory nature, about the unity of Hume's political and economic thinking and its relationship with his philosophical works. It is aimed at the informed general social science reader and seeks to be broad, while attempting to avoid mere superficiality, rather than deep.

I hope that the approach reveals something new about Hume's capacity to create a wide audience for economics writing, in his own time and even over time, given the link with Smith both analytically and rhetorically. I also hope that it reveals the intellectual effort that Hume made to find a way of communicating that created the philosophical–rhetorical partnership, suggested by Ciceronian practice and advice, which led in the fullness of time to the essays conventionally classified as economic. Hume's writing skills, always considerable, even in the much-maligned *Treatise*, at least as exemplified by those passages with economics content, were refined and focused within the small compass of the essay. Given his chosen genre he could not say all. He left some loose ends or some thoughts stranded without much of a context. Overall, the political and economic essays are works that are both efficient and effective. I hope that I have managed to convey something of the continuity of Hume's thought and of the significance of what I have called the rhetorical turn for the success of his writing, and managed to justify his confidence in the productivity of uniting abstruse and easy philosophy in a small compass.

There is some exploration of the rich and scholarly secondary literature on Hume at various places though the primary focus is on economic and related texts created by Hume. There is reference to some debates in that literature, though this is deliberately kept to a minimum, in keeping with the introductory nature of the volume. There is some though limited exploration of Hume's alleged reading of Cantillon, and there are references, sustained in the case of Adam Smith, to other of his contemporaries.

The first chapter provides an overview of Hume and his reputation and his biographical relationship to the *Treatise*. Chapter 2 may puzzle some readers. It raises issues of textual method, particularly concerning summarization and selection, and, to a much lesser extent, interpretation, of interest to historians of economic thought and others such as those interested in the study of rhetoric or communication. It is directly related to Hume as the *Abstract* and the *Enquiries* have at least according to many scholars a derivate relationship with the *Treatise*. His essays also call upon his philosophical writing in many diverse ways, though mainly in shorthand. Issues that are raised in general terms are confronted directly in Chapter 3, where the strategy exhibited in the writing of the *Abstract* is worked backwards through the *Treatise* and forwards through the *Enquiries*. This provides an idea of the general content and approach of Hume to philosophy. Hume's thinking on the origins of society and the nature of its economic base is explored, through the use of textual excerpts, in the fourth chapter. It shows the clarity and subtlety of Hume's economic understanding in the *Treatise* and illustrates that he has a significant starting point in understanding and communication for his later economics work. Chapter 5 looks at economics-related ideas as found in the two *Enquiries*.

Chapter 6 expands on Hume's rhetorical and Ciceronian turn. Hume's links with Cicero are many and what is achieved here simply scratches the surface of what must be a bigger enterprise. The chapter mainly explores essays that are classified as political but shows that, for Hume, the political and the economic intertwine. There is no hard and fast division of subject matter. Such an idea would have been alien to Hume's thought and to his notion of 'politics' as 'men united in society'. Chapter 7 explores, again textually, some of the essays normally classified, following Rotwein's pioneering work, as economic. The exploration in both chapters attempt to show the internal development of the essays as well as the implicit and explicit links with Hume's philosophical writing, including the significance for Hume of argument by analogy. Some consideration is given to interpretative themes in the secondary literature and to, in the case 'Of Public Credit' an unexpected link to Cicero. The book concludes with a long chapter that explores Hume's influence on the development of 'stadial theory'. 'Of the Populousness of Ancient Nations' is central to the chapter and a fitting place, given the incisive nature of the work and its influence on the Scottish Historical School, Adam Smith in particular, to terminate the book.

Abbreviations

ECHU   *David Hume An Enquiry concerning Human Understanding*
        edited by Tom L. Beauchamp, Oxford Philosophical Texts.
        Oxford: Oxford University Press 1999.

ECPM   *David Hume An Enquiry concerning the Principles of Morals*
        edited by Tom L. Beauchamp,The Clarendon Edition of the
        Works of David Hume. Oxford: Clarendon Press 1998.

Treatise *David Hume A Treatise of Human Nature* edited by David
        Fate Norton and Mary J. Norton, Oxford Philosophical Texts.
        Oxford: Oxford University Press 2005

Essays   *David Hume Essays Moral, Political and Literary* edited by
        Eugene F. Miller Indianapolis: Liberty Fund revised edition
        1987. Parts one and two. Essay titles are separately numbered
        in each part.

To read the references to *ECHU* and *ECPM* readers with access to the
Oxford material can omit the middle number in any sequence of three.
The middle number refers to the part of the relevant section and will help
locate references in other versions of the *Enquiries*.

WN   Adam Smith's *An Inquiry into the Nature and Causes of the
        Wealth of Nations* The Glasgow Edition of the Works and
        Correspondence of Adam smith [1776] (1976). Oxford:
        Clarendon Press

TMS   Adam Smith's *Theory of Moral Sentiments* The Glasgow
        Edition of the Works and Correspondence of Adam Smith
        [1759] (1976). Oxford: Clarendon Press.

LJ   Adam Smith's *Lectures on Jurisprudence* The Glasgow Edition
        of the Works and Correspondence of Adam Smith [unpub-
        lished] (1976). Oxford: Clarendon Press.

LRBL   Adam Smith's *Lectures of Rhetoric and Belles Lettres* The
        Glasgow Edition of the Works and Correspondence of Adam
        Smith [unpublished] (1983). Oxford: Oxford University Press.

1 David Hume

A biographical and critical overview

Biographical and critical overview

David Hume gained many contradictory epithets in his lifetime and later. To his religious and conservative-minded critics he was 'David Hume the atheist' (a term which carried with it strong implications of immorality) or the extreme 'sceptic', a negative thinker and a seeker after notoriety (the vulgar notion of 'fame'). To his literary rival, Johnson, he was a 'Blasphemer' (Sharbo, 1974, 32; Box, 1990, 5). Hume evoked, in his own time and since, 'antipathy or admiration' (Jessop, 1966, 35). In his own ironic mind he was Hume 'the great infidel', a disturber of 'zealots' (the Presbyterian spirit of Scotland in his youth was a significant context for the development of his secular morality and anti-religious convictions). Near the end of his life he held himself to be, with considerable justification, 'a man of great moderation' with respect to all of his 'passions', a judgment supported by Philip Vincent, relative of the 'lunatic' Marquis of Annandale, whom Hume worked with for 'a twelvemonth' (Murray, 1841, 14). He was certainly a naturalist and materialist. He may well have been an atheist (the question is in doubt) but if he were then he would probably be an example of a non-dogmatic one – someone who argues that there can be no convincing evidence for or against the existence of God but whom nevertheless believes that God does not exist. Yet, he toys with the notion of a divine mover, the 'Author' of nature. His normal everyday practices are not clear and, in defending his stand on religious abuses depicted in his *History of England*, he disliked the implication that being of no sect meant being of no religion (Calderwood, [1898] 1989, 74). He protected himself carefully. He had several friends among the moderate clergy, including his 'friendly adversary', George Campbell (Merrill, 2008, 66), and they gave him, in the end, a Christian burial. He could not reasonably be taken as an example of Shaftesbury's 'entheusiastical atheists'.

To salon society in France, during his diplomatic service in Paris – where his *Political Discourses* (1752) were warmly received in translation – he was 'le bon David'. Hume must have passed the own test of '*Is he polite? Has he wit*' (*ECPM*, 8.4) and was delighted with the outcomes. Even if his reputation in France, where things 'English' were already in vogue at the time, had an element of scandal because of his standing as a sceptic, Hume by his middle years had developed a formidable intellectual and literary reputation based on his output (Lucas, 1959, 18; Box, 1990, 3). To his modern-day admirers (there are also detractors) he is the embodiment of reasonableness, a rounded and 'many-sided genius' – for far too long misrepresented merely as a sceptical philosopher or one whose work was restricted to 'cause, induction, knowledge, necessity, the is–ought distinction and the like'. The epithets continue to grow. Hume now tends to be seen as a 'post-sceptical', and, hence, 'constructivist' philosopher' or one whose naturalism replaces the scepticism (Lucas, 1959, 3; Merill and Shahan, 1976, 1; Norton, 1993, 1). Hume as 'the Newton of the moral sciences' (Broadie, 2000, 60) has its supporters and critics. The modern, and expansive, view has taken a long time to develop and mature, although it was initiated (essentially) by Kemp Smith in the late 1930s.

To Adam Smith, his contemporary and friend, he was the very model of human perfection: 'Upon the whole, I have always considered him, both in his lifetime, and since his death, as approaching as nearly to the idea of a perfectly wise and virtuous man, as perhaps the nature of human frailty will admit'. Indeed Smith's judgment is significant for it readily affirms Hume as a man of virtue. In the *Moral Sentiments* Smith distinguishes the love of praise (a kind of vanity) from the desire to be 'praiseworthy' (*MS*, 1759), and it was surely to this end that Hume dedicates himself in his writing (Buckle, 2001, 17–18).

To some, as Potkay (1994, 9) points out, he remains a man of 'monumental ego' and there is no point in denying that he was proud of his own intellectual abilities. His judgment on those he disapproved of (zealots both religious and party, bigots, monks) could be harsh. He was prejudiced against the intellectual capacity of people of African descent, perhaps under the influence of a misguided geographical determinism, and, though he really did help Isaac de Pinto, he may have distrusted Jews. Hume was, like Adam Smith, no supporter of slavery. On the other hand, 'the most rude and barbarous of the whites, such as the ancient Germans, and the present Tartars, have still have something eminent about them' (I, Essay XXI, ft. 10, 208). Smith was also impressed by Tartar society.

Hume's 'love of fame', condemned so thoroughly and consistently by Kruse (1939), and also by some of his contemporary critics (Mossner, 1966, 7) perhaps needs to be understood in the context of Smith's notion, rooted in mid-eighteenth-century views of character and virtue ethics, of being 'praiseworthy'.[1] This is Smith's context. Smith's ideas were of course influenced by Hume's ideas, though Smith is not Hume by another name. Hume also wrote in the *Treatise* about fame and this too supplies a context within which Hume is to be understood. Hume felt, in 'Of the Passions' that 'reputation' and 'character' are of vast 'weight and importance' and their influence cannot be brought into play 'when not seconded by the opinions and sentiments of others' (*Treatise*, 2.1.1.11.1).

Hume sought to give intellectual coherence to the 'science of man' and ended up being personally accused of contradiction and wilful paradox. Hume lived his life in the light of his ideals, though he sometimes for reasons of prudence adjusted his actions, or complied with suggestions to adjust his actions, to social circumstances. He displayed his Stoic convictions, in the light of the failure of the *Treatise* to find an audience, in the face of threats of excommunication, for example, and even in his manner and composure demonstrated (and made public by Boswell with more than a little complicity on Hume's part) as death approached. Lucas puts it, delightfully, like this: 'By conviction a Sceptic, "le bon David" savoured life like a sensible Epicurean, and met death – much to the disappointment of bigots – as calmly as a Stoic, though with a humour and humanity that most Stoics have sadly lacked' (Lucas, 1959, 3). Hume latterly enjoyed cooking for his friends and made use of the pleasure–pain principle in the *Treatise*.

Rostow, in the introduction to his survey of the development of growth theory – he sees Hume as making a significant contribution to economic growth and developmental thinking – wonders whether the personalities of theorists matter. Rostow's view of Hume as a theorist of growth may have become commonplace or merely overlooked (for more attention is given nowadays to Hume's views on money), but it is one which may require re-examination. Rostow (1990, 9) quotes with a certain degree of approval Medawar's (1984, 263) views that 'academics lie outside the devastation area of the literary convention' by which suffering ennobles art. Medawar, however, was not only taking about 'academics' but specifically about academic 'scientists'. Hume is to be seen as a rounded social philosopher and social scientist and his work needs – needs because of its monumental significance and its impact on Hume himself – to be considered within the framework of the *Treatise*. Philosophy, despite Hume's desire to place it on a scientific footing, is not a science and even if it were this would not mean that scientific writing is not also literary. Ginsberg (1987, 7), drawing upon Richetti – in an edited work that explores *The Philosopher as Writer* – states that 'Philosophy insofar as it is written is a branch of literature'. Richetti, examining the boundary between literature and systematic discourse holds that: 'Locke, Berkeley and Hume provide a unique opportunity for an extraterritorial literary criticism precisely because for them that boundary was still uncertain and shifting' (Richetti, 1983, 2). This uncertain boundary can be traced in many places in the *Treatise*. Hume whose writing in the *Treatise* is characterized by, in Richetti's words, 'a continual return to the act of discovery' (Richetti, 1983, 21) attempted to discuss problems that cannot necessarily be captured clearly in writing. Hence the estimation of contemporary critics, and ultimately of Hume himself, that the work was full of unresolved paradox.

Box makes a similar point to Richetti when he considers Hume's literary reputation and states that 'we now have a much narrower notion as to what constitutes literature' than Hume and his contemporaries (Box, 1990, 4).

Kruse's judgment from the late 1930s is less accommodating. He holds that for Hume the love of literary fame overrode the philosophical 'consideration of truth' (Kruse, 1939, 8). This judgment has been softened in more modern literature. It underestimates the philosophical basis of his writing on politics, economics and criticism. A related point is made also by Buckle when he points out that Hume himself, in 'My Own Life' (Hume was 65 when he wrote this) mentions his 'passion for literature' in the context of his reading of classical philosophers such as 'Cicero and Virgil' (Buckle, 2001, 13). Cicero was both a philosopher and a rhetorician who attempted through virtuous rhetoric to move philosophy, for civic purposes, closer to an educated audience more widely defined. Such a 'rhetorical turn' was taken by Hume himself after 1739 and was, as will be shown, motivated by a desire to place philosophical reasoning into social discourse, to fill a gap in civil conversation.

Hume's desire for literary fame, such a feature of 'My Own Life', where he describes it as a ruling 'passion', does not in itself necessarily contradict a desire for philosophical fame, rather it is part of it. Mossner argues that this biographical sketch needs to be treated with caution as its language is ambiguous, especially for a modern-day reader (Mossner, 1966, 13–14). Hume is playing with his intended audience for Box and others have identified this as a reference to Alexander Pope's notion 'of the Ruling Passion as set out in the *Moral Essays*' (Box, 1990, 22). It is an ironic reference for Hume seeks to be a man of virtue and hence the ruling passion is part of the creative rather than the destructive drive.

Hume in the introduction to the *Treatise* is clear that the science of human nature also covers morals, politics and criticism. Although there are significant political ideas in the *Treatise* and certainly enough to make links with his later work – it would be hard to justify it as a source of economic ideas if politics had not also been covered in the sense of men acting cooperatively in society – he did not formally cover politics and criticism in separate books. By 'criticism' Hume intends aesthetics. The *Treatise* is in this sense incomplete, though there is still much of political significance within it (Wheelan, 1985, 3). Box suggests that Hume substituted the 'treatise by installment' with the developing genre of the essay as one way of stressing the continuation of Hume's original plans by other means (Box, 1990, 84). His essays of the early 1740s dealt with politics and criticism. The French term '*philosope*' and the similar English, eighteenth century conceptualization (the idea is older than the eighteenth century) of a 'man of letters' captures better Hume's position.

The essay, according to McCarthy, 'was a major vehicle of enlightenment' and the movement itself gave rise to new opportunities to write and hence to the profession of man of letters (McCarthy, 1989, 49). The notion that Hume abandons his originating work by turning to history, politics, economics or criticism is a gross misreading of Hume's intentions, and of the cultural context of European Enlightenment within which he also operated.

Leibniz, concerned in establishing a language of philosophy 'accessible to all', wrote philosophically informed essays as did Kant (McCarthy, 1989, 49). Hume shared Leibniz' concerns with the advancement of the sciences and the development of the arts. This sense of continuation in Hume's work has gradually come, over time, to be recognized (see for example Passmore, 1953, 3; Christensen, 1987; Danford, 1990). However, Kruse's judgment on the relationship between the essays and the *Treatise* – some do have a direct relationship, some do not and some are disputed – needs to be kept in mind (Kruse, 1939, 3). This will be a subject explored in Chapter 6. What he did do in making that turn was to pay more attention to audience. Such a concern for audience is seen to be a distinguishing feature of the essay as genre, even it its (then) elementary stages of development (McCarthy, 1989, 51). What is clear, as will be shown, is that in reflecting upon the needs, as he constructed them, of 'polite society' Hume drew upon personal experience and reflection of the failure of the *Treatise* to find a market and upon the ideas of Cicero and other classical writers concerned with the demands of effective communication. If we accept Cicero's point that valid rhetoric (rather than mere rhetoric) can be the servant of philosophy, then after 1739, Hume is extending his philosophical role through rhetorical adjustment to his intended audience. This is virtuous rhetoric versus vulgar popularization.

Rostow is inclined in most of the cases he considers to 'agree' with Medawar – whose position given what we know about how cultural and political assumptions can get inscribed even in scientific writing is extreme – but makes an exception for three (largely) economic theorists: Hume, J. S. Mill and Marx. These are big theorists in the sense that they each produced a number of significant works in political economy or with strong implications (in the case of Hume) for the development of political economy. It would seem that their particular circumstances, family background or depth of thinking requires some biographical context to be linked to the development of their work.

None of these thinkers was employed as academics. Mill, who never attended university and who never had an academic appointment (his appointment as Rector of Aberdeen was honorary and by its nature temporary), was educated at home under a scheme of rationale education constructed and enforced by his father. The scheme ignored the emotions and adversely marked Mill's adult life. Had James Mill a firmer grasp of Hume's ideas, J. S. Mill's personal history may well have been different. Marx built up his professional knowledge by extensive reading, particularly in the Reading Room of the British Museum.

Hume, who did attend University, twice attempted to gain an academic chair, once at the University of Edinburgh (1744) and once at the University of Glasgow (1751), and was rebuffed in both places, largely but not solely because of his sceptical views. Hutcheson did not support his application to a chair at Edinburgh on the grounds, essentially, that Hume could not meet the conditions. The terms of reference included defending the principles of Christianity. A significant role for the universities in Scotland at the time was the training of the clergy. University appointments were also 'politicized'. There were voices for as well as voices against, though Hume would have had to have had a significant amount of political support in order to overcome internal resistance, if he were to have been appointed (Emerson, 1994, 26).

Hume later complained about the shutting up of learning in 'Colleges and Cells' when it was better let loose on the world, and reflects, in writing, on how this could be achieved (see 'Of Essay Writing' and also 'Of the Different Species of Philosophy'; his essays are analysed in Chapter 6 onwards). However, the insight is somewhat exaggerated, certainly in so far as Scottish conditions were concerned: many Scottish professors participated in the numerous Enlightenment Clubs found in towns such as Edinburgh, Glasgow and Aberdeen. For Hume, philosophy had to be engaged with everyday life and experience. He needed to search for an income that would sustain him and make his literary work – as a historian and essayist as it transpired – at least possible.

Hume's life, whatever its vicissitudes, was not one lived within the narrowing confines of the academy nor within the narrow boundaries set by the Presbyterian beliefs and practices of his youth. This is not enough to exempt him, in my view, from Medawar's strictures. Hume, despite significant administrative posts, lived the life of a 'man of letters' (he applied the term to other *philosophes*) and hence though not shut up in an academic institution, acquired some of the features of an academic lifestyle. Think of his role as tutor to a marquis subsequently declared 'lunatic' or of his tenure as Keeper of the Advocates' Library (1752–57). It is the start of a case for exception. It was important to Hume that he maintained 'a just medium' between the (conventional) unworldly reputation of the philosopher and the partisan interests of the business man, or indeed, of the party zealot (see Danford, 1990, 11; also Buckle, 2001, 15; and 'Of Commerce'). The Enlightenment in Scotland was a phenomenon or rather a series of phenomena that though not limited to universities nevertheless found some of its highest forms of expression in the work of university teachers. Think of Francis Hutcheson and later Adam Smith at Glasgow (though Smith too had a varied life) and of the philosopher/sociologist Adam Ferguson. Even in the details of his life, Hume was exceptional. He made for himself a different career path through his writing and one that, as Christensen suggests, 'exploited, facilitated, and epitomized the operations of the society which it persuasively represented' (Christensen, 1987, 4). Hume's image, 'Historian and Philosopher' as painted by Allan Ramsay unites the opulence of the merchant represented by the magnificently embroidered scarlet cloth, edged with gold, of Hume's apparel and the philosopher by the simple device of having Hume portrayed with his left arm resting on a finely bound set of books. His face, as depicted by Ramsey, has both a 'far away' look and at the same time a superior sense of presence.

Hume's textual presence

There is an even stronger reason to include at least some reference to Hume's biography. Hume's claim to fame in the modern world, including his fame as a founder of modern economics, is built upon a foundation of thought created, even if the *direct* economic content is only marginally present, in his *Treatise of Human Nature*, a discourse that was so far ahead of its time that it hardly achieved in his lifetime the audience that it deserved. The *Treatise* is a vast and difficult work that has given rise to various interpretations over the years. It is a rich text and like all rich texts it is subject to alternative readings. It is a work that the author published anonymously and which he described as an 'attempt to introduce the experimental method of reasoning into moral subjects'. Hume's anonymity was not respected and as a result he was subjected to personal attacks. Hume, even when he is a difficult writer is also a careful writer. He calls the work an 'attempt'. In paragraph one of the *Abstract* he writes, 'But 'tis at least worth while to try if the science of man will not admit of the same accuracy which several parts of natural philosophy are found susceptible of' (*T, Abstract*, 1). Again Hume is putting an emphasis on the notion of attempting or trying. The convention of anonymity was meant to protect the author and to focus the attention of the critics upon the ideas presented for evaluation. His long title make is clear that the work was about 'moral subjects' though many then and since concentrated on his epistemology to the detriment of the work as a whole. The interplay between his work and his subsequent life was necessarily strong, so strong in fact that he both self-censored, by removing the passages on miracles before publication for fear of the adverse reaction, and ultimately rejected the *Treatise*.

The *Treatise* is a work of moral philosophy that aims to revolutionize the study of human nature and to reconstruct the science of man on a new foundation – in this respect it is as radical in its search to begin anew as the ambitions of Descartes: 'I compared the disquisitions of the ancient moralists to very towering and magnificent palaces with no better foundations than sand and mud'. Descartes also committed himself to the collection of a variety of experiences and to trusting the judgment of those who faced directly the consequences of their judgment rather than to secluded, armchair thinkers. For Descartes, the process was that of making himself an 'object of study'.

Hume's new foundation was anti-rationalist and empirical. Hume was also aware that he was working in the development of a tradition that started with Locke. [2] Richetti reminds us that the early modern philosophers had in common the notion of 'a new beginning rather than a continuation and modification of older thought' (Richetti, 1983, 7; see also Danford, 1990, 6). By the early eighteenth century, rejection of the principles and rhetorical practices of Aristotle and the 'schoolmen' (Descartes had talked of his scepticism concerning the utility of the syllogism for investigation of that which is not known) was almost a cultural expectation on the part of an educated readership. Descartes thought that he needed a new approach based on a work by a single hand. Perhaps this too suggested the comprehensive and exhaustive treatise as the vehicle for Hume's thought. Hume remained convinced of the value of the novel features of the *Treatise*.

In the Preface to the *Abstract* that he published in 1740 (see Chapter 2), Hume argues that 'bold attempts' to rethink philosophy, 'shake of the yoke of authority, accustom men to think for themselves' and further inquiry and discussion (*T, Abstract*, Preface 2). Hume differs from Descartes in as much as he puts the 'theory of human nature' at the roots of 'the moral sciences' whereas Descartes puts 'metaphysics' (Passmore, 1953, 12). Both Descartes and Hume (and Adam Smith for that matter) are concerned with 'assembling chains of propositions (Danford, 1990, 22) and this notion seems to be one that was culturally admired. Descartes admired the 'long chains of simple reasonings by means of which geometers are accustomed to reach the conclusions of their most difficult demonstrations' and holds that other phenomena are connected in the same way. Smith makes reference to such a 'chain' as part of Newtonianism as applied to social subjects, hence stressing its inductive nature, and his peers held Smith's ability to draw out implications for a few propositions (think of the use to which he puts the division of labour) through a whole chain of reasoning to be admirable. In the Preface to the *Abstract*, Hume acknowledges the problems caused for some readers in 'apprehending a chain of reasoning' where an argument 'is drawn out to a great length' and fortified and buttressed by reason and counter-reason. Hume uses both induction and deduction to make his web of connections and rejects the notion of certainty associated with the self-evident propositions of Descartes. It could be argued that Hume set out to establish the 'science of man' on a basis that would outshine both Descartes as well as Newton.

The *Treatise* is also a work that interweaves in subtle and less subtle ways Hume's as yet limited biographical experience. Hume is not averse to the use of the first person singular as part of the fabric of the writing. Postmodern literary criticism holds that the author is irrelevant to the interpretation of the work upon its publication and subsequent reading. Maybe, though it is the case that Hume felt the need to continue to come to the aid of the *Treatise* and the ideas that it contained. The *Treatise* is inscribed, either overtly or covertly in much of Hume's work after 1739. Hume is also inscribed in the *Treatise* through this 'characterization of the "I"' – Richetti talks of the 'speaker' – and this makes Hume's biography at least interesting. The use of the 'I' is not *always* personal but rather often constructed within the text as a general 'I' creating the sense in formal English as the equivalent to 'one'. It is not always easy to distinguish casually between the personal and impersonal uses. As will be shown, Hume generally, but not invariably, uses the first person singular to construct 'experimental' episodes, switching from the cooperative voice to the 'I' in doing so.

Richetti goes beyond even this view, seeing the 'I' as a 'visible mask, a personality manipulated for effect' (Richetti, 1983, 42). Jones makes a very telling point about Ciceronian influences in the structure of the *Treatise* when he writes: 'Hume models the structure of the first two books of the *Treatise* on that of *De Officiis*, where the first book is written from the reflexive point of view of an individual, and the second analyses his character from the point of view of others (Jones, 1982, 30). The writing is complex – 'a labyrinth' according to Jessop (1966, 41).

The issues, and indeed contradictions, involved can be illustrated in one of its strongest manifestations in the 'Conclusion of this book' (the end of part one of the *Treatise*) in passages in which Hume constructs his dangerous (and somewhat melodramatic) 'voyage' in very personal terms. Baier sees this as Hume's deliberate attempt to move the reader from a distorted reliance on 'the intellect' to an approach to philosophy that restores the balance by including the human passion and feelings (Baier, 1991, 1; see also Baillie, 2000, 37–39). The social dimension, including the capacity for friendship, is a necessary aspect of human nature and human development. Indeed the *Treatise* has been seen as a location where Hume's ideas were discovered and structured (or to borrow terms from the rhetorical canon, a location of 'invention' and 'arrangement') whereas his *Enquiries* can be seen as locations for the exercise of 'style' and 'delivery' (in the non-spoken sense). This would make the one properly 'philosophical' and the others *merely* 'rhetorical', nearly in the manner of Peter Ramus's division of the canons of argumentation – a way of thinking about Hume's *Enquiries* that Hume did not share and Buckle rejects.

Isolated, bewildered and oppressed by 'doubt and ignorance' occasioned by the uncertainties released by the philosophical enterprise in which he is engaged, Hume therefore walks in fear of 'error and absurdity'. Here Hume is making a strong attempt to portray his frame of mind in order to put, in an act of sympathy, his anticipated audience in a similar frame of mind. This is what Aristotle would have called 'pathos'. The 'I' here is personal and does not give way to the cooperative 'we'/'us'/'our' for nearly three paragraphs. There is a strong authorial voice at play here and the presence is direct. The passage is a puzzle: its personal nature, its drama and hyperbole suggest a work of literature or fiction rather than of (our latter-day view) serious philosophy. The reader is being excited or terrified by emotion rather than by reasoned argument. Although Hume wishes to place 'the science of man' on a new foundation, the writing here, although based on the face of it upon experience is not itself experienced scientifically (rationally) but dramatically (emotionally).

Hume attempts a reconciliation: 'For with what confidence can I venture upon such bold enterprises, when besides those numberless infirmities peculiar to myself, I find so many which are common to human nature' (*T*, 1.4.7.3). The scene shifts from that the struggling individual to common humanity, from the specific to the general, in line with his inductive orientation.

It is such 'infirmities' that limit human knowledge. Hume can be seen by as constructing himself in such passages as his own hero. The line between fact and fiction and between emotive and rational discourse is, in this textual episode, as Richetti suggests in general, blurred.

It is these common 'infirmities', the stuff of the epistemology of the *Treatise*, which allow Hume to move from the individual and personal to the general. Hume is textually creating an opportunity of the expression of sympathy by uniting to himself the feelings that he also imagines are engendered in the target reader. His bewilderment is also our bewilderment. If you read it without this idea of sympathy, or out of a context, developed by Hume in the *Treatise*, that reason is the servant of the passions, many unflattering interpretations become possible, including demonstrating his awareness of 'his own powers of mind' (Greig, 1934, 90). The conventional and somewhat disparaging review of the *Treatise* published in the *Works of the Learned* (1739) refers to the number of 'egotisms'. Hume's textual presence may account for a small part of the strength of the *ad hominem* attacks that he received.

These initial paragraphs give way, as they must if the content is to achieve validity, to a shared perplexity that is part of the human condition in general, and to a recapitulation of his basic philosophy. He refers to our disappointment 'when we learn, that the connexion, tie, or energy lies merely in ourselves, and is nothing but that determination of the mind, which is aquir'd by custom, and causes us to make a transition from an object to its usual attendant, and from the impression of one to the lively idea of the other?' (*T*, 1.4.7.5). This sentence is a very precise example of Hume's use of summarization to reintegrate the text and of his capacity to summarize complex ideas neatly. Hume may have exaggerated for the sake of liveliness, but the whole passage (meaning the first five paragraphs only) is nonetheless carefully constructed thereafter. Hume however returns to the personal and recovers his equilibrium by retreating from philosophical reflection into the grounded, stable and predictable sociability of everyday life: 'I dine, I play a game of back-gammon ...'. This was the essence of Hume's own escape from 'the disease of the learned' experienced during earlier periods of philosophical speculation that had initiated his thinking on the topics treated in the *Treatise*. The stress was not short-term and Hume writes candidly about his experience in a draft of a letter penned in the spring of 1734. The prospect of a 'new Scene of Thought' had overexcited his mind. He only recovered shortly before going to Bristol and from thence to France. His plans for writing the *Treatise* were, in the draft, already in formation: 'Having now Time and Leisure to cool my inflam'd Imaginations, I began to consider seriously, how I should proceed in my Philosophical Enquiries' (Hume's letters).

Hume is concerned in the *Treatise* and really throughout his life with observation including introspection and self-observation. Gathering such observations is, for him, an essential part of his scientific method. There are also other passages in the work that overtly and covertly deal with the substance of Hume's life. Baier, for example, sees in Hume's 'version of family relations' based on 'mutual love and easy intimacy' as an outcome of his childhood in a happy household run independently by his widowed mother (Baier, 1988, 771). Hume and his works are despite the relative absence of great 'devastation' – apart from his early and philosophically induced break down and its implications for his notion of the stability of the personality or in his infamous quarrel with Rousseau – in his life are bound up together. Kruse, it should be noted, constructs 'the complete fiasco of the Treatise', i.e. of the reception of the *Treatise*, as a sort of devastation (Kruse, 1939, 8). Hume, in 'My Own Life' (a 'funeral oration' of and to himself, not entirely devoid of 'vanity') talks, in contrast, of a comparative lack of 'calumny' in his experiences.

The reception of the *Treatise* irritated him, nonetheless. However much he may have complained about the lack of respect on the part of others for the convention, the strength of his presence in the text may have been one reason for the strength of the reaction. At the same time, it is hard to read Hume in the section in the *Treatise* on 'Of the Love of Fame' independently of his claim to have been motivated throughout his life by the desire for literary fame. Hume is very precise in placing the discussion of fame within the discussion of 'sympathy' and within the general notion of character: 'Our reputation, our character, our name are considerations of vast weight and importance, and even the other causes of pride; virtue, beauty and riches; have little influence when not seconded by the opinions and sentiments of others' (*T*, 2.1.11.1). Love of fame, moderated through 'sympathy' is related to nobility of character ('Our reputation, our character, our name...'). There is nothing demeaning here. In this context, Hume's 'love of fame' is not distorted, but normal. Fame after death does not, cannot, console any writer simply as a matter of common sense. See also, for example, Hume on the regard paid to 'a statesman or patriot' in his time or in distant ages (*ECPM*, 5.2.41). Such fame lacks the two-way process necessary to the sympathetic response.

Defending Hume's character – he defended it himself before he died – is not usually a principal concern of examining his texts but it is one that is necessary given the historical and persistent misinterpretations of Hume and his motivations.

Hume is the personalized 'narrator' of the *Treatise*, just as Descartes is the personalized narrator of the *Discourse on Method*. This presence must also be found in the textual detail and an extended example in the 'Of the Love of Fame' can be looked at in terms of Hume's biography. Hume as a younger son of a middle-ranking Border family, sustained in his early years by the frugality and care of his widowed mother, was not heir to a great fortune. When young he received only a modest allowance from his family.

He removed himself to France (1734) from Bristol, where he had worked with a Bristol merchant and had absorbed experientially some economic lessons, to live modestly – Hume like Smith was very impressed through direct experience and observation with the notion of frugality and primitive accumulation – on a small income and to write the *Treatise*. His plan, as reported in 'My Own Life' – a work in which Hume intended to fix his character for his peers and for posterity and hence not devoid of persuasive purposes – was simple: 'I resolved to make a very rigid frugality supply my deficiency of fortune, to maintain unimpaired my independency, and to regard every object as contemptible, except the improvement of my talents in literature' (xxxiv) (see also *ECPM*, 6.1,11). Cicero, whom Hume had read, suggested that 'economy is a great income.' (Cicero, *Paradoxa Stoicorum*, VI.3, 49). It is important, according to Cicero, not to confuse needs and desires (see, Colish, 1985, 131).

Hume first moves to Rheims but then removed himself to La Flèch, a place that housed the Jesuit Seminary in which Descartes, whose philosophical ambitions concerning the reconstruction of knowledge in the previous century rivalled, as we have seen, those of Hume, had been educated. The Jesuits, according to Schabas, quoting Hankins, were generally noted for an interest in scientific investigations (Schabas, 2001, 421) and this period there may have added to Hume's scientific understanding.

Consider the following passage:

> Nothing is more usual for men of good families, but narrow circumstances, to leave their friends and country, and rather seek their livelihood by mean and mechanical employments among strangers, than among those, who are acquainted with their birth and education.
>
> (*T*, 2.1.11.14)

This works biographically as much for his time apprenticed to a Bristol merchant as it does for his time in France. Hume of course sets these sentiments up as general and normal ('more usual') and not personal. The example is useful: 'In examining these sentiments, I find they afford many very convincing arguments for my present purpose'. Hume is using his own life, though 'masked' – to manipulate Richetti's notion – as an example. In the light of his scientific method and of his desire to leave no principle unsupported by exemplification and analysis, Hume, in order to explore the notion of sympathy, chose a situation with which he was very familiar. He then used it textually to evaluate a theoretical (in other words a hypothetical) proposition: 'All this appears very probable in theory; but in order to bestow a full certainty on this reasoning, we must examine the phenomena of the passions and see if they agree with it' (*T*, 2.1.11.10). This comes three paragraphs prior to the extend example.

The sense that this is an argument informed by personal experience remains strong.[3]

There are other passages too, such as when Hume in the *Treatise* talks about 'gaming' *(T,* 2.3.10. 9 and 10), or about sociability as an antidote to an overworked philosophy, where it is not unreasonable to conclude that in both instances, and given Hume's notion of human psychology, the general and the personal coincide.

If the *Treatise* is to be subjected to analysis then there is some need (more or less strong depending upon the conviction of the researcher) to say something about Hume's declared relationship to his own work. Hume completed a fairly advanced draft of the *Treatise* by the age of 26. Delays in finding a published encouraged him to revise the work. Originally it was to have included his argument concerning miracles (an argument partly prompted by a conversation with a Jesuit at the Seminary in La Flèch) (Greig, 1934, 94) but Hume decided to remove the argument from the work for fear of its likely reception. He sought no patron and although this was risky, it was also the path of independence. This sense of personal autonomy is an enduring aspect of Hume's life and aspirations. Tobias Smollett, his near contemporary whose social origins were similar to both that of Hume and Smith, was later to pursue just such independence in his literary career. The growth of education and of cultivated leisure and of consumerism meant that there were new opportunities for authorship and in the course of his productive life, Hume learned to exploit these to the fullest. However, Hume, in the haste of youth, made a poor bargain, even in his own reckoning, over the publication of the *Treatise*. He rarely made that mistake again. As his fame increased, so eventually did the income from his works published after the *Treatise*.

In 'My Own Life' Hume is somewhat sanguine about the failure of the *Treatise* to generate an audience. He says 'Never literary attempt was more unfortunate than my Treatise of Human Nature. It fell *dead-born from the press*, without reaching such a distinction, as even to excite a murmur among the zealots' (xxxiv). Some zealots were disturbed. Mossner (1966, 26) writes of the 'perverse vitality' of the *Treatise*, rather than of its death. Notice that Hume refers to his principle contribution to philosophy as 'literature' and he italicizes 'dead-born from the press'. The italicization is a clue that this is a quote. This is one of Hume's references to Alexander Pope, identified as a reference to dialogue two, line 226 of the 'Epilogue to the Satires' (Box, 1990, 22; Buckle, 2001, 8). The context is Pope's notion that all but truth suffers such a fate (Buckle, 2001, 8; Frasca-Spada, 1998, 86). There is not enough explicit evidence here, in my view, however to justify a strong sense of personal responsibility and philosophical error on Hume's part. Hume is dealing with the situation ironically. Hume adds in a later passage: '... my want of success in publishing the Treatise of Human Nature, had proceeded more from the manner than the matter, and that

I had been guilty of a very usual indiscretion, in going to the press too early'. Hume may have been predisposed to see it this way. Consider what Hume says in a complex paragraph in the *Treatise* about his task:

> ... 'tis very difficult to talk about the operations of the mind with perfect propriety and exactness; because common language has seldom made any very nice distinctions among them, but has generally call'd by the same term all such as nearly resemble each other. And as this is a source almost inevitable of obscurity and confusion in the author; so it may frequently give rise to doubts and objections in the reader, which otherwise he wou'd never have dream'd of.
>
> (*T*, 1.3.8.15)

The suggestion is when all this is taken together that Hume accepted that there were flaws and that, as Buckle insists, he had significant doubts about the validity of at least some of his arguments (Buckle, 2001, 9). That he subsequently developed his *Enquiry* and then his *Principles of Morals* as, essentially, popularizations of the key ideas in the *Treatise* is contested, with justification, by Buckle, as demeaning the works and Hume's character. A way out of this has already been suggested above.

Literary reconsiderations: an overview

Hume's explicit rejection of the *Treatise* is stated in very full terms in the Advertisement to his later works but one that is, according to Buckle, penned later that the production of the two *Enquiries* (1748 and 1751) and part of Hume's strategy of shaping his reputation for posterity. As the Advertisement constitutes a significant statement it is worthy of some close study:

> Most of the principles, and reasonings, contained in this volume, were published in a work in there volumes called *A Treatise of Human Nature*: A work which the Author projected before he left College, and which he wrote and published not long after. But not finding it successful, he was sensible of his error in going to the press too early, and he cast the whole anew in the following pieces, where some negligencies in his former reasoning and more in the expression, are, he hopes, corrected. Yet several writers, who have honoured the Author's Philosophy with answers, have taken care to direct all their batteries against that juvenile work, which the author never acknowledged, and have affected to triumph in any advantages, which, they imagined, they had obtained over it: A practice very contrary to all the rules of candour and fair-dealing, and a strong instance of those polemical artifices, which a bigoted zeal thinks itself authorized to employ. Henceforth, the Author desires, that the following Pieces may alone be regarded as containing his philosophical sentiments and principles.
>
> [italics removed]

This is a very simple statement and does not provide us with much to go on with respect to details of Hume's motivations. A closer reading, always a good idea when dealing with Hume's prose, is required. It is written in the third person with a strong sense of ironic distance. This stands in sharp contrast to the Advertisement to Book One of the *Treatise*, written through-out in the first person.

Before making a brief analysis of the passage it is useful to reproduce the Advertisement to the first two volumes of the *Treatise* as it shows the eager and perhaps naïf young Hume ('I') in contrast to the mature and more worldly-wise man ('the Author'):

> My design in the resent work is sufficiently explain'd in the Introduction. The reader must only observe, that all the subjects that I have there plann'd out to myself, are not treated of in these two volumes. The subjects of the Understanding and the Passions make a compleat chain of reasoning by themselves; and I was willing to take advantage of this natural division, in order to try the taste of the public. If I have good fortune to meet with success, I shall proceed to the examination of Morals, Politics and Criticism; which will compleat this Treatise of Human Nature. The approbation of the public I consider as the great-est reward of my labours; but I am determin'd to regard its judgment, whatever it be, as my best instruction.
>
> [italics removed] (*T*, 2)

Note the concluding statement. Earlier in the passage Hume suggests that he is writing 'in order to try the taste of the public'. Kruse saw this as 'a complete and unconditional surrender to fickle public opinion' (Kruse, 1939, 9). When the two sentences are taken together then the implication would seem to be that Hume is looking at the relationship between the public and writer as one in which lessons can be learned, both ways, some-thing that he articulates again later in his development as a writer. He is looking for a cooperative relationship, an enlightened conversation, whereas what he got was largely abuse. This two-way process becomes again signif-icant for Hume when he commits himself to easy writing (see Chapter 6).

Reading the new Advertisement rhetorically through its own internal structure and through that of the Advertisement to the *Treatise* yields some significant insight.

Hume is careful to observe the conventions here, in contrast, given that he is arguing that those who 'honoured the Author's Philosophy with answers' did not. The primacy of the *Treatise* is acknowledged: 'Most of the principles, and reasonings...' and 'negligencies in his former reasoning, and more in the expression, are, he hopes, corrected'. If the *Treatise* was judged unreadable, then he has, in line with what he committed himself to, addressed the issue. The *Treatise* is (face-savingly) constructed as youthful work. To emphasize the point, its inception and is placed in a time 'before he left College' and which was 'published not long after' (a telescoping of the time period). The next sentence seems to be written in fulfilment of the statement made in the Advertisement to the *Treatise*. There he was testing taste and willing to take instruction. Here he has learned his lesson: 'But not finding it successful, he was sensible of his error in going to the press too early, and he cast the whole anew in the following pieces ...'. Hume though of himself here as a 'youthful innovator' whose inconsistencies were 'frequent and blatant' – if I may be permitted to quote Passmore in a slightly different context from the one he intended (Passmore, 1953, 1). The problem, in terms of readership reception, may not be with expression (style) or even organization in the simplest sense but with methodology – Book One, according to Passmore, formulates Hume's social science methodology – and what I see as its implications for textual method or rhetoric (Passmore, 1953, 6). However, Hume sees the problems with the *Treatise* and its corrections as defined in terms of 'some negligences in his former reasoning' (a matter of logical detail?) 'and more in the expression'. Hume underestimates the problem that readers had in discerning the significance of the processes that he advocates. What is clear that Hume is arguing that the changes in expression outweigh the extent of the corrections of the reasoning.

The next long sentence in the sequence needs to be read with care. Hume is not universally ironic but it is as well to be sensitive to its possibility, even in a text as short as this. Those who noticed the *Treatise* in review, are treated with formal respect ('honoured the Author's Philosophy with answers') though there is a sense of irony for they have concentrated on 'that juvenile work'. They have offended against the convention of anonymity ('which the Author never acknowledged'). It is however in the tail that the sting is at its strongest. Such writers 'have affected to triumph in any advantages, which, they imagined they had obtained over it'. Hume is not here acknowledging that these critics have in fact obtained any significant intellectual advantage over the content of the *Treatise*. This sentence could be seen as a reference to Hume's concern about loose expression. In context, this suggests that Hume feels strongly that the fault is one of expression (a juvenile's lack of skill in the writing) and not essentially of analysis. He learned his lessons, as he had publicly promised in the Advertisement to the original work, and asks that this be acknowledged. Hume reinforces the sense of irony concerning the writers by pointing out the *mauvais-fois* in the use of 'polemical artifices, which a bigoted zeal thinks itself authorized to employ'. Selby-Bigge (1893, ix) reports that Grose, coeditor with Green (1889), perhaps with this phrase in mind, saw the Advertisement as 'the posthumous utterance of a splenetic invalid'. This is going too far.

Any rejection of the *Treatise* here must not be overstated even though he concludes with the request, directed to critics, 'that the following Pieces may alone be regarded as containing his philosophical sentiments and principles'. Hume wanted his ideas to be known directly rather than through the distorting lens of bigoted evaluation. Difficulties with and the lack of an audience for the *Treatise* stood in his way. The writing of the essays and of the *Enquiries* was a useful strategy for refining and recirculating his ideas, of inviting a proper rather than an entirely prejudicial debate. He could only really get this debate by widening his audience. The rejection of the *Treatise* in this reading is not absolute but relative to the *mauvais-fois* of zealot criticism as well as to the failings of style and expression that Hume felt he had discovered. Hume held generally that the actions and judgment of zealots, under the influence of a misguided enthusiasm must be either, at worst, deluded and extreme, and at best heavily compromised by a distorted imagination. The 'FEW' who actually judged him were 'apt to be corrupted by partiality and prejudice' as he had already put it in the Preface to the *Abstract* (published March 1740). That he wished for a broad and open-minded audience, rather than an audience of unenlightened zealots, is clear and in the *Enquiries* he wrote for, and probably helped to create, just such an audience. The *Treatise* may have asked for too much as it called for an audience or attempted to call into being an audience that could live with uncertainty, caution, perplexity and paradox. The *Treatise* remains, by academic convention and agreement, his most significant philosophical work.

These allegedly more 'popular' versions (and just how the text is simplified will be investigated and illustrated later in his volume) were also relatively 'unnoticed and unobserved' at least initially. Hume's sense of failure and his reflections upon it had a huge impact on his later writing including his motivation for switching to *genres* other than that of the sustainable and constantly expanding *Treatise*. He started essay writing before he published the first *Enquiry* (another genre type) (see Beauchamp, 1998, xviii) and there is little doubt that the early essays continue to discuss weighty matters that have a relationship with the *Treatise*. There was no way forward in constantly looking and defending backwards. Keep in mind that Hume had, with respect to public responses, 'fixed a resolution, which I inflexibly maintained, never to reply to anybody ...' (xxxvi), though he broke this rule at least twice. The essay as Hume developed it gave him flexibility and a capacity for further reflection and review than the more static form of treatise and its associated readership expectations, made possible. In the *ECHU* he notes, in a passage that reflects upon the 'easy' and 'profound' philosophy that 'Addison, perhaps will be read with pleasure, when Locke shall be entirely forgotten' (*ECHU*, 1. 4). This, though quite properly hedged, can be seen as praise for the ability of the essay format to circulate significant ideas (Brunius, 1952, 17). He constantly revised his essays, an extension of his idea of taking his instruction from the lessons generated by the public. These works, successful from the very first, had a huge significance for his economic well-being as well as for his intellectual reputation.

The extent to which there is much in the *Treatise* that allows biographical recovery must not be overstated, despite the narrative voice used by Hume.

One of Hume's early twentieth-century biographers, J. Y. T. Greig, holds that, 'Much may be learnt about the man Hume from those twenty-seven semi-popular but solid essays; more perhaps, than from the whole 1100 pages of the *Treatise*' and judges the essay form as composed by Hume to constitute 'a highly personal, revealing form of literature' (Greig, 1934, 115). Certainly they show Hume's liberal–commercial values and moderate stance in practice though whether they are any more revealing that the *Treatise* it is possible to debate. Greig illustrates for example how Hume's indirect text reveals how strongly he dissents from Rousseau's views on human sentiment without ever once mentioning Rousseau's name. In private, commenting upon Rousseau's style, he held that Rousseau's 'genius' was mixed with 'some degree of extravagance' (Richetti, 1983, 189). Could not the same be said for the opening paragraphs on the 'Conclusion of this book'? Or is this better viewed as a peroration that is both summative as well as emotive and which fulfils the demands of classical rhetoric, as recommended by Cicero, say, as well as Hume's concept of sympathy?

Greig uses the term 'semi-popular' with respect to the essays and immediately counters with the notion of 'solid' worth. The reputation for solidity, is also early attested to in the history of economic thought by Ingram. Ingram says of them that his main economics essays, 'should not be separated from the rest, for, notwithstanding the unconnected form of these little treatises, there runs through them a profound unity of thought, so that they indeed compose in a certain sense an economic system' (Ingram, 1910, 83). The judgments on the essays in general have tended to be agreed, with some lapses, by subsequent scholarship.

Take the essays usually described as having economic significance (the number varies according to what is included or excluded). Rostow reminds us that what is *normally* referred to as Hume's economics writing, excluding his essay on population, runs to not more than 100 printed pages (current standard page length). Even if there is more economics in the *Treatise* and in the essays not conventionally classified as economics, the 100 pages have made Hume's economic reputation. Hume's reputation in France was essentially established by his political and economic writing even if they were given, in translation, a significant French cultural spin (Shovlin, 2008). They have received critical attention from Rotwein, who published the economic collection in 1956, from Skinner, for example, and most recently in the Wennerlind and Schabas's (2008) edited volume on *David Hume's Political Economy*. These essays together with relevant sections of the *Treatise* provide Hume with a significant reputation as one of the founders, along with Adam Smith, of modern economic thought. Hume's contribution, in this respect, was early recognized by Macaulay, though he wished to overthrow the influence of Hume's *History* (Trevor-Roper, 1964, 381) and replace Hume's alleged 'Tory' version with his own Whig version. Macaulay (Macaulay, [] 1871, 262) also builds Hume up as 'undoubtedly one of the most profound political economists of his time' only to pull down his views on the consequences of the national debt and portray them as 'a memorable instance of the weakness from which the strongest minds are not exempt'.[4] Richetti (1983, 189) does not justify his view that 'Hume's opinions in the *Essays* are glossy commonplaces ...'. Richetti is not referring, however, to the later political and economic essays.

It is possible for works to be both 'popular', in some sense, and intellectually valid. 'Popularization' brings with it to modern sensibility the notion of 'vulgar' or of being devoid of critical or intellectual content. This need not be the case and it will be argued later in this work that 'audience' and the demands of a virtuous rhetoric may be a better way to understand Hume in this context. Hume's *Treatise* was ahead of its time in its method of argument and in the philosophical content. There was and is a lot going on within its covers. His writing thereafter, both by personal decision and the results of the passing of time and the accumulation of experience, changed. Buckle (2001, 7–12) is sensitive to the connotations of 'popular' and seeks to re-establish the philosophical validity of the *Enquiries*. Richetti (1983, 18) too sees the move from the *Treatise* to the *Enquiries* as both the outcome of and constituent part of a 'maturing process'. Here, we can accept, at least at this stage, that his later writings were both 'popular' in the *genre* sense, and hence a contribution to enhancing the intellectual content and significance of 'polite' conversation, and intellectually valid.

Approaching Hume's work: implications

It is clear that there are many versions of Hume the man and the thinker. Some of these interact with and colour how his work is viewed. Box puts it this way: 'Many more contradictory positions have been attributed to Hume than one would expect from a thinker who, unlike Emerson or Nietzsche, was attempting to build a self-consistent system' (Box, 1990, ix). Letwin (1998, xx), considering Hume in the company of Jeremy Bentham, John Stuart Mill and Beatrice Webb, puts the issues thus: 'In short, we are forcibly reminded that names and doctrines collect a variety of associations ...' not all of which are necessary helpful. There are many interpretations of Hume's work by scholars who have devoted years to the study of his works. Indeed even with respect to the *Treatise* there are almost as many interpretations as there are commentators. This is to be expected of texts that are 'rich'. The secondary literature on Hume is already vast, stimulating and complex. Hume's work was relatively neglected in the early to middle years of the twentieth century. This is not the case today. The end of the twentieth century saw a rapid expansion of interest in Hume and a series of attempts to adjust interpretation and to forge it anew against a surer background of eighteenth-century concerns or Hume's work more broadly situated within 'a living and vibrant debate in his own day'(Stewart and Wright, 1994, xii). Danford (1990) could point to the need to explore

Hume in order to assist the 'Recovering of the Human Sciences' and to gaps in our understanding of, among others, on 'how economics is related to human nature' (Danford, 1990, 1) – a problem that exercised Adam Smith, within his construction of the propensity to truck, barter and exchange, as well as David Hume. Interpreting Smith's downgrading of human reason and the status of Smith's 'propensities' requires some knowledge of Hume. Perplexities remain (Henderson and Samuels, 2004). Human nature and its relationship to economics remains an issue that is fought over by, for example, Austrian economists opposed to the vision of economic man constructed in conventional neoclassical economics or those who wish to contest the neatness but historical emptiness of mathematical analysis and modelling.

There is an extensive and valid secondary literature covering every aspect of Hume's writing, including his work on political economy – a significant gap has just been closed by the publication of *David Hume's Political Economy* edited by Wennerlind and Schabas – and even in his aesthetics ('criticism'). A new standard edition of the *Treatise* has recently been published (and reprinted with corrections several times) under the editorial care of David Fate Norton and Mary J. Norton (2005). This does not mean that there is any general agreement, only that there is lively interest.

Given all of this, what possible justification can there be for yet another book on Hume's corpus? Even in the 1950s, Passmore felt the need to answer this question. He did so in terms of a desire not to replace but to compliment the existing literature (Passmore, 1953, vii). What is proposed here is a general, rather than a highly specialist, book on Hume. His writing on religion will not be examined and his *History* mentioned only in passing. The central aim is to try and link Hume's socioeconomic thinking back to its intellectual origins in the *Treatise*. This is not entirely original – many of the contributors to Wennerlind and Schabas do just that for Hume's political economy.

The vexed question of Hume's methodology is one area that still exercises the scholarly community. There is much uncertainty in this area and Passmore's comment in the 1953 still feels relevant: 'Hume is one of the most exasperating philosophers' (Passmore, 1953, 1). Methodological considerations are important with respect to the development of the social sciences and it is not unreasonable to attempt an exploration of the subject, especially as one of the target audiences for this work is those interested in the intellectual history of economics, broadly defined. Here, an attempt will be made to distinguish 'methodology', 'textual method' (how the theoretical ideas concerning method are embodied in a body of writing) and 'rhetoric' (broadly defined but to include such notions as the ethos of the text). This will be done by focusing on sustained examples of Hume's writing. The aim is to remain close to Hume and outline his method of comparison and his associated use of analogy.

Then there is the question of audience. Hume scholarship is highly sophisticated and specialized. There is scope for a work that while it is oriented towards the intellectual history of economics (broadly defined to include the methodology and philosophy of economic thought) attempts to refocus on Hume's writing. Here there are a number of existing works of scholarship, the most significant being those of Richetti (1983), Box (1990) and Danford (1990). In this work extended passages in Hume will be subjected to some form of economically informed textual analysis. The focus will be on the writing and the analysis will be based on uncovering the textual strategy and implications and inner connections through a form of, for example, close reading. The approach has already been demonstrated in the analysis made above of the two Advertisements, the one to the *Treatise* and the other to the *Enquiries*. This approach needs to be justified and the justification will be worked through further in the next chapter. However, although close reading will be used, it will not used to the exclusion of all other ways of developing insight. What will be attempted here is the analysis of significant passages in order to explore not simply what Hume is saying but how and why he is saying it.

Although the 'attempt' (to borrow a word from Hume's long title to the *Treatise*) is that of developing a general and integrated of Hume's social and economic analysis, that intention will be carried by the analysis of representative passages rather than simply by critical summarization. The aim here is to draw others into the web of reading Hume and reflecting directly upon his writing. There is a problem with this, and it is one that is more acutely encountered by those who gather together anthologies. Medema and Samuels put the problem as one of confronting a 'smorgasbord of delights' while dieting: 'so many good things to sample and so little room to indulge' (Medema and Samuels, 2003, x). This problem will be overcome by some critical summarization and contextualization and by the fact that the writing examined will be Hume's throughout. Jones, who developed a survey of philosophy, with lengthy passages from original sources, from *Hobbes to Hume*, puts it this way: 'In revising, as in originally writing this history, I have been guided by four principles – concentration, selectivity, contextualism and the use of original sources' (Jones, 1982, viii). In making use of literary analysis, themes such as those identified by Jones will be kept in mind. It is a question of emphasis rather than exclusion.

2 Textual thinking

Summarization and simplification: overview

A literary-based analysis of Hume's work is likely to be considered unusual. McCloskey learned early in the debate on the rhetoric of economics that increased 'understanding' (a product of rhetorical awareness) was not enough in its self to satisfy her critics. Discovering the pleasure of reading Hume – overcoming the initial struggle can take time – as he sets out in the *Treatise* and in his other writings, a dynamic process of intellectual discovery and development, is not, conventionally, enough. Developing a capacity to specify the development of Hume's method or methods of writing – Hume's arguments as captured by his argumentation – if it is successful would be considered a significant pay-off. An aim is to show the unity in Hume's thinking, a well-worked theme in recent years.

The literary methods most often found in the pursuit of the intellectual history of economics are those that focus on intertextuality: textual interpretation and summarization. How themes, ideas, concepts, vocabulary developed in Hume's work relates to the work that came before or after him is the subject of intertextual investigation. In this present work, little attention will be devoted to intertextual investigation in the sense of examining texts external to Hume's writing. Some references will be made to Cicero, to Cantillon and to Adam Smith and to approaches taken to Hume in history of thought texts. Such contextual considerations are unavoidable, it is a question of emphasis rather than of exclusion.

Intertextuality, in a different sense, will be present. Hume's work or body of work (his corpus) is made up of variety of texts (according to subject matter: philosophy, history, essays on criticism or politics) and text types (*Treatise*; dialogues; essays; collected essays; abstracts). The relationship between these various subject matters and types of text is in the wider literature has been, and to some extent, remains problematic.

Summarization in the history of economic thought is one strategy used to introduce concepts and analyses in extensive and often remote texts to new readers. This is an inescapable aspect of professional work, particularly, but not solely, with respect to the development of book-length histories of thought.

Summarization is also a literary process whose rules are not self-evident and which require some reflection upon. This is an issue that goes beyond a study of Hume's writing but it is significant for Hume, particularly because of the production of the *Abstract*.

In turns out that providing a general account of the process of summarization is not straightforward. The relationships between originating text, intended readership, authorial motivation/point-of-view and so on are not immediately transparent. This chapter, while using examples, will reflect on the process in general. The following chapter will look in detail at the *Abstract* and its relationship with the *Treatise* and subsequent writing.

Interpretation

Reading old texts is a key activity for any exercise in the history of economic thought. Any kind of reading that is concerned with increasing understanding will also appreciate the made-quality of a text, the element of craft that creates the unity and persuasiveness of the writing, even in works with a scientific or analytical purpose. Such distinctive shaping establishes the writing as the work of an individual author. So in dealing with Hume, it is clear that he changed his writing strategy as he moved from the *Treatise* to other writings. It is also equally clear that he retained the habits of mind that he developed in the pursuit of his philosophical ideas. The purpose of professional reading is not simply to gain an insight into the text but to change it, to translate it into terms that speak to the modern-day reader or that sustain an interpretation of the writing from (say) the point of view of the shifting perspective of contemporary economic or political concerns. Reading can be both analytical and integrative and is usually more efficient when guided by a clear purpose or purposes. A creative restatement of source texts is a key purpose (not sole purpose) of reading in the history of economic thought. In what follows here, the complex processes involved in the analysis of 'summarization' will be used as the means of reflecting upon interpretation. There are other ways of working with reading/interpretation (Henderson, 2006) but these will be side-stepped here.

Before looking closely at summarization, it is worthwhile, however, making a quick (and necessarily episodic or sketchy) review of how Hume has been interpreted in histories of economic thought, i.e. looking at the results of interpretation rather than at the process. Such texts are general, and normally introductory in their aims and interests and their authors have to make decisions concerning the significance of one school in relation to another, one writer in relation to another, one text in relation to another. Interpretation is accompanied by both summarization (in some form) and selection. Placing Hume in (say) the context of conventional schools of thought is difficult, placing him thematically in economic terms swamps his contribution. Placing him in the Enlightenment is possibly a more comfortable context, though in terms of the Scottish Enlightenment Hume often stood apart. Hume was his own man.

Thus if a recent and well-thought of text is taken, that of Backhouse's *The Ordinary Business of Life* (2002), Hume, though mentioned elsewhere in the volume, is treated in a discrete section that is three pages long, in the context of the Enlightenment, whereas Smith is given nine pages. This of course represents the size and impact of their respective outputs – Hume's economics writing is conventionally referred to in terms of the nine essays as selected by Rotwein. Sir James Steuart is treated in a section slightly longer than Hume's. The review of Hume's work is mainly concerned with his *Political Discourses* (or part thereof) and though some mention is made of his philosophical approach, no mention is made of the economic content and approach of the *Treatise*. Perforce the treatment is simplified and introductory. Notice is taken on Hume's interest in the state and state power, in a liberal approach to commerce, to luxury as incentives to produce beyond the subsistence mode and of Hume's ideas on money. Hume's influence on Smith is not prioritized in this section. This span of attention is similar to that found in Landreth and Colander (1994, 47), where Hume is depicted as 'a liberal mercantilist' and where the development of his ideas on money are linked to those of John Locke. Economic and political liberty is highlighted as another significant topic and the passage closes with reference to Hume's methodological distinction between 'is' and 'ought' but no overt mention is made of any possible methodological links between the *Treatise* (the *Treatise* is not mentioned) and his political and economic essays.

A similar pattern is found in much earlier histories of economic thought. Gide and Rist (1948) mention Hume in a number of places but do not devote any sustained writing to his works. Compared with Smith, the treatment is meagre, as it is in Spann (1910), Catlin (1962) and Routh (1989). Routh (1989, 81), ever critical of the classical school, interprets Hume as a complacent optimist who waxes 'lyrical about the virtues of merchants and the benefits of commerce'. There is a hint of the caricature about Routh's short comments, for Hume's approach to merchants is to be contrasted with his belief in the idleness and vanity of landlords. Routh underestimates Hume's concern with sources of instability, though he does not underestimate his conservatism. Although there is an inevitable reductionist element in all of the writers considered, Routh seems the most critical.

Schumpeter links Hume with Condillac and Hartley and makes generalizations about all three. Schumpeter makes the historical links of Hume's thought with Bacon. Newton, strangely enough, is not mentioned alongside Bacon. Hume is linked with the intellectual work of Hobbes, and through Hobbes (despite the fact that Hume is often writing against Hobbes) links made with the natural law theorists (Grotius and Pufendorf). Schumpeter is of the view that as far as Hume's economics is concerned his philosophy of human nature can be dispensed with as unnecessary for Hume's reasoning in economics. Hume in his eyes 'claims our attention in three quite different and almost unconnected incarnations' – an economist outside the natural law tradition, historian, philosopher and metasociologist (Schumpeter,

1954, f3, 124). Hume's relationship with the natural law tradition is textually complex but in the *Treatise* it is very clear when discussing justice that Hume seems to reject both natural law and social contract (*T*. 3.2.8.4 and also *ECPM*, 3.1.12) In the second *Enquiry* he praises Grotius in a footnote to appendix three and throughout makes implicit references to Cicero. Schumpeter blows hot (sometime very hot) and cold about Hume, as he also does with Smith.

Hume wrote his essays as free-standing works and these can easily be the subject of autonomous reading. There is, then, no need to read Hume's *Treatise* to read his essays. But it can be counter-argued that we better understand the significance of his method should we do so. Hume's views on causation (and getting the appropriate causal links) and the intellectual problems posed by many possible causes, analogy and the psychology of human motivation, and his use of history are of some relevance to the development of his characteristic approach to political and economic questions. Schumpeter's notion that Hume failed because there is no 'mother science' of human nature is at odds with the fact that Hume's empirical approach led, even if by stages, to modern economics, political science, modern psychology and the modern study of history. It also underestimates the relationship between 'economics' and 'ethics'.

Spiegel (1971) examines links and contrasts between Hume and the Physiocrats, Hume and Steuart, Hume and Smith, and treats of his methodology and his psychology with respect to motivation. Spiegel's treatment is potentially more interesting than most, and not simply because it is more expansive than that of more condensed versions. Spiegel's aim is to 'strengthen the link between economics and the humanities' – Hume is ideal for the context. His text is, in addition, an advanced text. The coverage of Hume is detailed, organized and thoughtful. Backhouse's text, which also aims to be a valid history in the sense that it is addressed to the contexts within which economic arguments were articulated, is shorter and hence, perforce, constrained. Spiegel has space to explore specific links, even if still in reduced form, to the *Treatise* as well as to outline the contrasts between Hume and the Physiocrats. Spiegel's insights are fruitful even though the notion of Hume is that of a very liberal mercantilist. Spiegel addresses 'Hume's cosmopolitanism' – his ability to take a European-wide or even system-wide view of economic welfare, as evidenced by 'Of the Jealousies of Trade' – as well as his sense of Hume as a development economist who sees beyond the restrictions of mercantilist thought. These are in addition to Hume as an innovative monetarist.

This short exercise suggests that in histories of economic thought, where summarization is essential given the space devoted to Hume, there are likely to be both enduring consistencies and inconsistencies in the interpretation of the Hume. Wennerlind and Schabas, while exempting the last 25 years, put the whole period thus: 'For much of the twentieth century, however, Hume was treated as a relatively minor figure in the history of economics, occupying the nebulous territory between mercantilism, physiocracy, and classical political economy' (Wennerlind and Schabas, 2008, 1).

Summarization

What constitutes a good summarization will depend on assumptions made about what is central to the unfolding meaning of a text, about the intended reader's previous knowledge and the purposes of the writing within which the summarization is lodged. The development of modern-day economics provides a shifting perspective on past economics writings, though Backhouse has argued that this is being replaced, in histories of economics, by a concern to place historic texts in their cultural contexts – a move that brings the content of histories closer to Spiegel's approach. Hume was less fashionable when monetarism was out of favour, more fashionable when it was in. Purpose is a matter of choice within a wider context.

It is often assumed that a summarization is from the reader's point of view essentially a simplification and so the notion of the simplification of an economic text needs some critical exploration. This can be the case, though it requires considerable skill on the part of the creator of the summarization to ensure that this is in fact so. Economics is a very particular kind of subject even with respect to the development of historically significant works such as Smith's *Wealth of Nations* or Hume's economic ideas as set out in the *Treatise*, or in his essays. It did not take long in the early days of the development of classical economics for concerns to start to emerge about the need for consistent terminology, for explanations of definitions and for a need for ensuring public access even to the non-professionalized discussion of early classical texts. Malthus was one of the first in Britain to explore the question of definition and Ganilh in France to do likewise (Henderson, 2008). It also did not take long before educators (women educators in the case of early nineteenth-century economics) to point to the 'difficult' language of complex treatises and to the need to create simplified or popular versions of contemporary economic argument. These examples, from beyond Hume's time, remind us simply that what works for the writer does not always work for all readers, and that the reader's participation in the generation (or otherwise) of 'meaning' remains significant.

Today's economics as presented in any standard introductory university level text is written in a complex technical vocabulary, Latinate in origin, and much of the introductory work both to the text as a whole and in opening chapters deals with the educational socialization of that vocabulary, giving way as the text develops to intensive use of the vocabulary and concepts in making elementary analysis. A simplification of writing in the later stages of a university level introductory economics text for a newcomer to the subject could very well be *longer* than the original text, as technical and semi-technical vocabulary may have to be expanded in order to make the meaning transparent. A summarization, if convention is anything to go by, must normally be *shorter* than the original text. Synonyms for summarization include terms such as 'survey', 'abstract' (though the modern notion of 'abstract' is that a formal *genre* whose rules can be taught) and even 'review'. This extends the scope, within the subject in general, beyond simply the *genre* of 'histories of economic thought'. Summarization is normally achieved by turning a long text in to a *smaller* text. This is not enough for the smaller text – itself a new text – must have a relationship with the original text such that the smaller text 'stands for', in some sense, the larger one.

A 'synecdoche' is a trope (one of the 'four master tropes' along with metaphor, metonymy and irony) in which a part stands for a whole, e.g. 'There were many masts in the harbour' where 'masts' stands for 'sailing ships'. This trope may be a useful *starting* point for considering 'summarization' though it is clear that the relationship 'masts/ships' is an authentic relationship in the sense that the mast is a physical part of a sailing ship and integral with it but 'summarization/originating text' need not be. Of course, in such a phrase, any deletion of information is merely verbal and these deletions can be quickly recovered by explication. What is taking place is reasonably immediate or transparent and the status of the deletions understood: a ship that was all sail and no hull cannot work. The same is not true for deletions in summaries taken from or standing for extensive written texts. Any recovery of deletions requires exploration from the one text to the other. To make the example relevant to a study of Hume's works, if the *Enquiries* are simplifications of the *Treatise* and if there are deletions, then it is only by a textual investigation that we can know what these deletions are. Lots of useful effort has gone in to tracing the deletions between the *Treatise* and the *Enquiries*. Work has been initiated on the *Abstract*. The intellectual status of the deletions cannot be worked out simply in the light of the fact that they are deletions. More information is required. Synecdoche only takes us so far.

Synecdoche can be problematic where it degenerates to 'caricature and stereotyping' (Miller, 1992, 64). Synecdoche carries with it the idea of substitution (Jasinski, 2001, 556). It does not, however, allude to a significant aspect of summarization which is that of reworking a text in the light of the social needs (real or imaginary) of the readers. Hume reworked many of his texts in the light of his perception of readers and their needs. This reworking can be understood within the general notion of rhetoric. With this proviso, it remains worthwhile to continue the exploration.

The notion that Smith wrote the bible of capitalism is a summary idea that is also a caricature – a highly reductive account of a complex set or system of ideas. Capital had not fully emerged as a significant and independent factor of production in Smith's time; even so, Smith was aware of the negative aspects of the division of labour and the need for policies on education to counteract its effects. Experts on Smith would argue that he evaluated economic and social issues with respect to, what Smith called 'the system of natural liberty'. It was only later that this system became reduced, in the popular imagination at least, to that of the notion of 'laissez-faire'. This latter idea is probably in the popular versions (say in the works of Harriet Martineau) at any rate also a caricature of 'the system of natural liberty', deleting the many considerations by which Smith modified his views. The notion that Hume was merely a sceptical philosopher who made no positive contribution is also a caricature that deletes Hume's resolution of extreme scepticism through his understanding of the force of natural human instinct. Buckle identifies a tendency in the history of philosophy to construct Hume's arguments, especially in the *Enquiry*, in terms of 'warring schools of thought: rationalism and empiricism' (Buckle, 2001, 35) and which constructs Hume as challenging 'rationalists'. Buckle sees this tendency as distorting Hume's understanding of the 'complex interrelations' between these two alleged camps.

When dealing with summarization the rhetorical issue is that of representation. Clearly in the representation of one large text by a smaller but related text, there will be 'gaps' and even 'misrepresentation', a fact highlighted by 'poststructuralist' accounts of (non-textual) representation (Jasinski, 2001, 486).

Summarization within a work is a task directed by the author and its aim is to reinforce key points in an argument or interpretation and implicitly at least to announce a new stage in the development of the text. Summarization within works by the author is known as 'accumulation', of which there are many instances in Hume's *Treatise*. This action is merely one of good manners: it helps readers know where they are in an argument. Because of his awareness, even in the *Treatise*, of the implications for his readers of his 'compleat chain of reasoning', Hume resorts to internal summarization, though he rarely gives advanced notice of the stages in an argument and of its final outcome.

Summarization from a work is usually, but not uniquely, a task undertaken by someone other than the author. An abstract, though often external to a given text, is usually prepared by the author of the full text or, in the case of journals, by professional writers. The issue is a general one but it is not a matter of indifference to the study of Hume, as Hume produced, in a separate work written in the third person, 'An Abstract of a Book lately Published, entitled, *A Treatise of Human Nature*, &c'. Norton claims that the 'Abstract' is not 'an abridgement of the *Treatise*, but an attempt to make this long work clearer by outlining the 'CHIEF ARGUMENT' of *Treatise* 1(Abs. title)' (Norton, 2000, 197). Norton points out that Hume published the *Abstract* before he published Book III. It is not an abstract in the modern sense but rather an attempt to guide readers through a complex work.

There are also then problems with the lexis: 'summary', 'abridgement', 'abstract' or even 'guide' (this is what Norton seems to be suggesting as the

Abstract's role) and many other synonyms with respect to the process as well as the product. The same sort of issue could arise in terms of the status of the *Enquiries* with respect to the *Treatise*. The distinctions are not merely verbal if there are different *genre* expectations about the work that is being done. Does it make a difference if we think of the *Abstract* as an abstract, a summarization or a book review? What is probably more important is an empirical investigation of the *Abstract* in relation to the other texts involved but this needs some sort of starting point. The *Abstract* will be treated here as in the general functional sense of a summary, i.e. the intentional remodelling of a work to meet an identifiable need on the part of an audience. Part of the detailed work of the next chapter (Chapter 3) will be to trace the links between the *Abstract*, the *Treatise* and the *Enquiries*.

Hume points out in the body of the work that 'The author has finished what regards logic, and has laid the foundation of the other parts in his account of the passions' (*T*, *Abstract*, 4). Hume on the Preface talks of his 'extraordinary' expectations in that his 'intentions are to render a larger work more intelligible to ordinary capacities, by abridging it' (*T*, Abstract Preface, 1). In the final paragraph he tells us how he achieved his aim: 'I have chosen one simple argument, which I have carefully traced from the beginning to the end'. An abridgement is a shorter, balanced version of a longer work that covers that longer work in its entirety. Producing an outline in the manner that Hume describes is an act of summarization (also of simplification) in which the basis for the summarization is spelled out.

Bazerman sees the process of abstraction as 'turning the article into an object' and of looking at a whole and then making a 'representation of it' (Bazerman, 1988, 220, 221). Hume engages in this objectifying process especially in the use of the third person to refer to the originator of the *Treatise*, and is a basic part of a controlling textual strategy that runs all the way through the writing and which will be illustrated here by two instances from many. The third person references to the author, creates a sense of distance and objectivity throughout the *Abstract* that is further reinforced by detail. The opening sentence is at once interesting and disingenuous: 'This book seems to be wrote upon the same plan with several other works that have had a great vogue of late years in *England*'. Other examples can be provided: 'thro' this whole book, there are great pretentions to new discoveries in philosophy; but if any thing can entitle the author to so glorious a name as that of an inventor 'tis the use he makes of the principle of association of ideas, which enters into most of his philosophy' (*T*, *Abstract*, 35). This sentence implies, for example, a sense of objectivity careful reading and hence judicious discrimination.

The notion of objectivity is further reinforced by the notion of active selection on the part of the author of the 'Abstract': 'The second principle, which I propose to take notice of, is with regard to geometry' (*T*, *Abstract*, 29). The distancing language here, in both cases cited, also reinforces the idea of selection ('thro' this whole book/but if anything …'; 'which I propose to take notice of') that is essential to summarization. There are numerous instances of language which suggest careful and justifiable selectivity. At the end of paragraph four, for example, he writes: 'We shall therefore chiefly confine ourselves to his explication of our reasonings from cause and effect. If we can make this intelligible to the reader, it may serve as a specimen for the whole' (*T, Abstract*, 4). A part here stands for the whole. Hume selects and seemingly independently recommends his own work and frames how the original should be read. He is very careful, for example, to show that the position of the 'very sceptical' philosophy is modified by human nature: 'Our author insists upon several other sceptical topics; and upon the whole concludes, that we assent to our faculties, and employ our reason only because we cannot help it. Philosophy would render us entirely *Pyrrhonian*, were not nature too strong for it' (*T*, Abstract, 27).

The sense of 'part' is with respect to any summary is problematic in the context of 'representation' and limits the help that we can derive from synecdoche. The 'new' text must have a very distinctive relationship with the source text. The new and smaller text is made up of parts (in some sense) of the larger text. It is arrived at by a process of actual deletion (though the originating text is left intact) or may be even involving 'deflection', a kind of turning away from material that is difficult to handle. Representation, in the poststructuralist depiction, can '*reveal* as well as *conceal*' (Jasinski, 2001, 486). Metaphor, and hence the other master tropes, perhaps with the exception of irony, reveals or highlights the positive analogies and suppresses negative analogies. We have to be on our guard. Popular words from everyday conversation, uninformed by poststructuralist theories, for the process – 'reducing', 'condensing' or even 'boiling-down' – can carry a sense of intellectual disapproval. Kruses' disapproval of Hume's desire to 'popularize' is based on this sense of intellectual reduction. Jones, in reflecting on the needs of a survey text and of students, rejects 'boiled-down' summaries in favour of the idea that it is better to understand a few critical ideas than 'to be superficially acquainted with a great many' (Jones, 1969, viii). He opts for extensive extracts rather than summaries. In the cooking process (the unifying metaphor here?) such activities add to the flavour of the dish but they also, by implication, tend to make the final 'dish' easier to swallow.

A good summarization therefore creates a new text that has, however, an authentic, justifiable and traceable relationship with the originating text, even if it also distorts. In principle someone who has read the summary could then read the source text and find the 'meaning' indicated by the summary in the processing (reading and reflection) made of the source text – Hume's intention as set out in the Preface to the *Abstract*. There is always the possibility that summarization leads to an 'authoritarian' reading in that the summary gives rise 'to a right way to read a work of literature' (Miller, 1993, 100). Clearly, there is a difference in intention between helping to provide a 'handle' on a text that eases the novice in to the work and the provision of a 'monopoly-view'. Ideally, a reader will also find other 'meanings', some of which may be in conflict with the 'meaning' predicted by the summary or will at the very least restore the 'deletions'. In principle, someone who has read the summary should find the reading of the source text is made easier in some way.

However, if a summarization excludes all source text efforts to socialize the text, to make the content familiar and interesting to the reader or to gain the reader's assent, a summarization may not feel, even if shorter, like a simplification, to the novice reader. The dimensions of a persuasive text such as its concern for audience, its deliberative strategies and dialectic structures (for example Hume's consistent use of questions to develop and test his ideas in the *Treatise*) and its attractiveness as writing – what makes the writing interesting and special and perhaps even problematic for a modern-day reader – may well be what is deleted. Hume's *Treatise* is a written product that is both located in time and taken as having enduring meaning. The issue of what is deleted, and why, is something that will need to be considered.

No systematic writing on historical texts of interest in the intellectual history of economics can proceed without some summarization. This is not the issue. Scholarship is no longer concerned solely with annotating the writings of the masters as intended to be in the Middle Ages. It is surprising how little reflection there is, within the discipline, on the nature and purpose of summarization, given that the types of texts normally subject to summarization are texts that are 'rich' – in the sense that a range of interpretations are possible – or are texts that were constructed to persuade readers to view or construct the world in a particular way. Hume's *Treatise* is one such example – and many of Hume's persuasive strategies are easily identified – as is Smith's *Wealth of Nations*. Given the range of interpretations available on those works (both overall and with respect to significant parts), there is obviously a need to reflect upon and justify any particular exercise in summarization.

Equally, the nature of the 'whole' is to be brought into consideration when considering a part/whole relationship (Miller, 1992, 64). Is the summary a summary of what is written (the 'what' of the text) or what is intended (the 'why' of the text) or of the rhetoric (the 'how' of the text) or of any combination of these possible textual elements?

The purpose and subsequent use made of the summarization (either by the reader or the writer) may vary. The writer may intend the summarization to be used as a means of encouraging the novice reader to approach, thereafter, the originating text, as Hume, for example, clearly intended when producing the *Abstract*. Or the summary writer may be developing the new text as a means of bypassing the source text so that together they can explore a topic that moves beyond the originating text in some way. Readers (and authors) are free to choose either way. Hume's *Abstract* could serve, whatever Hume's intentions, the reader either way according to choices made. Reading the *Abstract* is not an equivalent experience to a full reading of *Treatise* 1, but a considered reading of the *Abstract* will provide some insight into a key concept (causality) in Hume's philosophy. One of the aims of this volume is to help those coming new to a study of Hume to approach a sustained reading of Hume in the original or through sustained pieces taken from the corpus.

Take as another example of the nature and purpose of summarization, Rostow's interest in the development of growth theory. His vantage point is the growth theory of his day. He starts with Hume, and it is useful to be reminded that Hume's concerns can be integrated or interpreted in this way. Hume's essays are concerned with topics related to economic growth and (for example) the role of luxury in the stimulation of agricultural production for the market rather than merely for subsistence. Hume is also concerned with the growth of an active middle class and hence with the link between economic growth and the significant Enlightenment topic of progress, including moral progress. Interpretation requires a context and in this case a double context: that of the originating work and that of the new work. Even if he had not justified Hume as his starting point there is an implicit message that there is nothing of much interest with respect to growth theory before Hume, and not simply so far as Rostow is concerned. Conventionally, modern economic thought is taken to start with Hume (Cantillon has been pushed vigorously in more recent literature) and growth theory is a modern subject that arises historically out of the experience of reflecting upon sustained and noticeable growth.[1] As Rostow is interested in the development of growth theory then any presentation, interpretation or summarization of Hume in Rostow's work must therefore reflect both Hume's originating texts or ideas (in some way) while at the same time be directly related to the development of Rostow's main interest.

Rostow's aim is to 'survey growth theory from the mid-eighteenth century to the late 1980s' (Rostow, 1990, 3). Survey work or survey articles summarize a whole series of texts and can be readily found in the field. Rostow (1990, 5) sets out the criteria for the summarization in terms of a series of questions about the originating views and a relationship to some 'noneconomic doctrine' or philosophy; the economic experience that the theorists observed and the relationship to their thought; and did they use either implicitly or explicitly the basic growth equation.[2]

Hume's work is summarized and redescribed in terms of a relationship with the 'universal equation or production function' and Hume's thought is a means to an end rather than an end it itself. This is not a criticism of Rostow, merely a specification of how Rostow and Rostow's intended readers could relate to Hume's original texts. Rostow makes his survey and its methods and purposes as transparent as he can and this is methodologically appropriate. He is aware of the potential reductionism. He demonstrates his professionalism by setting out his criteria and we understand that although there are distortions, they are useful or purposeful. They are open and can be argued over. Given the choice between 'true' and 'useful' as investigated by Burke (1945) then Rostow can be seen as choosing 'useful'. Summary in this sense can be thought of as a type of hinge that allows for a two-way movement, one swinging back to the originating text and another pointing away to the new and developing text, constructed, in this case, for a different, but not radically different, purpose.

A similar kind of phenomenon is found in relation to Hume's *Abstract*, which aims 'to render a larger work more intelligible to ordinary capacities, by abridging it' though here the new text is to help readers negotiate significant aspects of the originating text. At the same time Rostow makes (limited) use of sustained passages from Hume's writing, contextualized by also using sustained passages from secondary sources on Hume. This illustrates another aspect of the writing of the history of economic ideas and that is that works primarily based on summarization cannot dispense entirely with the originating texts. Othmar Spann, a pioneer figure in the discipline, put it this way in 1910: '... in economics no less than in philosophy we are often concerned with passing judgment on extremely intricate and difficult trains of reasoning. There are cases in which we must let the masters speak for themselves' (Spann, 1930, 7). Difficult texts, however, rarely speak for themselves and the intellectual historian's role is to assist with exposition and interpretation and mediate between an old text, other related old texts and modern considerations. The general significance of Spann's point is that the relationship between a summary and an originating text is always under some tension as different interpretations (readings, the 'stuff' of analysis) are always possible. It is almost as if the links need to be re-established by direct quotes to maintain stability or authenticity.

Hume's writing in economics may not exhibit the complexities of modern economics (though it is bound by the very nature of conventions in writing to have complexities of its own) but the issue, that a summarization may not be also a simplification at least in language terms, still stands. Summarization by implication is smaller in length than an original and it helps where it is in fact simpler than the original.

Hume's writing after the *Treatise* is shaped within a particular understanding of intended reader and so on. Neither summarization nor simplification can capture the many layers of meaning. An intention of summarization is to assist the development of a knowledge basis that makes the handling of ideas in the text, at some future stage, easier to access. Another possible intention is to sort out what is of lasting theoretical value in the text from what is ephemeral or historically conditional. A third intention is to make a whole sweep of ideas available in a manageable form, again so that the reader is exposed to a range of ideas in a more effective way than reading through a huge collection of primary material. The significance of summarization is that a lot of ground can be covered in very quick time, though aspects of the original are lost both intentionally and inadvertently.

By focusing on the original text, or on selected passages of text, the new reader encounters that complexity in many of its aspects, even if he or she can only grasp some of the complexity in an initial or indeed in any one reading. Grasping at 'meaning' is more complex, though the effort (say) that students make to understand becomes more intense. Some of the problems inherent in summarization can be overcome by looking at the original text. This leads to a direct and more intense exposure to the work under review but is clearly impractical for newcomers to Hume or Smith. If the aim is to increase the reader's capacity to operate independently with an author's works, then that capacity is not likely to develop all at once. To read an economics text with understanding requires adoption of a set of schema that develops to match the needs of becoming a reader of economics. The same is true for approaching historical writing in political economy. It takes time to develop what might be called the 'matching criteria' as the actual reader of a historical text comes, more and more, to resemble the implied reader. This is a problem that Hume thought about when he set out to write his essays, and his thinking is encapsulated in 'Of Essay Writing', which will be the subject of investigation as part of Chapter 6.

Selectivity

Focusing on the original text or collection of texts brings its own problems or dilemmas for there is the same sort of relationship to be considered. Under normal circumstances a selected text stands for other texts found in a bigger corpus. Synecdoche is, once again, relevant. Such reading/analysis can only ever be of particular passages in particular contexts. The method must therefore be highly selective, and this problem is one that confronts those scholars in the history of economic thought who prepare 'readers' or selected anthologies. Samuels and Medema put the selection problem this way: 'The task of putting together a reader ... is like confronting an endless smorgasbord of delights when on a highly restrictive diet ...' (Medema and Samuels, 2003, x). Their justification (or 'hope') is that what has been selected is 'sufficient to provide an overview of some of the major themes' as developed by 'giants'. They acknowledge that the selections 'are no substitute for reading the original works in their entirety', which is no doubt pious but only relevant if the reader is going for 'mastery' rather than with, for example, 'familiarity'. Studying a reader can be a means to an end or an end it itself. Their method of selection has an empirical element: course reading lists, discussion with colleagues and, of course, personal judgment or 'intuition'. Their readings on Hume consist of his 'three classic essays on money, interest and the balance of trade' (Medema and Samuels, 2003, 133) or what could be thought of as clearly defined economic topics. It is in fact difficult to separate Hume's economics from his political essays, as Hume's own definition of politics is that of 'men cooperating in society' and hence economics is implied.

Rogers' anthology on the topic of *Self-Interest* functions in a similar basis though Rogers provides a justification for inclusion (texts supportive of a 'broad perspective') but also for exclusion ('the crowding of texts in the early modern period implied even stricter selectivity') (Rogers, 1997, 4). Rogers provides two extracts from the *Treatise* and three from the *ECPM*. A similar appeal to that found in Medema and Samuels, almost in defiance of the notion of a division of labour, is made to the reader, who is requested to 'delve into the full range of historical materials on self-interest' and to treat the anthology as 'an initial step'. Readers, naturally, will make other choices depending on their purposes. Both Medema and Samuels and Rogers provide careful contextualization for each individual author selected. Both provide a direct engagement with originating texts.

If we consider Hume's *Treatise* alone, then it is simply not possible to use a sustained textual analysis of the kinds considered in this work to be presented and assimilated in the span of one book. To make the idea of refocusing on the text viable as an educational exercise requires selectivity. Selection must be guided by some principles either implicit or explicit and by judgment. Suppose the aim is to increase the familiarity or mastery (two ideas that are not identical) of the author's key ideas or of work as a whole. Passages for analysis need to be selected on the grounds that they are in some sense significant to the development of key concepts or for the development of the work as a whole. This leads to a further problem, for the significance of particular passages will depend on judgments that the selecting author makes about such passages. The selecting author is not neutral with respect to the target author's work. This is inevitable and indeed it is part of what we hope, normally, that an intended author will do: use his or her professional judgment and knowledge of the subject to guide the development of our thinking or to assist in shaping some of the schema required to undertake a sustained and direct engagement of, in this case, Hume's writing.

Blackburn, who provides the novice reader with an experience of engaging in short readings and a guided evaluation of Hume's text, identifies then 'ten of the most important moments in Hume's philosophy' and chooses as the integrative element Hume's significant concept of the 'the science of human nature' (Blackburn, 2008, 3). Other quotes in opening positions refer to empiricism (all simple ideas derived from simple impressions), causation, perception, the self, passion and morals, conventions and obligation, miracles, natural religion and taste. He admits a leading quote from one of the essays 'Of the Standard of Taste' (an interesting demonstration of Hume's empirical method as applied to aesthetics), and refers to others. Blackburn and Jones generally agree on the core areas to be considered, but there is in fact very little overlap in the passages that they choose to select as illustrative. Blackburn does not refer to the economic writing in any direct way other than in the Introduction, where he states that the foundation to all of Hume's writing, including economics and politics, is the 'science of human nature' (Blackburn, 2008, 3). Schumpeter's judgment, in this respect, has long been left behind.

Blackburn's work is summative, evaluative but also approving not only of Hume's ideas but of his later style. He says of the *ECPM* that it has 'an air of relaxed sunshine' and approves of Hume's desire to reach a wide audience. Historically, not everyone has. The introduction to the series makes it clear that it is offering guides, in the form of 'first-hand encounters' and 'keys that will enable readers to go on to make discoveries of their own' ('Editor's foreword' in Blackburn, 2008, vii). Once again the pointer is to the original texts but given the degree of explication and critical comment there is also an implicit pointer to secondary works. Hume speaks but he does not speak on his own.

Selectivity is not entirely avoided by summarization (think of the problem of how much or how little detail is required) nor is it avoided where use is made of one-sentence quotes from (say) supporting passages. It is as true for single-sentence quotes as it is for sustained passages that context alters meaning. This was illustrated in the previous chapter in terms of Macaulay's ironic view of Hume as an economist. Contextualization is essential, either textually or culturally. Macaulay builds Hume up in order to cast himself, rather than Hume, as having the superior insight into the question of the consequences of the size of the national debt. With writers such a Hume and Smith the aphorisms and epigrams must be carefully examined in context. Meaning is rarely in a given sentence, being rather constructed within a sweep of sentences in a surrounding discourse. What is required is a justification for the selection of specific passages and the omission of others but also contextualization of the passages chosen. It is difficult to exemplifying the possibilities but in general terms some justification of the selection in terms of relevance to the development of the original point of view being explored. In the case of the work presented here, a key aim is to textually illustrate the significance the arguments in the *Treatise* to the development of Hume's approach to social and political analysis over time. Some passages will have more relevance than others (and the decision is not clear-cut) and the decision may not be independent of the imagination or of the experience of the intended author.

Another possibility in general that can help guide the selection is the notion of 'typicality'. If we are interested in argumentation then there has to be some assurance that the passages selected are 'typical' in some sense. Circularity has to be avoided, as what is taken as typical will in part be determined by past experience of what has been seen to be typical. Refocusing on the text ought at least to have the possibility some critical edge with respect to the established representation of Hume's writing. If at least some conventional judgments are not challenged then the exercise is simply educational rather than also scholarly.

The notion of 'typicality' can be based on the assumption that arguments and the form through which they are delivered (sometimes called 'argumentation') are repeated throughout a text. Hume, to take a very simple example, says that all knowledge is based upon comparisons. Even if he is referring to similarities perceived in the brain (inferences from 'cause' to 'effect' based upon the 'the comparison of ideas' or upon analogies experienced through the repetition of phenomena) it is a safe bet that the comparative method will be used to organize sustained textual episodes when dealing with 'matters of fact'.

Hume also makes other significant methodological statements in the Introduction to the *Treatise*, where, as he claims, his 'design in the present work is sufficiently explain'd' (Advertisement). It would be cheating to take the word 'design' and apply it directly to textual patterning but it is clear in the Introduction that his aims (his sense of 'design') is to work on philosophical ideas in a particular way that he sees as the 'experimental method' by gathering together experimental data (everyday experiences considered from different angles or points of view) to handle the data in a scientific and inductive manner and to take nothing for granted. Such a 'design' has textual implications. It could be predicted from these statements alone that the text will engage the reader in repeated and systematic ways.

It would be very surprising if the *Treatise*, in the light of what Hume says does not frequently utilize examples, especially examples of human behaviour or of the human condition, in either historical or contemporary terms. Even without prior knowledge of the text it could be suggested that 'taking nothing for granted' implies a certain rigorous even exhaustive quality to the writing or the supply of an amplitude of reasons. There is also Hume's commitment to 'a compleat chain of reasoning', a commitment that recurs in various places. He refers to the 'chain of reasoning' even in the Preface to the *Abstract* where he thinks that it causes problems for inexperienced readers. It is interesting that he hardly refers to such a chain in his later writing. Even in the text of the *Abstract* he contrasts ancient philosophers who were more content with 'greatness of soul' rather than with 'following out steadily a chain of propositions, or forming the several truths into a regular science' (*T*, Abstract, 1) It may not be wholly transparent what this term implies for it is neither a technical term in Hume nor is it predictive of a familiar textual pattern such a compare and contrast. It could suggest a 'series structure' as identified as one of the textual patterns commonly found in argumentation. It could be something other than that, such as a recurrent logic but whatever it is it is suggestive of textual design. It will be the subject of one of the chapter's later in this work. It does seem to suggest a series of stages in an argument (one 'link' at a time) that is sustained over a number of stages (a number of such 'links' in a chain) and which unite 'one common principle' with 'another'.

Hume is very clear in the *Abstract* about the implications with respect to argument: 'If in examining several phaenomena, we find they resolve themselves into one common principle, and can trace this principle into another, we shall at last arrive at those few simple principles, on which all the rest depend' (*T*, Abstract, 1). At the very least it suggests then that readers may be expected to carry forward information, particularly with respect to principles, from one extended episode in the unfolding argument, to another. It also suggests that Hume will be aware of the need for 'accumulation', i.e. the gathering up (accumulation) of key points in summary form at predictable moments in the text. Another term is 'recapitulation'.

'Typical passages' then, for the time being, could be taken as passages that evidence Hume's Newtonianism or Hume's rhetorical strategies for presenting Newtonian thinking in the context of 'the science of man'. Or they could demonstrate how Hume was responding to intellectual problems of his own day. Hume insisted on a relationship between 'abstruse philosophy' and everyday life, the context for his essays. For the *Treatise*, there is some agreement that the 'science of man' is a significant overarching context. This is an interpretative stand, a kind of anticipation of patterns in the text, but one that points back to Hume's own text by way of justification. It assumes that Hume will stick to the style suggested by his statements, which then serve us as stable structures of reason. Such structures make textual moves predictable. Whether he does or does not maintain the patterns can be subjected to textual exploration. If the original text were Smith's *Wealth of Nations* and if 'typical' passages were to be selected from that work then a justification, similar to that of Rostow, could be built around the selection of passages that illustrate Smith's theory of growth.

Reading Hume: textual methods

The work in the rest of the book will be based around the notion that Hume did not abandon his philosophy but extended it through *genres* other than the serially published treatise. The idea of a *genre* is not self-evident, especially when *genres* were in evolution as it were. Hume contributed to the development of the essay as *genre*. If Hume had a particular set of communication goals in writing a treatise there may be some difficulties in imagining that he had the same communicative goals in writing an essay. An essay may be expected to share more communicative goals with other essays rather than with a serially published treatise (this and other things relating to *genre* is adapted loosely from Swales (1990)). The developing *genre* will itself change the style of communication so there must at least be some acknowledgement of audience and expectations. Not only that, but Hume wrote over a span of time during which by his own judgment he matured as an author. This growing maturity can be witnessed in the 'tone' of the *Abstract* (mature, measured, distanced) compared with that of the *Treatise* (by his own account full of youthful enthusiasm).

In switching *genres*, Hume is already writing in a different way. His notion of what is was to write history is driven by his philosophical interests concerning human motivation and observation, but details of the style and argumentation will vary over the *genres*. His notion of history remained significant in the market for two generations though there were others available only to be fully challenged in the early nineteenth century by Macaulay. Hume also took the essay and used it to introduce a wider range of topics into 'polite conversation', including political and economic subject matter that was or had been otherwise the 'stuff' of faction where discussion was likely to induce conflict and so to end with powdered wigs on the green. He also used the essay format to discuss historical themes, to write philosophical sketches and to treat of criticism or aesthetics. The *Treatise* since it is a treatise had to conform to some extent at least to what was at the time expected of a treatise. His readers will have expected it to conform to the requirements of a philosophical treatise and Hume was not able to conform in this respect. His essays had to achieve their communicative purpose in a short span of reading time. In looking a Hume's arguments and argumentation then, it is essential to keep in mind that the notion of *genre* suggests that there are implications for 'structure, style, content and intended audience' (Swales, 1990, 58). That he pursued his philosophical ideas on human nature by other means is not a new idea, but it has not been fully explored either textually in terms of characteristic argumentation in Hume or with respect to samples drawn from the whole of his economic reasoning. The process will not be neutral, as the analyses will be carried out within self-contained chapters that have each a theme, each theme contributing towards the whole. How significant this is remains to be seen.

In a general sense the following chapters will explore, using samples of text, the literary and philosophical unity of Hume's work. A main concern will be with what is called 'argumentation' and this will be seen as an area of concern that incorporates questions of logic (here meaning informal logic but also Hume's 'logic' as set out in Book one of the *Treatise*); dialectic (here meaning Hume's characteristic use of questions to further the analysis); rhetoric (here encompassing Hume's concern for audience). The exploration of argumentation is not an end it itself but is rather a means to an end. Sustained passages will be analysed within the context of specific chapters addressing specific aspects of Hume's work, e.g. a survey of the economic content (broadly defined) in the *Treatise*; exploration of the notion of a 'compleat chain of reasoning'; comparisons between passages with some economic content in the *Treatise* and *Enquiries*; an examination of his 'economic' essays to reveal linkages with his philosophical writing.

That Hume produced persuasive texts is not a contentious issue. Box and Danford both attest to the significance of Hume's rhetoric as does Richetti. It is not unreasonable therefore to search for Hume's characteristic ways or ways of developing arguments in written form. Argumentation is taken to mean written communication that is designed to persuade through reason giving. Hume can be taken to be, even from the limited material examined thus far, a writer who is self-consciously interested in the nature and success of the process of communicating. Hume rejected the formal reason of the 'school men' and displaced the search for certainty with probabilistic reasoning.

In trying to communicate his understanding of this type of reasoning he produced a primary text that was seen as filled with paradoxes and which lacks closure or at least the kinds of closure that his contemporaries were accustomed to look for in a philosophical work. He produced complex arguments over long stretches of text, even in his own judgment. If there is a typical pattern of moves in Hume's writing, or parts of Hume's writing, not adequately specified before, this will be a useful addition to knowledge, especially if such patterns can be shown to exist throughout his writing.

The analysis will be supported by 'close reading', and will provide an encounter with Hume as he engages in his philosophical activity but directed towards a preliminary exploration of the origins in the *Treatise* of Hume's economic and political thinking (the basis for selectivity. The technique calls for close attention to the lexical and other linguistic details of the text. Such a reading demands working with extracts, hence the amount of time that has been already devoted to selection. A series of such close readings can lead to understanding of inter and intra textual relationships but strictly speaking it is a method of reading and hence of analysis that isolates one text from another. To some extent, without any formal statement of the process, the method has been used with respect to the analyses of the Advertisements and to the *Abstract* that have already been presented. The *Abstract* will be examined in greater detail and compared in its approach to fuller passages in the *Treatise*.

3 Reading Hume's *Treatise* through the *Abstract*

Hume's economics, as will be shown in Chapter 4, originates in the *Treatise* but his publicly successful economics writing also originates in a rhetorical turn (see Chapter 6 for the development of his essays, an extension of the rhetorical turn considered here) initiated when Hume contemplated the failure of the *Treatise* to find an audience. The extent of Hume's reflections on this failure has significant consequences for the format and presentation of his economic thought.

This chapter will examine Hume's textual strategy in the writing of the *Abstract* of his *Treatise* and compare it with his strategy in writing the originating text and other later writing. The chapter will first consider the notion, mentioned several times by Hume in the *Treatise,* of a 'compleat chain of reasoning' as providing a key to the textual method used by Hume in the conceptualization of the writing of the *Treatise*. It will then consider the *Abstract* and the structure and insights of the *Abstract* with respect both to the *Treatise* and to the *Enquiries*. It differs from that undertaken by Beauchamp concerning sentence fragments from the *Treatise* and found in the *ECPM* in that the mediating instrument is the *Abstract*.

'A compleat chain of reasoning'

David Hume was disappointed with the lack of attention paid to the *Treatise* on its first appearance and later rejected the work on the basis, among other things, of what he came to see as its prolixity and juvenile qualities. Some philosophers have tended, in the past, to look at the *Treatise* as a work of epistemology and overlook the social philosophy – the analysis of human social potential from the point of view of both the understanding and the passions – that the work contains. 'Morals, politics and criticism' (economic considerations are included implicitly within the definition of political) are a full part of Hume's intentions as he makes clear in the 'Advertisement to Books I and II' as well as in the work's long title. At the same time recognition of Hume's literary aspirations has tended to be focused on his later writings, especially on his political and economic essays. Kemp Smith, confirmed by later researchers, has shown that although

Hume modified his philosophical views, the *Treatise* remains significant as a source for much of his later ideas, even these are presented in an altered form, in just about all aspects of his writing (Kemp Smith, 1941; Whelan, 1985; for a contrasting view see Danford, 1990, 27). Hume also held literary aspirations for the *Treatise*.

In the Introduction proper to the *Treatise* Hume dismissed 'eloquence' or 'speculation' (armchair reasoning *a priori*) and promoted 'reason' (i.e. reasoning from observation or empirical evidence). His aim, in setting out a 'compleat chain of reasoning', is the development of 'the science of man' through observation and experimentation:[1]

> We must therefore glean up our experiments in this science from a cautious observation of human life, and take them as they appear in the common course of the world, by men's behaviour in company, in affairs, and in their pleasures. Where experiments of this kind are judiciously collected and compar'd, we may hope to establish on them a science, which will not be inferior in certainty, and will be much superior in utility to any other human comprehension.
>
> (*T*, Introduction, 10)

This is an ambitious agenda and suggests that the 'science of man' would match the achievement of Newtonian physics with respect to the certainty of its conclusions and outstrip it with respect to its usefulness (a quality Hume admired strongly). It is possible to take the notion of the science of man as some superior and overarching social science but Hume is concerned with putting moral philosophy, as he or Adam Smith understood the subject matter, on a new basis. Hume's approach is based on 'a cautious observation' – caution, careful consideration and reconsideration of the first appearance of things, being essential.

It is useful to also consider that Hume held that: 'All kinds of reasoning consist in nothing but a *comparison*, and a discovery of those relations, either constant or inconstant, which two or more objects bear to each other (*T*, 1.3.2.2). There are two aspects to Hume's interest in comparison. The mind internally works by comparisons and associations. Externally, observation and matters of fact can be understood by the comparative method.

Hume tells us that the experimental method and the comparative method will be significant. His interest, manifest in his way of writing, according to Box, is to 'excite the calm passion of curiosity' in his readers by 'helping them to enjoy the experience of the investigation' (Box, 1990, 58). This chapter will show that although the notion of a 'compleat chain of reason' is related to Hume's version of Newtonianism, the notion itself can yield insight into Hume's textual organization with respect to the *Treatise* and has significance for the specification of Hume's textual strategy. It provides an integrative framework for his commitment to developing on the part of his readers the empirical way of thinking. It is this extensive textual organization, based on the application and reapplication, of elements in his system of thinking, and implied by his notion of a very strict induction, that is effectively abandoned in his writing, outside of completing the *Treatise*, after the production of the *Abstract*. Hume's essays, including the chapters in his *Enquiries*, are, more-or-less, self-contained and adopt argument by example, in the Ciceronian manner, in place of a more fully specified complete inductive process.

Reference to a 'long chain of reasoning' is also to be found, as expected, in the opening paragraph of Book III, where Hume outlines the problems of writing and reading philosophy ('all abstruse reasoning'). The problem of maintaining 'conviction' is 'still more conspicuous in a long chain of reasoning, where we must preserve to the end the evidence of the first propositions...' (*T*, 3.1.1.1). It is clear that he hopes that his 'reasonings concerning *morals* will collabourate whatever has been said concerning the *understanding* and the *passions*'. Hume's use of the notion of 'a chain of reasoning' in the first Advertisement is not, then, accidental. Hume is aiming at a way of thinking and hence also of writing that promotes order, induction, logical sequence, clarity and the accumulation of evidence and application ('new force as it advances') and integration of ideas.[2] Any chain is only as strong as its weakest link. The conceptualization commits Hume to an exhaustive work.

That he had self-consciously thought out the implications of a sustained 'chain' there can be little doubt. In discussing 'reasonings concerning cause and effect' Hume also calls upon the notion of a chain:

> 'Tis obvious all this chain of argument or connexion of causes and effects, is at first founded on those characters or letters, which are seen or remember'd, and that without the authority either of the memory or senses our whole reasoning wou'd be chimerical and without foundation. Every link in the chain wou'd in that case hang upon another; but there wou'd not be any thing fix'd to one end of it, capable of sustaining the whole; and consequently there would be no belief nor evidence. And this actually is the case with all *hypothetical* arguments, or reasonings upon a supposition; there being in them, neither any present impression, nor belief of real existence.
>
> (*T*, 1.3.4.2)

This statement illuminates Hume's understanding of Newton's desire, to avoid hypotheses. Hume's sense of the word is clear: reasoning upon supposition rather than reasoning based on 'phenomena' (Kupyers, 1966, 16). The modern sense of the term carries the notion of an idea that is set up to be explored experimentally, as part of a series of experiments in a research project, though Hume's search for analogies sometimes corresponds to just that. It also shows that Hume's idea of a chain is not merely decorative for here it is integrated to substantive matter in the text. Hume does in fact sometimes use the term hypothesis in this modern sense. What is fixed to the end (i.e. the beginning or stating point) is experience. Hume is clear that *'all our simple ideas are in the first appearance are deriv'd from simple impressions which are correspondent to them, and which they exactly represent'*. (*T*, 1.1.1.8). What is in the mind concerning matters of fact has its origins in the senses. Hume's empiricism is founded upon the notion that thought, human understanding, can be subjected to the sensory test. However, the senses may or may not lead to accurate knowledge of the world. In practice, in the course of clear thinking, what may be fixed at one end of any given chain of reasoning, i.e. any investigative episode in the *Treatise*, is a clearly formulated question, arrived at by inference, or, textually more frequently, pairs of questions that are subjected to exhaustive investigation. With respect to direct human experience, distance produces a reduction in 'vivacity' (*T*, 1.3.13.3), a conviction can only be maintained by 'firm imagination'.

In furthering the discussion of historical evidence, Hume states clearly that historical proofs are 'perfectly resembling'. When Hume is exploring propositions about the *consequences* of human nature, he often draws examples from historical as well as from contemporary experience. He also is, on the basis of his view as the constancy and universality of human nature, read backwards from contemporary evidence to under-reported historical circumstances: like causes will give rise to like consequences. This is an operation that he uses, for example, later, in writing 'Of the Populousness of Ancient Nations'.

The only area of knowledge in which it is possible to have certainty is with respect to algebra and arithmetic: 'the only sciences in which we can carry on a chain of reasoning to any degree of intricacy, and yet preserve a perfect exactness and certainty' (*T*, 1.3.1.5).

Hume's claim to Newtonianism has, of course, long been recognized (Kemp Smith, 1941, 53–62) and the sense of senses in which it is related to or in contradiction or even in competition with Newton is still being established. A close analysis of the implications of a 'chain of reasoning' for the content and structure of Hume's writing is not so readily available.[3] Box for example, as far as I can establish, mentions the phrase only in passing (Box, 1990, 85 and indirectly 99). Given these considerations it seems reasonable to undertake an analysis of Hume's output to reveal the way in which Hume structures his writing in order to execute his argument and achieve his aims. If the concern is with his Logic, i.e. with the implications of Book One for the 'science of human nature' then any short investigation needs to be restricted to '*identity, the situations in time and place*, and *causation*' (*T*, 1.3.2.1). The concern here is therefore with both structure and content. The idea of examining structure is significant especially when we consider the attempts to base knowledge upon induction. Hume is aware, in as much as he had read Cicero, and other classical writers, of the requirements of formal argument.[4] Newton may be the source of his scientific thinking but in putting this into writing, other influences are possible. Hume was aware that the argument from example is an established form of argument, supported by and developed by Cicero. Scientific induction, if we keep Newton in mind, requires something stronger. Ideally, it requires a complete consideration of all related aspects of the phenomenon under investigation. In the *Treatise*, but not, as will be shown in due course, in the essays, Hume attempts to go beyond merely selecting instances.

The notion of a long 'chain of reasoning' is one that was shared by other writers, including, later, Hume's friend Adam Smith. Of course, the dangers of overgeneralization were recognized. Smith's students and contemporaries are said to have admired Smith's capacity to unite a number of ideas/problems under one long chain of reasoning, punctuated, since experience was significant, with engaging examples (Henderson, 2006). Think of Smith's audacious use of the division of labour as a simple causal explanation for a number of different economic phenomena. In his *LRBL* Smith talks of Newton and of the Newtonian method of accounting 'for the several phenomena, connecting all together by the same chain' and, again, in the same passage, 'It gives us pleasure to see the phenomena which we reckoned the most accountable, all deduced from some principle (commonly a well-known one) and all united in a chain, far superior to what we feel from the unconnected method, where everything is accounted for by itself, without any reference to the others' (*LRBL*, ii 134). By referring to Newton, Smith is stressing that this method is based upon empiricism, rather than on the Cartesian method of deduction. Think of Descartes' 'whole chain of truths'. Smith's use of the 'division of labour' as a vigorous explanatory concept is, in this sense, rooted in this view of the Newtonian ideal. Smith's comments may suggest an array of cultural expectations rooted in the contemporary understanding of Newtonian ideas and of their application to human society.

Hume makes the link between reasoning about human nature and scientific reasoning very clear: '… we find in the course of nature, that tho' the effects be many, the principles, from which they arise, are commonly but few and simple, and that 'tis the sign of an unskilful naturalist to have recourse to a different quality, in order to explain every different operation. How much more must this be true with regard to the human mind …' (*T*, 2.1.3.6). He also makes clear specifically in relation to his epistemology that tracing an idea back to its original impression is significant. This may only be a short chain, but this linking is fundamental to his philosophical method. Concern as to the way or ways in which the notion of a 'chain of reasoning' is achieved in writing is not therefore a restricted problem but one that may have more general significance in the context of eighteenth-century arguments and of the Scottish Enlightenment.

All systematic and original writing can be expected to be linear. This may be a cultural assumption that is itself a product of the Enlightenment. However, a notion such as that of a 'compleat chain of reasoning' suggests, if the metaphor is taken seriously, very careful attention to the episodic links in the chain: no gaps, no leaps of faith, no link untested, a discourse that can be followed on a consistent and hence predictable step-by-step basis. This is a set of aspirations and may not have been consistently achieved in practice. Hume tells us, in the *Treatise*, the *Enquiries* and in a number of his essays, that he aims at clarity rather than merely abstruseness so it does not seem unreasonable to look at how he achieves this clarity through composition. The concern here is not with the macro-structure of the text (a structure than many have found wanting) but with sustained episodes of argumentation.

Experimental reporting and cause and effect

A chain of reasoning suggests interconnected ideas and predictable out-comes or conclusions or implications and has associations with Newtonian principles, including the intellectual power of a few simple but significant propositions. Hume may have been over-impressed by the power of his division between impression and ideas but this paper is not evaluating so much his philosophy, as his writing. If his understanding of cause and effect is his major innovation, as he claims in the *Abstract*, then the first-step must come in 'an impression of the memory or senses' (*T*, 1.3.4.1). The chain of inferences must terminate somewhere and that must be when the argument is exhausted. It also suggests recognition of the linearity of writing as a form of argument. Hume is in a sense endorsing an approach to writing that many of his peers had sought in clarity of purpose and simplicity in execution (see Box, 1990, 20–40). Complex ideas and propositions need to be set out step by step, if we take the metaphor seriously, in a chain (the literal equivalent of which being a series of systematically linked passages), that is, somehow, discernable by the reader. Step-by-step (the replacement of a 'chain' with a means of stable locomotion: mixing metaphors may be disallowed but the collision of images can be fun – Hume also switches from 'chain' to 'steps', and to, indeed, 'footsteps') is itself a metaphor and there will be a need, also, to reflect upon what this means. So the reading is answering questions such as 'What is Hume doing in the writing at this or that point?' and 'How is what he is doing, linked to the idea of a chain of reasoning?' What Hume is doing may be something quite simple such as 'asking a question' (questions, and the precise framing of questions, are basic to his method) or 'proposing an answer' or 'providing an example' or 'tracing an implication', even if the material is philosophically difficult or dense.

Hume states his treatment of causality at *T*, 1.3.2.1. There he reactivates distinctions first made in Part one, Section one. This is already a long gap between the introduction and definition of the relevant categories and their activation and use in the context of discussing probable knowledge. This originating taxonomy is not clear and Hume has additional work to do.

Hume distinguishes those that do not depend on order or timing (that which is necessarily true or matters of relation, though this is using the clearer language of the *ECHU*) from those that do (those that cannot be known *a priori* or matters of fact) and focuses on '*identity, situations in time* and place and *causation*'. The focus here will be on passages dealing with 'causation'.

> To begin regularly, we must consider the idea of *causation*, and see from what origin it is deriv'd.[sentence one] 'Tis impossible to reason justly, without understanding perfectly the idea concerning which we reason; and 'tis impossible perfectly to understand any idea, without tracing it up to its origin, and examining that primary impression, from which it arises.[sentence two] The examination of the impression bestows a clearness on the idea; and the examination of the idea bestows a like clearness in all our reason.[sentence three]
>
> Let us therefore cast our eye on any two objects, which we call cause and effect, and turn them on all sides, in order to find that impression, which produces the idea of such prodigious consequence [sentence four] At first sight I perceive, that I must not search for it in any of the particular *qualities* of the objects; since, which-ever of these qualities I pitch on, I find some object, that is not possest of it, and yet falls under the denomination of cause or effect.[sentence five] And indeed there is nothing existent, either externally or internally, which is not to be consider'd either as a cause or an effect; tho' 'tis plain that there is no one quality, which universally belongs to all beings, and gives them a title to that denomination. [sentence six].
>
> (*T*, 1.3.2.4)

Sentence one is evidently not a question but it can be readily transformed into one without any major violence being done to its meaning. A sequence of evaluative reasoning is usually signalled by a statement of this type. This statement is signalling the start of a chain of reasoning, a discussion of the idea of causation and of its origin. Causation has already been established as one of those ideas that are about matters of fact. Sentence two is a reaffirmation of what it is to 'reason justly' in Humean terms. Causation is an idea and to understand an idea it must be traced back, according to the 'first principle of the science of human nature' (established at *T*, 1.1.1.11–1.1.1.12; see also *T*, 1.1.1.7), to an originating impression. This is a very short recapitulation of a concept first introduced many sections before. Sentence three provides the justification in hermeneutical terms. To reason justly is to reason clearly. Hume never abandons his commitment to the notion of clarity, especially with respect to the framing of originating questions, as will be shown later in this book.

With sentence four, the search for an originating experience, giving rise to an originating impression commences. The cooperative reader is asked to join

Hume in contemplating 'any two objects'. The mind experiment here or the practical experiment (if the reader is active) is perfectly general. The advanced reader can think in terms of object A and object B (as suggested by Norton), the novice by something altogether more concrete. The search is for the 'impression'. Sentence five switches the focus from that of a cooperative activity to one that is reported upon as a matter of personal experience. This not the egotistical use of 'I' but the functional use. It is about understanding and a sequence or chain of related understandings perhaps couched in rather too ready terms: 'at first sight I perceive ...'. This is a form of structured guidance to the reader, shaping the reader's way of approaching the experimental nature of the experience that is being verbally contrived. Experiments in science were first demonstrated to a small audience and then the conventions for writing up or recording experiments evolved from the demonstration. How are the results of experiments in 'the science of human nature' to be written up and recorded? This is, in a sense, what Hume is resolving textually.

The active reader has also to keep in mind the notion of qualities for all that is suggested here is that there is a range of qualities. The sense is of extending the range of objects though this is only by implication. There is no one property that is universal. Sentence six is again not perhaps as clear as it could be for the novice reader. There is 'no one quality' which is universal and gives rise to 'cause'. There is neither 'impression' nor its corresponding 'idea' though this notion is to be carried forward by implication from sentence three in the previous paragraph.

Even in this short stretch of text, considered in context, any reader is engaged in reactivating a number of concepts (this we should be expected as the chain is always fixed to one end, in principle at least, at the same point, and elements have to be reapplied to a new context) as well as understanding the requirements of using them purposefully through participating in an experiential piece of learning as guided by Hume. A lot is being asked of the general reader.

Hume then explores '*contiguity*' and '*succession*' and finds that these do not offer a complete account. The next move (*T*.1.3.2.11) is characteristically by a question:

> Shall we then rest contented with these two relations of contiguity and succession, as affording a compleat idea of causation? By no means. An object may be contiguous and prior to another, without being considered as its cause. There is a NECESSARY CONNEXION to be taken into consideration; and that relation is of much greater importance, than any of the other two above-mention'd.

What happens next is a repeat of the experiment, this time with respect to the new idea, i.e. turning 'the object on all sides, in order to discover the nature of this necessary connexion, and find the impression, or impressions, from which its idea may be deriv'd'.

In the introductory move the focus is on cooperation: 'we'. In the execution, the focus is on the personal experience: 'I' and the experience and experiential moves established according to predefined terms for earlier in the discourse: '*known qualities*' and '*relations*'. Yet again, the chain requires the reactivation of earlier knowledge and application according to steps already established. This pattern of switching from a cooperative act to individuated reporting recurs time and again when Hume is conducting an experiment or relating an experience, e.g. the transition of pronouns at *T*, 1.3.8.5.

The chain starts again but no clear starting point is discovered. To proceed, Hume starts four new questions – announced confusingly as '*First*' and '*Secondly*' and careful attention needs to be paid to the italicized terms ('*necessary*'; '*inference*'; '*belief*') as these are the main elements that are investigated in the following sections – and initiates a further set of inquiries. In exploring the issues, Hume reactivates the distinction between relations and matters of fact. Hume, from the investigation, arrives at a conclusion: 'Since it is not from knowledge or any scientific reasoning, that we derive the opinion of the necessity of a cause to every new production, that opinion must necessarily arise from observation and experience'. The intellectual pay-off from beating about 'all the neighbouring fields' is not fully made clear to the reader until *T*, 1.3.6.3. This is a substantial stretch from start to end and gain requires a significant capacity on the part of the reader. These questions, modified from their initial framing at *T*, 1.3.3.9 in turn give rise to another set of investigation and the writing starts once again along similar lines.

The significant outcome, the big pay-pay off for the whole discussion, a set of 'rules by which to judge of causes and effects' does not come until *T*, 1.3.15. Hume establishes eight rules of reasoning about cause and effect and declares that 'here is all the Logic I think proper to employ in my reasoning …'. Because he sticks rigorously to the idea of a chain of reasoning, and of experimentalism, Hume *rarely* allows the reader to anticipate results or to see where the steps are likely to lead. There is integration but that integration is normally concerned with the reapplication of previously established principles rather than upon any anticipated outcomes stated and anticipated in advance over long sections of text. An almost perfect example is found after the treatment 'Of the probability of chances'. The pay-off is discovered after the fact of the initial exploration:

> What I have said concerning the probability of chances can serve to no other purpose, than to assist us in explaining the probability of causes; since 'tis commonly allow'd by philosophers, that what the vulgar call chance is nothing but a secret and conceal'd cause. That species of probability, therefore, is what we must chiefly examine.
>
> (*T*, 1.3.12.1)

How Hume shapes experiments in writing in the *Treatise* has been commented above but some fuller exploration is required. Hume usually, but not invariably, starts with a cooperative pronoun ('we'), switches to 'I' especially when the subject matter need shaping in a way that is beyond the commonplace and then, in concluding, switches back to cooperative mode (see another set of examples at *T*, 1.2.3.1–4).

Hume is aware that his approach is built on rigorously applied chains of reasoning with repeated elements in which the link between impressions and ideas is foundational. This is an implication of not working *a priori*, of taking nothing at first sight. Experiments punctuate the text of Book One. Hume is also aware, though he tells us somewhat late in the exercise, when dealing with causality, that he has to struggle with language:

> I must not conclude the subject without observing, that 'tis very difficult to talk of the operations of the mind with perfect propriety and exactness; because common language has seldom made any very nice distinctions among them, but has generally call'd by the same term all such as nearly resemble each other.
>
> (*T*, 1.3.8.15)

Hume was aware of his methods and had thought through how these demands were to be met in reporting on the results. He had a model of sorts in natural philosophy but in so far as the demands of 'the science of man' were concerned he had to be initiator, experimenter and recorder, working within the demands of a very strict set of requirements: no untested propositions, no *a priori* thinking in relation to matter of fact. The reader is accommodated by a variety of strategies (cooperative activity including directed cooperative activity; textual reapplication of ideas and points of summary) but with very little looking forward or explanation of the purpose and sequence of ideas nor any strong hint of 'pay-off', of the relationship, otherwise so important to Hume, between effort and reward. When the *Treatise* failed to find an actual audience that matched Hume's intended audience – it did find an audience of a type that Hume roundly rejected – Hume radically reconsidered his approach to the writing-up of his experimental results. He did so in a very short paper known in shorthand as the *Abstract*.

The *Abstract*

The authorship was once disputed – it was thought to have been the work of a very young Adam Smith – though it is now accepted that Hume did in fact write the *Abstract*. In the Annotations to the *Abstract*, Norton has identified, very helpfully, those sections and passages of the *Treatise* that are referred to in the *Abstract*. It could be thought that the *Abstract* should be considered as a work on its own, i.e. it ought to be read independently of the *Treatise*.[5] It is important to do this, and this in fact corresponds roughly with how the initial readings for this research were undertaken. Ideally, it might be possible to then read the *Treatise* and make direct comparisons of the relevant passages. This is only likely to work in a few instances. Why it is not likely to work is implicit in what happened when we considered in the last chapter that the *Abstract* is not an abridgement. This is significant for the 'abstract as *genre*' in today's terms is a literary *genre* in which fidelity to the source text is of absolute significance. The Summary is a remodelling of a text in which fidelity to the originating text is less significant than consideration of its effectiveness for a target audience.

Hume's *Abstract* is a summary, a new work – something like a sympathetic book review though more sophisticated than most as published at the time. Reviews at the time, and for some time well into the nineteenth century, published verbatim long tracts of material from the original source with some challenging commentary (see Fieser, 1996, 647). Hume's *Abstract* also more or less points to the originating text but not writing that necessary parallels elements of the originating text. An early reviewer of the version edited by Keynes and Sraffa – the edition which effectively established Hume's authorship – refers to the *Abstract* as 'a very brilliant piece of condensation and summary' and goes on to assert, nonetheless, that it does not 'qualify the point of view expounded in the *Treatise*' (S.P.L., 1938, 640). It does however add some interesting examples and concerns.

Hume simplified (by selection as well as other methods) and the simplifications are huge. Indeed the writing strategy is completely different, as we shall see, in that an open, discursive style of the *Treatise* gives way to a tighter, focused, purposeful style of the *Abstract*. The first example is a salutary one, as the introductory moves in the first four paragraphs on the *Abstract* cover material developed over 10 paragraphs in the original. What can be done is to illustrate elements of the *Treatise* that relate to the *Abstract* where and when it is appropriate to do so. This may be interleaved with discussion of the *Abstract* or undertaken in a separate section depending solely upon convenience. In may be thought that this topic has been exhausted by the treatment given to it in Keynes and Straffa's Introduction to the rediscovered work. This Introduction is referred to as a guide in this chapter but the analysis is informed rather than constrained by the earlier work. By the end of the investigation, it might be possible to show how Hume simplified (an important activity and relevant to the development of his economics) and perhaps illuminate why. The idea behind the analysis is that understanding the writing and more significantly understanding Hume's growing sense of audience is a significant aid to understanding the thinking.

Diminishing returns are likely to be at work in this exercise and so that part of the *Abstract* which deals with the operation of the mind and of passions, essentially material relating to Book II and which does not occupy much space in the *Abstract*, will not be included in this close analysis. Concentration will be placed on the issue of 'cause and effect' since this, together with his ideas of belief and custom, are identified in the *Abstract* as being of key significance to his arguments in the *Treatise*.

The *Abstract*: opening moves

It is a drawback for reporting on the outcome of a close reading that it requires a high level of interaction with the original text. The *Abstract* can be found in David Hume *A Treatise of Human Nature* (2000) Oxford: Oxford University Press, from pages 403–417. The Annotations on the *Abstract* are to be found in the same volume at pages 566–569. These have proven to be helpful in making an analysis of the composition of the *Abstract*. It would be helpful if the reader has access to the text of the *Abstract*, though every effort will be made to ensure that readers without this access can follow what is going on. Although the primary purpose is to point out the inner workings of the *Abstract* as a piece of writing, and perhaps predictive of other writings, there will be some comment on its content other than simply relabelling.

Hume makes his motives clear in the Preface. He justifies his arrangement in terms of helping 'ordinary capacities' follow the lengthy 'thread of argument'. He is very clear in the Preface as to the strategy adopted in the *Treatise*, where the argument was 'drawn out' and where 'each part fortified with all the arguments, guarded against all the objections, and illustrated with all the views, which occur to a writer in the diligent survey of his subject' (*T, Preface to Abstract*, 1). Put like this it is easy to feel that the writing as developed in the *Treatise* has a capacity to overburden the reader. In creating the *Abstract* Hume is working towards 'a chain of reasoning, that is more single and concise' that will allow 'the connexion to be more easily traced from the first principles to the last conclusion'. In order to do this he states: 'I have chosen one simple argument, which I have carefully traced from the beginning to the end.' He adds that 'This is the only point I have taken care to finish'. The *Abstract* itself quickly establishes (see below) this chain of reasoning to be reasoning about 'cause and effect'. Benefits to be expected from undertaking the effort of reading the *Treatise* are established at the end of the second paragraph, including an alteration in the foundation of sciences; an ability to shake off orthodoxy; a capacity to think for ones self and so on. Significantly Hume, as mentioned in an earlier chapter, accepts by the writing of the *Abstract* that there is a communication problem, identified as due to length as much as 'abstractedness'. His concerns were in evidence in his personal correspondence much earlier. The hostile review in the *History of the Works of the Learned* (1739), which made such a fuss about the lack of a transparent design for the work, seems to have infuriated him and put him off publishing in the journal concerned (T, Annotations to *Abstract*, Preface, 2). It appears, however, that he had drafted the *Abstract* before he saw the offending review (Mossner, 1966, 121).[6]

The opening paragraphs of the body of the *Abstract* concentrate upon the context within which the *Treatise* was written. Hume claims, in a conventional move, that his work follows 'upon the same plan' as others who have also 'started a new kind of philosophy'. He identifies what is new about this 'new kind of philosophy' by comparing the (as yet unidentified) new philosophy with that of the 'philosophers of antiquity'. He gives a positive and a negative evaluation of the ancient philosophers. In a positive light, they 'have shewn more of a delicacy of sentiment, a just sense of morals, or a greatness of soul' and negatively in that they lacked a 'depth of reasoning and reflection'. What does Hume mean by a 'depth or reasoning and reflection'? He tells us in the next sentence. Such reasoning requires 'following out a steady chain of propositions, or forming the several truths into a regular science' (*Abstract* 1). It is a short step in the text from the introduction of the word 'science' to 'the science of *man*'. Hume then tells us what following out a steady chain of propositions actually means (notice that the word 'steady' and the word 'regular' point to the same kind of experience). It means resolving 'several phaenomena' into one set of 'simple principles'. This is Hume's interpretation of Newton's approach.

The statements thus far are general. Hume moves carefully from the general (the new philosophers; regular science) to the *Treatise* (to the particular) as an example and a particular one at that. Hume specifies an overall principle that the author follows: 'he proposes to anatomize human nature in a regular manner, and promises to draw no conclusions but where he is authorized by experience' (*Abstract* 2). The move is from the general to the specific both with respect to the focus of the *Abstract* and with respect to the kinds of general principles that are being dealt with. Anatomy is a science that developed by careful observation and direct experience of cutting up bodies. In a very significant sense, 'anatomy' is a 'science of man' though this is implicit rather than explicit in the text. 'Experience' is then contrasted with 'hypotheses' (by which he means metaphysical speculation or principles derived *a priori*) and the stress on experience in the *Treatise* justified in the *Abstract* in terms of Locke, Shaftesbury, Mandeville, Hutcheson and Butler, who, despite disagreements, founded 'their accurate disquisitions of human nature entirely upon experience'. The stress is on continuity of exploration leading towards the development of a 'regular science' and the 'science of *man*' first mentioned in the middle of the first paragraph.

The third paragraph, and the last of the general contextualizations for the *Treatise*, acts both to specify the content for the science of man and to open the discourse out again. The content is taken from Hume's original Introduction to the *Treatise*: '*the sole end of* logic *is to explain the principles and operations of the reasoning faculty, and the nature of our ideas;* morals and criticism *regard our tastes and sentiments; and* politics *consider men as united in society, and dependent on each other*' (*Abstract* 3). The *Treatise* does not italicize and the italics signal that this is a quotation. The punctuation differs in detail from Norton and Norton's edition of the *Treatise*. The science of man then draws logic, morals, aesthetics, politics and (as we shall see) economics into its fold. The content is therefore specified. Hume however opens the issue out by specifying the *Treatise* as seemingly 'intended for a system of the sciences'. This deserves comment for if philosophy hitherto had essentially served the interests of theology, here Hume is showing his truly radical hand in making it serve the interests of a broadly defined social science (see Schatz, [1902] 1972). In one short sweep of paragraphs, philosophy has been reinvented and repositioned. Its 'Logic' (i.e. Book One of the *Treatise*) is to serve what we would call social science, though care has to be taken here. Hume, like Smith, is concerned with moral philosophy and hence about human behaviour. Moral actions are just as important as maxims.

The fourth paragraph is also interesting in that it is still making comparisons essentially but no longer uniquely between the 'old' and 'new' philosophy. Hume cites 'Leibnitz' (an example of a new philosopher) as a critic of 'the common systems of logic' (built on syllogisms) as 'very copious' when dealing with 'demonstrations' but 'too concise when they treat of probabilities'. Hume here talks of 'those measures of evidence on which life and action entirely depend'. Locke is easy to identify from the list of titles then supplied. Norton names Malebranche and Arnauld and Nicole as the authors of the other two works cited. The 'common systems of logic' (Aristotelian and the 'school men') are at fault but so too are some modern philosophers in this respect. Hume's own work in the *Treatise* is then considered: 'The author of the *Treatise of Human Nature* seems to have been sensible of this defect, in these philosophers and has endeavoured, as much as he can, to supply it'. The *Treatise*'s basis for an independent contribution to the development of the philosophical literature is therefore established by this claim.[7] Hume in the *Abstract* will confine his attention primarily to 'his explication of our reasons from cause to effect'. This is to be understood as a demonstration of the logic as it deals with 'probabilities', though this is by implication rather than explicit. Hume also makes it clear that the regular connection of ideas is significant: 'In a word, nature has bestow'd a kind of attraction on certain impressions and ideas, by which one of them, *upon its appearance*, naturally introduces *its* correlative.' (T, 2.1.4.8). The association of ideas, explored further in the *ECHU*, a significant aspect of his empirical project.

This is a 'nice' tight structure, and writing that has been very carefully crafted to make a persuasive case. In one short paragraph Hume has decoupled the linking of reasoning about probabilities from the study of the existing systems of logic and identified not only the *Treatise*'s claim to originality of contribution in general but its strongest individual argument to that end. All of this is achieved by a remarkable economy of language, an economy only made possible by the fact that all of the hard work had already been done in the *Treatise* itself.

The *Treatise*: comparison with the opening moves

The four paragraphs cannot be readily directly compared with the ten, at least not in any simple sense. There is much that is deleted. This does not help us for the significant questions concern what and how. Hume gives us a clue: length and degree of abstractedness. That there is a reduction in length is self-evident but as to how it is achieved, this is slightly more difficult. Take the depiction of the 'philosophers of antiquity'. There is nothing quite as simple as this in the Introduction to the *Treatise* as might be expected. The mention of the English philosophers is undertaken in a footnote in the *Treatise* and nothing much is left of the originating passage except a phrase 'some late philosophers in England' is changed into 'our late philosophers' ('our' is a backwards reference to 'England' that appears in the first sentence of the *Abstract* (*T*, Introduction, 7). But there is plenty of evidence of intel-lectual confusion (also a theme in Descartes) in the ranks of philosophers. Hume simplifies most of paragraph one into his notions of 'regular science'.

Take the following sentence, the last in the first paragraph of the Intro-duction: 'Principles taken upon trust, consequences lamely deduc'd from them, want of coherence in the parts, and of evidence in the whole, these are everywhere to be met with in the systems of the most eminent philosophers ...' (*T*, Introduction, 1). This becomes the lack of a 'chain of propositions, or forming the several truths into a regular science'. Take most of paragraph two which is taken up by the development of a series of noisy metaphors culminating in the notion that 'the victory is not gain'd by the men at arms, who manage the pike and sword; but by the trumpeters, drummers, and musicians of the army' (*T*, Introduction 1). This becomes in the *Abstract*: 'They content themselves with representing the common sense of mankind, and with the best turn of thought and expression ...'. The *Abstract* is calm where the Introduction to the *Treatise* is full of noise and show with its armies and drummers, castles, and slow and 'lingering' sieges. This in the *Treatise* could be taken as an example of Blair's Ciceronian notion of faults arising from 'too great attention to ornament' (Blair, [1783] 2005, Lecture 18, 196). Hume in the *Treatise* argues for marching up 'directly to human nature' but it is only in the opening moves of the *Abstract* that he does this 'marching' in relatively straightforward language. Elaborate and extended metaphors are eliminated and the style could be classified in eighteenth-century terms as 'plain'. However there is an outbreak of (moderated) imagery right at the end of the *Abstract* where Hume is talking about the principles of association': 'For as it is by means of thought only that anything operates upon our passions, and as these are the only ties of our thoughts, they are really *to us* the cement of the universe, and all the opera-tions of the mind must, in a great measure, depend on them'.

Even with respect to the notion of experimentation and experience, the directness of the *Abstract* in relation to the relevant passages in the *Treatise* is remarkable. The *Abstract* says: 'If in examining several phaenomena, we find that they resolve themselves into one common principle, and can trace this principle into another, we shall at last arrive at those few simple principles, on which all the rest depend. And tho' we can never arrive at the ultimate principles, 'tis a satisfaction to go as far as our faculties will allow us' (*Abstract* 1). The *Treatise* says: 'And though we must endeavour to render all our principles as universal as possible, by tracing up our experiments to the utmost, and explaining all effects to the simplest and fewest causes, 'tis certain that we cannot go beyond experience; and any hypothesis, that pretends to discover the ultimate original qualities of human nature, ought at first to be rejected as presumptuous and chimerical' (*T*, Introduction 8) and much more besides. A long statement about observation and experimentation over parts of two paragraphs in the *Treatise* becomes one in which the author: 'promises to draw no conclusions but where he is authorized by experience'.

It is an irony that it has taken, thus far, longer than four paragraphs to illustrate Hume's textual method in so far as the introductory moves found in the *Abstract* are concerned. It is not going to be possible to move forward in the same way with the rest of the *Abstract*. Something slightly less exhaustive will be attempted. What has been illustrated thus far is that Hume, having decided that the problem is length and 'abstractedness', commits himself in the writing of the *Abstract* to a process that deals with both faults. Expression is shortened and tightened and the order in which notions are presented is simplified. There is particular care taken with developing a less abstract language to introduce the theme of the *Treatise* through consideration of the *Abstract*. If we take abstract/concrete as opposites then Hume substitutes, in the first four paragraphs, concrete expressions and examples for abstract ones. Box refers to Blair's ideas of diffuse and concise but the principles are the same (Box, 1990, 30). Overstated metaphor is removed. He does the same with the pair general/specific. Philosophers in general are replaced with 'antient' and 'late', and recent philosophers are named in the text.

The *Abstract* and *Treatise*: the three paragraphs from paragraph five

The *Treatise* proper starts with a distinction made between Impressions and Ideas. Hume defines and leaves the activity unlabelled. The *Abstract* comes straight to the point: 'Our author begins with some definitions'. Norton, in the Annotations to the *Abstract*, talks of this as a paraphrase (*T*, Annotations to *Abstract*, 5). What kind of paraphrase is it and how is it arrived at? Definitions are provided for 'perception', 'impressions'; and 'ideas' and the textual pattern is easily identified as that of rule/example. This is the same pattern as found in the *Treatise* (*T*, 1.1.1.1) though executed in the *Abstract* in less than half the words. The economy of Hume's *Abstract* can be illustrated, further, in the treatment of the strength of impression as compared to ideas:

> *Abstract*: *Impressions*, therefore are our lively and strong perceptions; *ideas* are fainter and weaker. This distinction is evident; as evident as that betwixt feeling and thinking. (*Abstract* 5)

Treatise: I believe it will not be necessary to employ many words in explaining this distinction. Every one of himself will readily perceive the difference betwixt feeling and thinking. The common degrees of these are easily distinguish'd; tho' it is not impossible but in particular instances they may very nearly approach one another. ... (*T*, 1.1.1.1).

The passages are not strictly equivalent, as the excerpt from the *Treatise* does not deal with the exemplification of the terms involved. However, there is enough to illustrate that Hume in producing the *Abstract*, as he tells us indirectly in the Preface, simplifies the 'thread of the argument' be removing all of the 'fortified' arguments necessary for a 'diligent survey'. There is no mention of 'sleep' or 'madness' in the *Abstract*. At the same time, the phrase 'Every one of himself will readily perceive ...' is efficiently reduced to 'This distinction is evident'. The two documents differ in expression over this narrow range but not in the function performed by the writing. Both establish and socialize the definitions through exemplification. Hume tells us as much with respect at least to the *Treatise* though he does so *retrospectively* (a tendency referred to above): 'Having by these divisions given an order and arrangement to our objects, we may now apply ourselves to consider with the more accuracy their qualities and relations' (*T*, 1.1.1.3). Notice that this is in itself a form of internal summarization. He sums up what has gone before in order to introduce a new stage in the investigation.

Definitions are relatively easy. The next paragraph of the *Abstract* examines Hume's 'first proposition'. The opening sentence is: 'The first proposition he advances is, that all our ideas, or weak perceptions, are derived from our impressions, or strong perceptions ....' (*Abstract* 6). This corresponds to two early statements in the *Treatise* (at *T*, 1.1.1.7 and *T*, 1.1.1.12) only one of which is signalled (again, after the event) as 'the first principle' (*T*, 1.1.1.12). Both statements in the *Treatise* are more complex than the version in the *Abstract* and in both cases the complexity is reduced by deleting the term 'simple' as the *Abstract* at this point does not elaborate on the difference between simple and complex ideas. Indeed the development of the paragraph seems to have no direct equivalent in the *Treatise* at this point other than the fact that Hume chooses to concentrate his attention on a footnote to the first paragraph of the *Treatise*.[8] This contains a criticism of Locke for treating 'idea' as if it stood for all 'perceptions'. In the *Abstract* Hume elevates this to a main point. This seems like a significant departure. Can we account for it? Hume seems to be trying to reinforce further links (either positive or negative) between his philosophy and those who pursued similar ideas and who came before him (Locke; Malebranch). This modifies the sense of the 'new' and may be a response to his critics in which case there is a further element of intellectual defence in the *Abstract* that goes beyond Hume's desire to simplify. His hope, expressed in the *Treatise*, that he had 'by a clear stating of the question' removed all disputes over 'innate ideas' would seem on this evidence to have been a vain one (*T*, 1.1.1.12).

In the next paragraph, Hume quotes directly from the *Treatise*: 'no discovery could be made more happily for the deciding of all controversies concerning ideas, than this, that impressions always take the precedency of them, and that every idea, with which the imagination is furnished, first makes its appearance in a corresponding impression. ...'. The strength of the *Abstract* here is that Hume puts this 'discovery' to work immediately. If a 'philosophical term' has 'no idea annexed to it' then 'he always asks *from what impression that pretended idea is derived?*' This is taken by Fogelin (1985, 9) as a positivistic statement, though he downplays Hume as a positivist. It is a simplification of a much more complex idea of 'substance' in the *Treatise* (Fogelin, 1985, 10). If the answer is none, then the 'term is altogether insignificant'. This is a general proposition which is then backed by a specific application in the *Treatise* ''tis after this manner he examines our idea of substance and essence'. The lack of hedging and the telescoping of the *Treatise* in this section of the *Abstract* may have philosophical disadvantages, hinted at by Fogelin, but it has the educational advantage of immediacy. The target text to which Hume intends to direct readers is the *Treatise*. Any disputes about Hume's ideas must be considered in relation to the substantive text. There is a pay-off in understating the 'precedency' of impression over ideas. The 'new kind of philosophy', which Hume is justifying, according to the Preface, 'promises more both to the entertainment and advantage of mankind'. Some useful purpose is necessary and here it is delivered quickly.

Abstract: paragraphs eight to twenty-one, cause and effect

Cause and effect is first mentioned in the context of impression and ideas (*T*, 1.1.1.6) but this is dropped in the *Abstract*. The switch from matters of the mind, to 'matter of fact' is therefore somewhat abrupt. Something else happens in the transition. Hitherto the fictions necessary to identify the author of the *Abstract* as different from the author of the *Treatise* have been maintained in every paragraph thus far. From paragraph eight to the end of paragraph twenty-one, there is no mention made of the author of the *Treatise*. It would seem unlikely that this is simply a slip of the pen. Such a shift, even if it is intended that we carry forward the notion of the 'author', requires some investigation and reflection for it seems to imply that the author of the *Abstract* has taken extensive control over the material of the text in a way not implied hitherto in the writing. That control is not handed back until paragraphs twenty-two and twenty-three. It is not that Hume no longer paraphrases, for there Norton has identified some match between the *Treatise* and the *Abstract*, though the stretches of text that are involved in the originating text is more extended than was the case earlier. Hume can be thought of here as fulfilling his desire, set out in the Preface to the*Abstract*, of bringing parts of an argument together (by omitting details) so that 'parts lying nearer together can be better compared'. This requires the restatement of the 'thread of the argument' and Hume resorts to the style of restatement with which he is most comfortable for dealing with psychological subject matter: that of the first person narrative. He does not however start with an 'I' but with 'we'. Hume and the intended readers of the *Abstract* are working together in the present (the tenses tend to be present tenses). This joint development of knowledge is sustained through the paragraphs but it is the 'I' that does most of the difficult work. In a sense the relationship between the 'I' and the 'we' in both works is similar.

The first sentence of paragraph eight introduces the topic of 'cause and effect'. This is significant. Hume chooses this as a key element of his work. In the *Treatise* he refers to his eight rules as his 'Logic' but this is done in the middle of a section, where it could be easily overlooked, and *retrospectively* at the end of the whole consideration. The second sentence introduces the manner in which it will be explored: 'In order therefore to understand these reasonings, we must be perfectly acquainted with the idea of a cause; and in order to that, must look about us to find something that is the cause of the other'. Hume is signalling the need for an active example and this he supplies in the opening sentence of the next paragraph: 'Here is a billiard-ball' ...'. This is almost casual in its manner and again is evidence of the immediacy that informs other aspects of the *Abstract*. It is chosen because it is an example that is simple and easy to imagine and well within the experience of most of his readers. The example does not exist explicitly in the *Treatise* but it is implicit in the example given at *T*, 1.3.2.9 (see also the Note by Norton for that paragraph *T*, Annotations, 448).

At the end of paragraph ten the reason for a clear example is given: 'if we can explain the inference from the shock of two balls, we shall be able to account for this operation of the mind in all instances'. The 'we' and 'us' and the extended example together with the pay-off as it were heighten the immediacy of the *Abstract* at this point. This is an active exploration of a developing idea rather than a reporting on a main text, even if the two texts are linked. But the sentence prior opens with: 'This is the inference from cause to effect; and of this nature are all our reasonings in the conduct of life'. The pay-off is clear but the phrase 'in the conduct of life' is a backwards reference 'to those other measures of evidence on which life and action entirely depend' (paragraph four and a reference to Leibnitz). Danford, in commenting on the fact that in the *Abstract* Hume chooses cause and effect as central, states that: 'It may seem strange in view of this consensus to claim that the full implications of this momentous discovery, as Hume understood them, are rarely brought out. One reason is the relative obscurity in which the implications are buried in the *Treatise* itself '(Danford, 1990, 60). The 'consensus' that Danford is referring to is that of a standard college philosophy course, in the United States, such as 'Philosophy 1'. Hume's notion of life and action means that causality is central both to the everyday aspects of life as to social investigation. Later, in his political and economic essays Hume will explore often by explicit analogy the issue of causality in economic life.

The motion of billiard balls is presented as perfect 'instance of the relation of cause and effect'. In examining the motion, a list of circumstances is created as 'requisite' to the 'operation of all causes': first contiguity; then priority and then constant conjunction. Now in the *Treatise* the first relevant section only lists two (contiguity and priority). The 'third' is only mentioned much later. These three elements are all that Hume (writing consistently in the first person singular, perhaps in order to keep the active or immediate notion alive) can discover in the cause. The use of the narrative 'I' is a strong step towards the *Treatise*. Any conclusion that goes from movement of one billiard ball to movement of another is an 'inference' – the text had moved from 'matter of fact' back to matter of mind – and that is explored in paragraph ten.

Hume in opening paragraph eleven introduces '*Adam*' newly created 'in the full vigour of understanding' (*Abstract*, 11). 'Adam' is a very useful device for he is 'a creature that has understanding' (in the sense that Hume thinks of understanding) but who being recently created has no 'experience'. Experience only comes from living and observing and from experiencing sensations. His introduction suggests Hume thought some of the issues through anew. 'Adam' is so useful as an expository device that the extended example is sustained over three paragraphs. Paragraph twelve is taken up with the need for 'Adam' (divine intervention denied) to be exposed to the experience of witnessing several instances to arrive at the link from cause to effect. In the end, Adam's 'understanding would anticipate his sight, and form a conclusion suitable to his past experience'. Hume has introduced the notion of inference by a device not available in the *Treatise*. It is a formidable device as 'Adam is the perfect Cartesian' (Robison, 2006, 30) and Hume shows then 'that knowledge of the world is not possible on Cartesian grounds'. It is a good device in context as it saves the expenditure of many words. It is however a dangerous device as 'Adam' was made, in religious teaching, in the image of God. Hume was concentrating on human nature and wanted to avoid any discussion that linked human nature with divine nature so this has also the potential to muddy the waters.

He uses 'Adam' in a direct way, only once, as far as I can establish, in the *Enquiries*. This episode does illustrate (further) a point made earlier that a summary is both different from (new) and the same as the originating work. In the paragraphs under review here Hume has departed significantly from the means of telling the story in the *Treatise* while the content remains recognizably the same. Given the short span of paragraphs involved this can hardly count as a major alteration in rhetoric. 'Adam' does however serve, once again, to humanize and concretize the discourse.

Inference is not based upon reason (i.e. the formal reasoning of the syllogism or demonstration) but upon experience and analogy (see below). The mind can imagine many causes (the word imagine or imagination is not used). Possible reasoning is not the same as certainty and certainty is implied by a demonstration. The argument about demonstration is clearly a shorthand version of what is found in the *Treatise* but the execution here is effective and economical. Hume buttresses his claim by appeal to others: 'and this is a principle, which is generally allowed by philosophers'. This is also a backwards reference to 'Leibnitz', whose criticism of the school men has already been presented, and to the others listed earlier.

'Adam' provides a good basis for illustration in a very simple context. The first sentence of paragraph 13 consists in an implication, conventionally signalled: 'It follows, then, that all reasonings concerning cause and effect are founded on experience, ...'. Another implication (of the first implication) follows within the same sentence: 'and that all reasonings from experience are founded on the supposition, that the course of nature will continue uniformly the same' (*Abstract*, 13). This idea is further expanded in the first sentence of the next paragraph: 'and that the future must be conformable to the past'. This is a key element of Hume's argument in the *Treatise* – this is the problem that Hume sees with induction, that it might dramatically fail us – here spelled out in the span of a few paragraphs.

From the *Abstract* to the *Enquiries*

This exercise serves to illustrate in an extended piece of writing by Hume the reflections on summarization and its use in the history of economic thought that took place in Chapter 2. Hume is in this account engaged with the same problems facing any act of summarization. The preface sets out the problem – the long 'thread' or chain of argument and the abstractedness of the writing that hinders some readers understanding the significance of what they are reading – that the *Abstract* is meant to help solve. The general principles that seem to have informed his writing in the *Treatise* – and analysed semi-independently in the first section of this chapter – and central to his scientific purpose, seem, in his own analysis, to have gotten in the way of clear communication with the reader. His writing then proceeds to select key events from the *Treatise* and to illustrate them in simple, mainly concrete ways (philosophers named; context spelled out; examples made immediate; pay-off linked directly to the brief analysis) or even if the language is different, textual functions may be the same (introducing; contextualizing; defining). Hume accepts in the Preface that there are faults with the writing (mainly length and complexity and the degree of 'abstractedness') and with the *Abstract* finds a way of modifying the text that makes part of the work feel more reader-friendly. It could still be used as a simplifying device to help inexperienced readers understand how to approach a first reading of at least parts of the *Treatise*. As this is his first recorded rethink, it is worthwhile at least understanding the textual strategy adopted by Hume in the *Abstract*. It is slightly puzzling, however, that Hume, in the Appendix, talks about not being able to 'discover any very considerable mistakes in the reasonings...' and maintains that 'some of my expressions have not been so well chosen' (*T*, Appendix, 396). No mention is made of what may be termed the structural problem, only of 'expressions'. Kruse, however critical, and however dated, is also very accurate, particularly in this respect. On the needs of 'popularization' he writes: '... these considerations required two sacrifices: an abbreviation and the surrender of all systematic arrangement' (Kruse, 1939, 34). As has been shown, there is a coherent rhetorical system in the *Abstract* though of course Kruse is referring to the rigor of a full inductive process as attempted in the *Treatise*. Kruse (unusual in his judgment at the time) perceived the structure of the *Treatise* and its division into Logic and progressive application as a unity.

The Appendix is written 'chiefly to remedy this defect' in expression. However, the Appendix is divided into two parts and the second part contains revisions of 'errors' of content. Keynes and Sraffa state that 'On comparison we find that the *Abstract* anticipates most of the points discussed in the first part of the appendix, but none of those, and particularly not the corrections, in the second part' (Keynes and Sraffa, 1938, xxv). Keynes and Sraffa are engaged in searching for internal textual evidence that Hume is the author of the *Abstract*. Here the emphasis is on the interrelationship more generally though the internal evidence that they cite is relevant. Both texts mention that belief entails a feeling that is different from the 'mere *reveries* of the imagination' (Appendix) or 'mere reverie of the imagination' (*Abstract*). Both texts, or rather at least the first part of the Appendix, as Keynes and Sraffa suggest, were produced at roughly similar times and yet are very different. A very significant statement in the Appendix is, in the respect, the following:

> I had entertain'd some hopes, that however deficient our theory of the intellectual world might be, it wou'd be free from those contradictions, and absurdities, which seem to attend every explication, that human reason can give of the material world. But upon a more strict view of the section concerning *personal identify*, I find myself involv'd in such a labyrinth, that, I must confess, I neither know how to correct my former opinions, nor how to render them consistent.
>
> (*T*, Appendix, 10)

This is followed by a statement that this condition is a 'sufficient' reason for scepticism. The route from the Appendix to the *Enquiries*, if there is one, is philosophical rather than merely literary.

What, if anything, is the relationship between the *Abstract* and the *Enquiries*? There may not be much that is specific with respect to the

ECHU except in the question of length, the self-contained nature of each contributing essay, and the degree of 'abstractedness' although Hume's concern that effort should be rewarded by benefits of knowledge and pleasure is also related to the general immediacy of the *Abstract*. The *Abstract* points to Hume's written argument as achieved in his later writings. This was spotted early by Laing in the early debate on the authorship of the *Abstract*: 'Yet a short and concise Abstract might be expected to reveal something of the author's main purpose and argument. One gets the impression, for instance, that the Abstract in structure and in phraseology, is largely an anticipation of the *Enquiry* of which it is a miniature' (Laing, 1939, 116). Laing leaves this at the impressionistic level.

The opening chapter of the *ECHU*, which must serve as a rough equivalent to the Introduction to the *Treatise*, avoids the martial and noisy metaphors that occupy so much space in the originating work. Metaphors, including a restrained mention of the military metaphor, remain in play but they are relatively straightforward and unelaborated. In the *ECHU*, Hume, reserves 'the flowers of rhetoric for subjects which are more adapted to them' (*ECHU*, 7.2.30) 'Adam' makes a very brief direct appearance (4.1. 6), though the idea of such a person is extended (someone 'brought on a sudden into this world') and the notion associated with an Adam is used at least twice more in the *ECHU*: 'We fancy, that were we *brought on a sudden into the world*, we could at first have inferred that one Billiard-ball would communicate motion to another on impulse; ...' [my italics] (see also *ECHU*, 5.1.3). There are other surviving fragments from the details of *Abstract*. Thus the phrase '*from what impression that pretended idea is derived?*' is found in the *ECHU* as '*from what impression is that supposed idea derived*' (also italicized). His statement in the *Abstract* that ''Tis not, therefore, reason, which is the guide of life, but custom' becomes in the *ECHU*, 'Custom, then is the great guide of human life' (5.1.5). The example of the collision of the billiard balls is used very effectively in the *Abstract*, not directly in the *Treatise* but is mentioned in the *ECHU* (4.1.7–9). His challenge to Locke with respect to 'innate' ideas in the sixth paragraph of the *Abstract* is expanded and written as a footnote at the end of Section II of the *ECHU*. Further, relations of ideas and matters of fact are brought into immediate contact in the *ECHU* (4.1) and the sentence in the *Abstract* which reads: ''Tis evident, that all reasonings concerning *matter of fact* are founded on the relation of cause and effect ...' becomes in the *ECHU*, 'All reasonings concerning matter of fact seem to be founded on the relation of *Cause and Effect*' The phrase 'matter of fact' is present in the *Treatise* at 1.3.7.2 but it does not seem to be given any prominence and is yet again introduced retrospectively.

His statement in the *Abstract* that 'Philosophy would render us entirely Pyrrhonian, were not nature too strong for it' becomes in the *ECHU* personified as 'a Pyrrhonian' and the problem expanded (*ECHU*, 12.2.23). The consequence of such an extreme scepticism is depicted as the cessation of 'all action', lethargy and universal death. This is not to be dreaded as likely for 'Nature is always too strong for principle'. Hume's statement of his notion of scepticism is taken to be clearer that that found in the *Treatise* and more consistent with his attempts to unseat 'superstition and metaphysics' (Immerwahr, 1976, 238) and there may be a hint of this transition in the *Abstract*. Here the summary becomes expanded into a substantive text and suggests that the idea of a 'hinge' that we explored when looking at summarization is still appropriate even if the text did not exist at the time the *Abstract* was produced. In dealing with the issue of length and proximity of ideas and with the question of overly hedging or developing, the *ECHU* maintains the notion of immediacy that we have identified in the *Abstract*. Hume had already tried his hand in the *Abstract* and would seem to have learned appropriate lessons, as far as elements of rhetoric in the *ECHU* is concerned, at any rate.

It is useful to give a short passage from *ECHU* illustrative of the collapse of the length of the chain of reasoning and of the increased concern to bring the location of questions and answers together under the idea of immediacy. Properly formulated questions, suitably italicized, as in the *Treatise*, still form the basis for the exploration. Questions are posed to be answered rather than extensively explored, and any demonstration of the basis on which the answer is supplied comes later. What Hume is doing is presenting results rather than argument, what is deleted is the finely detailed psychological analysis of causality:

> ... When it is asked, *What is the nature of all our reasonings concerning matter of fact?* The proper answer seems to be, that they are founded on the relation of cause and effect. When again it is asked, *What is the foundation of all our reasonings and conclusions concerning that relation?* it may be replied in one word, EXPERIENCE.
>
> (*ECHU*, 4.2.14)

The same sort of rethinking, this time explicit, the nature of the 'chain of reasoning' is found in Section VII, 'Of the Idea of Necessary Connection'. Hume considers mathematical and moral sciences. The mathematical sciences are 'clear and determinate' whereas as the moral sciences suffers from 'ambiguity' stemming from the difficulty of holding the 'finer sentiments of the mind' distinct when considered by 'reflection'. But Hume argues that the two sciences when looked at in terms of their 'advantages and disadvantages' balance out: 'If the mind, with greater facility, retains the idea of geometry clear and determinate, it must carry on a much longer and more intricate chain of reasoning, and compare ideas much wider of each other, in order to reach the abstruser truths of that science' (*ECHU*, 7.1.2.). The steps in moral science are fewer. The problem there is not the length of the required chain of reasoning but 'the obscurity of ideas, and the ambiguity of terms'.[9] Hence the desire for caution and for careful expression. This seems to be a major change in if nothing else, the rhetoric. Fixing the meaning of the terms '*power, force, energy* or necessary *connexion*' becomes significant. Hume wants to avoid the substitution of synonyms for clear definitions. His method is to start with one of the terms, reduce it to a simple idea and trace the idea to an originating impression. If there is no originating impression, then the term is empty of meaning.

The *Abstract* does not seem, then, to point directly to the new works that Hume wrote to clarify both the language and the conceptual apparatus of the *Treatise* in the sense mentioned in the past chapter. It is not too strong a claim to suggest that the *Abstract* and the thought process behind its writing, hints at the possibility of the *Enquiries* and the textual method of the essays. The *Abstract*, rather than a 'miniature' of the *ECHU*, is suggestive of it, for that work is subtle and finely worked. Hume remains sensitive to the needs of the reader with respect to the difficulties of long chains of reasoning, both implicitly and explicitly. In the constructing the conclusion to his argument concerning 'necessary connection' Hume writes: 'But to hasten to a conclusion of this argument, which is already drawn out to too great a length ...' (*ECHU*, 7.2.26).

The textual method in the *Abstract* is significant for most of Hume's 'political/economics writing' beyond the economic ideas in the *Treatise*, is developed within the framework of the political economy essay. The reflection on writing continued and those essays conventionally classified as 'economic' were written later than those conventionally classified as 'political'. The turn from 'diffuse' to 'concise', as stated by Danford (though the degree of conciseness must be relative as the essay is a discursive mode and not all of his essays are short and 'plain'), writing styles gives rise to the style and hence to the accessibility and popularity of his economic essays. The first *Enquiry* too was published *after* Hume had engaged in significant essay writing (the essays published in 1742 contain both political and philosophical material) and by that time his writing style had already a chance to mature. Indeed the critical, but perceptive, Kruse argues, using a letter from Hume to 'Henry Home of June 1742' that Hume deliberately set out to create a public for his essays to better further the marketability of his subsequent*Enquiries* (Kruse, 1939, 11). Kruse is wholly unsympathetic to Hume's attitude towards literary fame and denigrates the *Enquiries* as a having abandoned the 'systematic structure of the three books of the Treatise' (Kruse, 1939, 12). Modern commentators tend to display more understanding.

It is a part of the essay-writing *genre* – and seems to have been since the time of *genre*'s originators, Bacon and Montaigne – that it deals with a problematic context/content and that it is 'marked by a definite concern for the reader's response to the written word' (McCarthy, 1989, 63 and 51). Hume clearly understood and delighted in this approach. Box at least would agree that Hume subsequently took the idea of concision seriously: 'In condensing whole books of the *Treatise* into collections of linked essays, Hume shortens the chain of reasoning within and between sections, making the interconnections more apparent and helping prevent the reader from failing to see the forest from the trees' (Box, 1990, 175). However, the intellectual effort made in the *Treatise* to communicate the 'science of man' within the constraints Hume sets for a scientific project must be recognized in something more discerning than simple the 'abstruse' style. His *textual* method is not in itself aiming at abstruseness but for a systematic, step-by-step scrutiny of propositions and inferences, for the clarification of questions and for the careful evaluation of evidence. It is an attempt to model his experimental methodology in a systematic written format. We can point to how it may be difficult for novice readers (then and now) to develop the schemata for successful reading. The *Treatise* is constructed, exhaustively, with 'science' and a full inductive process in mind. We will see in Chapter 6 how Hume furthers his move, in his essays, from 'science' to 'rhetoric'.

Hume in the *Abstract* is still pushing strongly, and somewhat crudely, the radical and innovative nature of his ideas (Danford, 1990, 22). It is easy to see why those who are unsympathetic to Hume's character may find this self-recommendation distasteful: 'Thr' this whole book, there are great pretensions to new discoveries in philosophy; but if anything can entitle the author to so glorious a name as that of an *inventor*, 'tis the use he makes of the principle of the association of ideas, which enters into most philosophy' (*Abstract*, 35).[10] Where criticisms of the author's views in the *Treatise* appear to be offered by the author of the *Abstract*, they are immediately modified by subsequent phrases or sentences. It is as well to remember, as Mossner says, in contrast to moralizing found elsewhere, that the practice of 'puffing' (the term 'puff' seems to have been used of the *Abstract* originally by Keynes and Straffa and has been repeated in the literature since) one's own work was not unusual at this time and later. Malthus indulged in the same practice. The tone of the *ECHU* reflects the elements of the simplification process found in the *Abstract* and is less strident though still clear on the claims that are being made for Hume's philosophy. Hume is also less present than in the *Treatise*. If Box is right and Hume switched from a diffuse to a concise style in the essays and *ECHU,* then the *Abstract* is the first systematic attempt at achieving concision. It still maintains the notion of a long 'chain of reasoning' (the *Treatise* is still the target text) but accepts the difficulties that this gives to non-philosophical readers. Hume is moving however from philosophy to rhetoric in the sense that he is starting to very carefully take on board the nature of audience. This transition will only be completed in his *History of England* or in his essays. The final paragraph of the Section I of *ECHU* reflects the motivation behind the writing of the *Abstract* and is telling with respect to the overall 'tone' of his new approach to writing, including his future economics essays:

But as, after all, the abstractedness of these speculations is no recommendation, but rather a disadvantage to them, and as this difficulty may perhaps be surmounted by care and art, and the avoiding of unnecessary detail, we have, in the following enquiry, attempted to throw some light upon subjects, from which uncertainty has hitherto deterred the wise and obscurity the ignorant. Happy, if we can unite the boundaries of the different species of philosophy, by reconciling profound enquiry with clearness, and truth with novelty! And still more happy if, reasoning in this manner, we can undermine the foundations of an abstruse philosophy, which seems to have hitherto served only as a shelter to superstition, and a cover to absurdity and error!

4 The *Treatise*

Shaping social and economic life

In what sense or senses may we consider the *Treatise* to be a foundation for Hume's 'economic' ideas worked upon only a few years later? Schatz, writing in 1902 and however dated in other respects, makes a significant general point about Hume's economics and the *Treatise*: 'C'est sa philosophie qui fait de Hume un économiste ... Ses *Discours politiques* viennent seulement après que cette évolution s'est produite et après qu'une notable partie, peut-être la plus importante, de son oeuvre économique, a déjà été élucidée et exposée dans son oeuvre philosophique' (Schatz, 1902, 5). This is in stark contrast with Schumpeter's later judgment (see Chapter 2). Relevant passages in the *Treatise* have been worked over, of course, by political theorists but I have not seen a close analysis nor an economics interpretation of *all* of the passages to be reviewed.

Rotwein, for example, locates the later economics in aspects of the psychological concerns of the *Treatise* as well as in his historical understanding – a view not accepted by Schumpeter (Rotwein, 1955; Schumpeter, 1954, 447). Rotwein's treatment is general rather than specific and does not deal in any significant detail with Hume's Newtonian methodology (Rotwein, 1955). Skinner also makes significant use of the *Treatise* to illustrate Hume's understating of the social psychology of economic life (Skinner, 1993). The recently published, *Blackwell Guide to Hume's Treatise* only makes direct reference to Hume's economics as 'post-*Treatise*' writing (Robison, 2006, 35–37).

The emphasis here will be on the fine details of the writing as well as on the 'scientific' methodology of Hume's approach, though the issue of classifying Hume's methodology in terms of 'logical positivism' or 'sceptical realism' or even 'interactionism' will be side-stepped (see Dow, 2002, 412; Nakano, 2006, 688). The stress is on what is potentially available of an economic nature in the *Treatise*. The relationship with the economic essays will be indicated here but an analysis postponed until Chapters 6, 7 and 8.

'Economic ideas' will be interpreted fairly widely to include for example those motivations and conventions that Hume seems as significant for the development and coherence of society such as justice, property and promises (and hence, contracts, essential for the functioning of a market economy) including issues of motivation as well as what may be thought of nowadays as economic sociology.

The method used will be textual analysis. This will take the form of a close reading. A 'close reading' looks into a text and hence isolates it from other texts, in the first instance, in the hope that we emerge with a clearer understanding of the examined text as written (Henderson, 2006, 111). Strict adherence to the methodology of a close reading will not be maintained as comments are made on features of the writing that may be taken to be typical of features encountered elsewhere in the *Treatise*. The focus is rather on the coherence of textual episodes. Some ideas will also be introduced out of sequence as discovered in the text as we will only be dealing with short passages rather than the section as a whole.

The urge to society

Extract one

The first strong statement on the origins of society is found, not in Book III, where the bulk of his comments on society and what he would have called 'oeconomy' are to be found, but in Part III of Book II. The main subject is 'Of liberty and necessity' and the opening concerns of the section are with the 'operations of external bodies', 'the communication of their motion' and 'their attraction and mutual cohesion', a reference to Newtonian concepts. Hume reactivates his notion of *cause* and *effect* (based on the perception or, rather, inference of 'constant union') and illustrates his point with respect to 'human affairs' in two related passages, reproduced below. It will soon become obvious why the topic is introduced in Book II (*OF THE PASSIONS*):

> To this end a very slight and general view of the common course of human affairs will be sufficient. [sentence one] There is no light, in which we can take them, that does not confirm this principle. [sentence two] Whether we consider mankind according to the difference of sexes, ages, governments, conditions, or methods of education; the same uniformity and regular operation of natural principles are discernible. [sentence three] Like causes still produce like effects; in the same manner as in the natural actions of the elements and powers of nature. [sentence four]
>
> There are different trees, which regularly produce fruit, whose relish is different from each other; and this regularity will be admitted as an instance of necessity and causes in external bodies. [sentence five] But are the products of *Guienne* and of *Champagne* more regularly different than the sentiments, actions and passions of the two sexes, of which the one are distinguish'd by their force and maturity, the other by their delicacy and softness? [sentence six]

Are the changes of our body from infancy to old age more regular and certain than those of our mind and conduct? [sentence seven] And wou'd a man be more ridiculous, who wou'd expect that an infant of four years old will raise a weight of three hundred pound, than one, who from a person of the same age, wou'd look for a philosophical reasoning, or a prudent and well-concerted action? [sentence eight]

We must certainly allow, that the cohesion of the parts of matter arises from natural and necessary principles, whatever difficulty we may find in explaining them: And for a like reason we must allow, that human society is founded on like principles; and our reason in the latter case, is better than even that in the former; because we not only observe, that men *always* seek society, but can also explain the principles, on which this universal propensity is founded. [sentence nine] For is it more certain that two flat pieces of marble will unite together, than that two young savages of different sexes will copulate? [sentence ten] Do the children arise from this copulation more uniformly, than does the parents care for their safety and preservation? [sentence eleven] And after they have arriv'd at years of discretion by the care of their parents, are the inconveniences attending their separation more certain that their foresight of these inconveniences, and their care of avoiding them by a close union and confederacy? [sentence twelve]

(*T*, 2.3.1.5–9)

Sentence one contains Hume's commitment to explore the idea of uniformity. His commitment is merely to that of a 'slight and general review' and this is confirmed by the following paragraphs (seven if this present one is included) that deal with a series of near-related illustrations. Sentence two reinforces Hume's conviction as to the truth of his proposition, or rather propositions, put in a clear form in sentences three and four. His propositions are that we can detect in social life the regular operation of natural principles and that these with respect to 'cause' and 'effects' work 'in the same manner as in the mutual action of the elements and powers of nature'. The idea of causal links thus described, together with his empiricism is of considerable significance for the future development of Hume's economic understanding. Robison (2006, 35–37) holds correctly, for example, that this notion of causality is central to Hume's economics. The list in sentence two suggests a series of systematic investigations.

This link between human nature and natural philosophy is one that is made in many different places in the *Treatise*. The detail of the linkages is not spelled out within the sentence but as the passage is introductory, it can be expected to be supplied later. (It is to evidence such as that we would look for support for Kemp Smith's view that, in Ayer's words, Hume's intent was to 'assimilate natural to moral philosophy' (Ayer, 2000, 26). Hume seems to be consistent in the ways on which he creates and then fulfils a reader's expectations even if he does not always provide an overall plan in advance to assist the reader. Indeed such an expectation is specifically fulfilled by the elements of the next sentence. Sentence four carries the idea of the passages that have gone before in which Hume makes the point that 'external bodies' move in accordance with necessity. The ideas contained in sentence four shape in fine detail the structure, content and presentation of the ideas developed in the next three paragraphs. It is very important to Hume to fix the idea of the 'cohesion of parts of matter' through the careful manipulation of details of his writing.

Sentence five is divided into two parts. The first consists of a general statement of 'scientific' fact (an observed and established 'regularity') and the second is an evaluation of the status of the fact with respect to the train of thought that Hume is developing. It is presented as an example of 'necessity and causes in external bodies'. In such textual detail Hume achieves his notion of a 'chain of reasoning'. The sentence starting with 'But' (sentence six) exemplifies 'trees' with reference to tropical and more temperate produce (*'Guienne'* and *'Champagne'*: the reader is left to fill in the missing details)[1] and draws a parallel between natural products and the division and 'sentiments', 'passions' and other attributes of the sexes – the 'immaturity' of the one and the 'softness' of the other – in humankind. Hume is consistent in later writing and holds that female company softens manners and hence promotes 'polite' society. (He rarely makes the mistake of underestimating female intelligence.) This is presented as a rhetorical question or at least one on which the reader can pass a judgment that agrees with Hume's point of view. Questions play a significant role in shaping details of Hume's discourse throughout the *Treatise* and the clarification of questions is central to his method. No analysis, of the 'sentiments' or 'passions', is made at this point. Note also that Hume is using both 'natural philosophy' in the Newtonian sense and 'nature' and in the sense of 'biological nature'.

The third paragraph gives further emphasis, presented as a series of questions that by their rhetorical structure imply their corresponding answers. Hume's articulation and development of questions is one of the most significant ways in which the 'chain of reasoning' is advanced. The construction is in many ways similar to that of the sentences in the preceding paragraph and with respect to the final sentence in the first paragraph (sentence four). The writing is all of a piece – observation is of key significance – and follows an integrated pattern of development. The emphasis shifts from external nature (the world beyond humans) to the human experience of development and of ageing over time and to associated human mental capacities. Physical nature and the mind – Hume draws here on classical sources – are tied up together in Hume's account. Sentence seven is general and repeats the pattern of the opening sentence in the preceding paragraph. The parallels between 'body' and 'mind' are drawn with considerable detail in sentence eight, which is the counterpart in structure and intent to sentence six. The statements are based on observations or rather expectations. There is a link between individual human characteristics, including age and character, and expected human activities (see also the third person dimension to this at *T.* 2.3.2.2)

The opening sentence of the final paragraph of the excerpt is complex and made more so by the colon. Although it has been numbered as sentence nine it is best considered in three sections. The first section (from the initial capital letter to the colon) is both a summary of what has been consistently demonstrated before and an implication. Notice the tail: 'whatever difficulty we may find in explaining them', i.e. 'them' being 'the natural and necessary principles' that inform the behaviour of parts of matter. The second section runs from the capital 'A' of 'And' to the semi-colon. This section sums up the main force of the preceding examples. The repetition of 'like reason'/'like principles' strengthens the phrase. The final section (also internally complex) runs from the lower case 'a' of the 'and' to the end at the full stop. The phrase 'and our reason in the latter case, is better than even that in the former' is significant. Here Hume is contrasting knowledge with respect to the working of human nature with knowledge concerning the workings of physical nature. The 'whatever difficulty we have in explaining them' (knowledge of physical nature) is not to be applied to our knowledge of human nature in this respect. The fact that 'men *always* seek society' (the unspoken assumption of sentence two) can be explained with reference to simple principles set out in the rest of the passage. Keeping sentence two in mind, we can expect an explanation in terms of 'the same uniformity and regular operation of natural principles', though this time they will be specifically identified. The 'science of man' has by implication some advantages over natural science. Hume has, clearly, high hopes for its success.

Sentence ten maintains the parallelism, essentially an argument by analogy. Argument by analogy will be shown to have significance for Hume in social and historical analysis in general (see Chapters 7 and 8). This analogy may be one that could be questioned as physical nature and emotional nature seem so very different. Here we have Newton and Hutcheson in close juxtaposition (though with respect to method, Newton wins out) between 'external bodies' and 'human nature' that informed the structure of much of the previous writing and provides it with its cumulative impact. Hume uses the question format to explore the degree of certainty of a natural union between 'two flat pieces of marble' and 'two young savages of different sexes'. Human nature is predictable, human desires lead to action in the world. 'Copulation' is the key to social formation as is the production of children and raising them through the operation of 'natural affection' (explored also as a question in sentence eleven). Hume is consistent with his view of human nature in this regard (consider, for example, the following: 'We blame a father for neglecting his child. Why? Because it shews a want of natural affection, which is the duty of every parent' (*T*, 3.2.1.5). Given the need for cooperation in the rearing of children, anarchy by implication is not an option. Sentence twelve then traces out the steps that go from initial family formation to 'a close union and confederacy' – Hume's rather weak way of going from feelings to a widespread social convention. Here 'foresight' does have a part to play, according the Hume.

The outcome of the 'copulation' of 'two young savages of different sexes', whom we must presume were intent on their pleasure or at least on the satisfaction of their bodily 'appetites' and not on such an end, is the formation of society.[2] This is of course a specific example of a general feature of social argument among the Scottish 'literati', that of 'unintended consequences'. Adam Smith makes very particular use, along Humean lines, of unintended consequences in Book one, Chapter II of the *Wealth of Nations*. It also embodies Cicero's notion that the family is 'the nursery … of the state' (*De Officiis*, I, 54).

In the middle of the next paragraph Hume writes:

> Men cannot live without society, and cannot be associated without government. Government makes a distinction of property, and establishes the different ranks of men. This produces industry, traffic, manufactures, law-suits, war, leagues, alliances, voyages, travels, cities, fleets, ports, and all those other actions and objectives, which cause such a diversity, and at the same time maintain such a uniformity in human life.
>
> (*T*, 2.3.1.9)

This is a very curious list and mixes government and market in almost equal proportions. Activity (to meet needs/wants; to evade the solitary condition and to find fulfilment in living) is necessary part and consequence of human nature but structured and sustained cooperative activity requires appropriate institutional arrangements. In this passage, Hume may have deleted direct human action but it is of course implied. It is the distinction of property and hence of interests that creates the action. The list constitutes the kind of useful external objects upon which people, given the means, universally, fix their practical concerns. The action-oriented human agent is in Smith's account the consequence of a certain tendency/propensity in human nature 'to truck, barter and exchange' (*WN*, I.ii.1).

Hume's notion of a necessary balance between action (in various forms) and indolence (or repose) will be looked at again when considering the *Enquiries* and the *Essays*. Action on the one part and harmony and balance on the other are two sides of the same coin. This notion of 'balance', a notion that is general in Hume in the sense that it occurs and recurs in a variety of contexts: at the level of the individual life (the 'mixed kind of life'); in the political life of a nation (the balance of interests within a constitution or state; moderation as a political virtue); in relations between nations ('Of the Balance of Power') and in trade and related monetary matters ('Of the Balance of Trade' and how it is to be politically evaluated). It is also found in moral matters in the sense of temperance, prudence and caution: 'a due medium, says the Peripatetics, is the character of virtue' (*ECPM*, 6.1.1). Such a medium is 'determined by utility'.

Essay V, 'Of the Origin of Government', merges Hume's insights from the sociobiological, with economic necessity (discussed in the next section) and custom to give: 'Man, born in a family, is compelled to maintain society, from necessity, from natural inclination, and from habit' (I, Essay V, 36). For Hume, stable economic activity is the outcome of ordered relationships, property relations in particular, and ordered relationships are the concern of government. Property is prior to government and both property and justice are prior to commercial economic life. This stance is maintained in his later writing, where, according to Velk and Riggs (1985, 154), even Hume's later argument for free trade 'left the government with room to manoeuvre'. His ideas developed in 'Of Commerce', while challenging aspects of mercantilist thinking nevertheless incorporates mercantilist patterns of thought, as perhaps the quote just given from the *Treatise* also does. Hume's thought while it has a market element nonetheless manages also to be focused on government. In this sense then government and institutional arrangements are foundational though clearly subject to adjustment and change as society develops.

Deleule (1979, 14) argues that Hume was appreciated in France and interpreted at the time as a writer who achieved 'tantôt la synthèses de la pensée néo-mercantiliste, tantôt les prémises du libéralisme'. How the link between society, government and economics comes about is the subject of the next analysis, taken from Book III. Smith would develop similar views though constructed around the idea of 'unintended consequences'.

Notice that Hume talks of 'Government' as making the distinction of property (by implication through 'law') and of establishing 'the different ranks of men'. Social categories in this sense are ordered by the distinction of property (e.g. those who have property and those who have not: a necessary consequence of Hume's notion of scarcity, examined below). This is a long way from the market-place and the individualization of economic behaviour. The passage is collapsing a whole process of human social evolution into an over-shortened time span. Hume was historically aware with respect to the origins and purposes of social hierarchy and such a passage alone cannot tell us very much about Hume's tendency to liberalism or conservatism. The framework of institutions and conventions is primary for social development and creates, from Hume's analysis, as we shall see, the possibilities of a stable approach to economic life.

It should be noted that Hume argues a counter-case based on the observation that 'necessity is regular and certain' and human nature and conduct 'irregular and uncertain' (*T*, 2.3.1.11). This is a typical, and perhaps overworked, move in the wider discourse and one that is in keeping with the idea, found in the introduction, that principles are not be taken on trust. The move is also in keeping with the idea that finding a strong basis for generalization requires 'number' and 'variety' with respect to 'experiments' (Kemp Smith, [1941] 1964, 62). It is precision such as this, the implication of a scientific induction rather than mere argument from example, in

Hume's approach to the analysis of his topics, which can overwhelm the reader. In looking at the counter-case, he is testing out the stability of 'stable objects' (mentioned in the quote from Whelan). Variable human reaction has been the concern of philosophers since the time of Plato, Aristotle and Xenophon, philosophers with an interest in what could be called, post-Adam Smith, the visible hand of management. Hume finds the counter-case wanting on the grounds that 'one single contrariety of experiment' does not 'destroy all reasoning' and that 'mind' proceeds 'with that degree of assurance on evidence which remains' (*T*, 2.3.1.12). He is not therefore dealing with certainties, or, to put it another way, with absolutely stable objects, but, rather, with general tendencies, probabilities. A version of the inference from the counter-example is found in 'Of the Rise of Arts and Sciences': 'What depends on a few persons is, in a great measure, to be ascribed to chance, or secret and unknown causes: What arises from a great number, may often be accounted for by determinate and known causes' (I, Essay XIV, 112).

The urge to economic life: a second set of extracts

This set is taken from Book III, Part II, Section II, 'Of the Origin of Justice and Property'. Biologically, society, Hume has established, is implied by our human needs for emotional support and for the care of our long-dependent offspring. Humans need cooperative action in society in order to survive but human nature is complex, and benevolence and self-interest both need to be explored and accommodated with respect to social formation. The products of economic cooperation (various forms of property) are, even with social formation, scarce and such scarcity can lead to conflicts that prevent social formation. Hume is concerned with two questions, the establishment of the rules of justice and the link between the rules of justice and 'moral beauty' (here the influence of Hutcheson is very close to the surface).

There is a much to consider in this section and attention will only be given in detail to selected highlights. Before he considers the origin of the rules of justice (essential to his conceptualization of economic life) Hume compares human and animal nature with respect to natural 'wants' and the 'means' available for their satisfaction. In this set of comparisons, the human animal considered on an isolated basis, 'is provided neither with arms, nor force, nor other natural abilities, which are in any degree answerable to so many necessities'. Hume's view, throughout, is that human nature is, what Alanen calls, 'animal and social' (Alanen, 2006, 179). The conflict between the mechanistic and the biological in Hume's philosophy and economics is central to Deleule's (1979) work on Hume. Nowhere in this section does he really consider the social basis of animal life, nor does he move much beyond a conventional presentation of animal life. Nonetheless, the passage is worth a close reading. The significance of cooperation and trade is also drawn attention to elsewhere in the *Treatise* (see *T*, 3.2.4.1).

'Of the origin of justice and of property'

We now proceed to examine two questions, viz. *concerning the manner, in which the rules of justice are establish'd by the artifice of men*; and *concerning the reasons, which determine us to attribute to the observance or neglect of these rules a moral beauty and deformity*. [sentence one] These questions will appear afterwards to be distinct. [sentence two] We shall begin with the former. [sentence three].

Of all the animals, with which the globe is peopled, there is none towards whom nature seems, at first sight, to have exercis'd more cruelty than towards man, in the numberless wants and necessities, with which she had loaded him, and in the slender means, which she affords to the relieving these necessities. [sentence four] In other creatures these two particulars generally compensate each other. [sentence five] If we consider the lion as a voracious and carnivorous animal, we shall easily discover him to be very necessitous; but if we turn our eye to his make and temper, his agility, his courage, his arms, and his force, we shall find, that his advantages hold proportion with his wants. [sentence six] The sheep and ox are depriv'd of all these advantages; but their appetites are moderate, and their food is of easy purchase. [sentence seven] In man alone, this unnatural conjunction of infirmity, and of necessity, may be observ'd in its greatest perfection. [sentence eight] Not only the food, which is required for his sustenance, flies his search and approach, or at least requires his labour to be produc'd, but he must be possess'd of cloaths and lodging, to defend himself against the injuries of the weather; tho' to consider him only in himself, he is provided neither with arms, nor force, nor other natural abilities, which are in any degree answerable to so many necessities. [sentence nine]

'Tis by society alone he is able to supply his defects, and raise himself up to an equality with his fellow-creatures, and even acquire a superiority above them. [sentence ten] By society all his infirmities are compensated; and tho' in that situation his wants multiply every moment upon him, yet his abilities are still more augmented, and leave him in every respect more satisfy'd and happy, than 'tis possible for him, in his savage and solitary condition, ever to become. [sentence eleven] When every individual person labours apart, and only for himself, his force is too small to execute any considerable work; his labour being employ'd in supplying all his different necessities, he never attains a perfection in any particular art; and as his force and success are not at all times equal, the least failure in either of these particulars must be attended with inevitable ruin and misery. [sentence twelve] Society provides a remedy for these *three* inconveniences. [sentence thirteen] By the conjunction of forces, our power is augmented: By the partition of employments, our ability encreases: and by our mutual succour we are less expos'd to fortune and accidents. [sentence fourteen] 'Tis by this additional *force, ability*, and *security*, that this society becomes advantageous. [sentence fifteen]

$$(T, 3.2.2.1–3.2.2.3)$$

Sentences one to three constitute the introductory paragraph to the section as a whole. The extracts here will deal with the origins of the division of labour. The origins of justice will be dealt with by summarization.

Hume is setting out the topic of the section and divides it into two questions, highlighted by the use of italics (a helpful convention encountered in reading earlier parts of the *Treatise* – for a further example see the third paragraph of Book III, Part I, Section I, where Hume also states that the question actually posed, 'will immediately cut off all loose discourses' – and which Hume also occasionally applied to significant propositions within a topic as it develops). In the earlier section, I argued that sensory experience is normally one end of the chain and that Hume avoided *a priori* reasoning. However, as with all writers, Hume has to start somewhere. What he does, and he does this throughout the *Treatise*, is sets up a question or series of questions for investigation and then threads (another term used later in the *Abstract*) the exploration through the subsequent discourse. The chaining that will be illustrated here is not so much that of the articulation and reapplication of the empirical test as established earlier, but of a carefully contrived coherence within a series of passages devoted to the same theme. The passages looked at here achieve a perfect fusion of content and expression.

Hume's language is very careful: '*the artifice of men*', hinting to the notion of justice as an 'artificial virtue'. Hume also states in sentence two that the two questions 'will appear afterwards to be distinct'. This is a signal that the answer to each question will be composed of different elements and anticipates Hume's division between the first stage of establishing justice (before, as it were, social formation) and then the moral approval of justice, based upon utility – an idea given its fullest and simplest textual expression in the *Enquiries* – in the development of society subsequently. Sentence three, then, though there is no explicit numbering system, sets out the order in which the topic will be developed and answered. Hume makes use of a variety of devices, often subtle and easily missed, for the advanced organization of an episode, but he often fails to do this for very long stages in an argument (e.g. in the treatment of the entire topic of cause and effect for example). The notion of a chain of reasoning suggests predictable moves but readers have to work at understanding how to anticipate the developments. The present example is very clearly organized and simply signalled (questions–answers).

Sentence four locates 'man' in 'nature' and sets up an initial contrast between 'man' and other 'animals' with respect to the provision of natural wants. There is in this passage no claim to direct access to experience as there was in the first set of passages analysed: the statement is taken, to some extent, as already justified by experience though its claims are justified, as any discerning reader of Hume would now expect, by exemplification. As a statement of the plight of human kind, it is as telling as the neoclassical notion that 'scarcity' is everywhere the fundamental economic problem. Scarcity, absolute in the case of the indigent savage, and relative in the case of any social formation that falls short of universal abundance, is a significant notion for Hume (see Chapter 5).

Very great care is taken to ensure that the series of contrasts that are later provided are vividly articulated as they form a basis for Hume's argument against the notion of an original 'state of nature'. Hume is careful to add 'seems, at first sight' and this signals that there will be at least a second look at the proposition later in the text. Contrasts are made between men and beasts in terms of a second contrast between 'wants and necessities' on the one hand and the 'means' of 'relieving these necessities' (i.e. natural advantages) on the other. The contrasts and continuities between human nature and circumstances and animal nature and circumstances will have been encountered earlier in the discourse – in what Whelan refers to as 'the curious *Treatise* chapters on animals' (Whelan, 1985, 68). Such comparative episodes would have come as no surprise to educated eighteenth-century readers. Humans were conventionally seen as part animal, part divine, with reason seen as the differentiating feature and the link with God. Stressing links between human nature and animal nature with respect to the reasoning capacity of animals was part of the process of divorcing the discussion of human nature from divine nature. This was a primary concern of Hume's, and hence part of the process of shifting the discussion – developed also, though much more cautiously, by Smith, who was even more careful to hide behind the smokescreen of Deism – of what it is to be human, from theology to social science.

Sentence five sets up a general proposition that in other animals the needs and means of satisfying them 'compensate each other'.[3] This is both a rider to the first idea set out in sentence four and a proposition that is further supported and investigated in the set of sentences that follow. The focus goes from animal to man and back to animal. In sentence six the move is back to animal but this time it is to a particular animal, the 'lion'. The use of a series of particular animals in contrasting circumstances lends strong justification to Hume's proposition. 'Wants' are set out for the 'lion' in terms of his 'very necessitous' condition and the 'means' set out in terms of his 'make and temper' and other conventional natural attributes. The 'lion' represents carnivorous animals in general. Lexical items move in parallel even although the words are adapted to suit the 'lion' as a particular kind of animal.

In sentence seven, herbivores provide a natural contrast to the condition of the 'lion'. The parallelism is maintained but simplified, 'their appetites are moderate, and their food is of easy purchase'. 'Appetites' matches the originating 'wants' and 'food of easy purchase' matches the originating 'means … to the relieving these necessities' and so the elements are balanced.

Human appetites are complex (a mixture of basic needs and elaborated desires, based in the imagination) and not fixed. They involve a negotiation of sorts between the interior and exterior aspects of human nature. Implicit in this way of setting up the problem is the notion of an animal economy, an idea that was to find its fullest expression in the works of Charles Darwin. And this is not a casual thought in Hume, he repeats in 'Of Polygamy and Divorces' in a slightly different context. Mating in animals, regulated, surprisingly, by 'the supreme legislator', suggests that nature's circumstances shape the animal mating practices: 'Where she furnishes, with ease, food and defence to the newborn animal, the present embrace terminates the marriage; and care of the offspring is committed entirely to the female. Where the food is of more difficult purchase, the marriage continues for one season, till the common progeny can provide for itself; and then the union immediately dissolves ...' (I, Essay XIX, 183). The implications of the long dependency of human offspring are clear.

Sentence eight puts forward the main idea of sentence four in a more concise form and as a proposition. As a proposition then, in Hume's scheme of arguing, it needs to be immediately justified by an example. The textual patterning is simple but the elaboration within the whole passage is skilful. The next sentence (sentence nine) is divided into two equal parts: the first deals with the set of human needs and these are, as may be expected, more elaborately developed than the needs of the animals; the second deals with the relative lack of means, when compared implicitly to the animals, to answering 'so many necessities'. The items parallel and detail those of sentence four, in the same way as has been observed for the sentences on the 'lion' and on the 'sheep and ox'. However, Hume is careful to add 'tho" to consider him only in himself' (recall the 'at first sight' of sentence four). This predicts the opening move in the subsequent paragraph. Hume has focused on the human predicament and the need to work for, at first, survival. Everything that human's have in life is gained by work. Nature's gifts have to be appropriated and transformed by work to provide initially basic food, shelter and clothing. Hume develops this idea and locates the motivation to work in the active principle of human nature and located the active principles in the passions. Smith was to borrow and refine this idea and located the animating principle in the 'propensity to truck, barter and exchange'.

Sentence ten marks the start of Hume's analysis of the benefits of society. The whole passage is very rich and well wrought and anticipates by several decades Smith's published views in the WN in the significance of the division of labour. Hume, unlike Smith, does not make use of the notion as a formidable analytical device or as part of the foundations for a theory of growth. Nor does he integrate the notion with other sustained aspects of theory-building. Smith unites the division of labour with his complex version of stadial theory (see Chapter 8) to account for the growth of wealth in and social transformation towards commercial society. Hume merely states the advantages. However, overall the passage is a relatively underdeveloped form of stadial storytelling and it is hardly likely even to be acknowledged as such without knowledge of Smith's model. This particular sentence is carefully arranged in a hierarchy of benefits that runs from supplying 'defects' to 'equality with his fellow-creatures' through to 'superiority above them'. This implies a hierarchy of social conditions. It is the appreciation of potential of such benefits (utility) in the understanding that makes, for Hume, society possible.

By moving from the negative to the positive, Hume intends to impress his readership with the positive attributes of social life and at the same time suggest a sort of social evolution not just with respect to means of living but with respect to experience. In the *ECHU* Hume makes it clear that human reasoning capacity with respect to inferences and causality is differentiated from that of the animals and enhanced by experience (including in developed society by education and reading, aspects, particularly reading, stressed in the *ECPM*). Consider the view of human experience and original limitations in the *NHR*: 'But a barbarous, necessitous animal (such as man in the first origin of society), pressed by such numerous wants and passions, has no leisure to admire the regular face of nature ...' (Hume, *NHR*, 24). Admiring the regular face of nature implies careful observation and causal reasoning. Human understanding, the capacity to reason from cause and effect and establishing a chain of reasoning, develops with the development of, in this case, expanded economic experience. When Adam Smith links the division of labour to learning, he is also drawing, to some extent, upon Hume.

Sentence eleven further elaborates the claims that Hume makes concerning the benefits of social life. There is an internal contrast between the compensation for his 'infirmities' in society and his potential condition in the context of a 'savage and solitary condition' (the imagined alternative condition).[4] This reference prepares the reader for the criticisms that Hume will later make of the Hobbesian notion of the state of nature. Because he is intent of making a thorough and different analysis than that made by the state of nature theorist, Hume invests strongly in his analysis of the origins of justice and property, and later uses it as the basis for the origins of government. However, Hume does not lose sight of the nature of economic life in society and he carefully balances the multiplication of wants (new and stimulated by general commerce but also latent as it were, 'conceal'd in the soul' till articulated by economic change) to be expected in society with the fact that 'his abilities are still more augmented'. Later, in developing his views on 'luxury', prefigured here in the multiplication of wants, Hume will make use of the notion of improvement as an incentive to further productivity (see 'Of Commerce', for example). Human nature itself and its interaction with the external environment simply, under normal circumstances, disallows Plato's state, set out in the *Republic*, of an endless reproduction of the same. In this process, there is the potential for an improving dynamic and hence for society rising above the 'necessitous'. The 'solitary state' here, given what happens later in the section, should be thought of as providing a means of comparison (i.e. an analytical device rather than necessarily a historical fact). The next part of the sentence (a claim at this stage and not as yet evidenced by a principle or set of principles) balances out, by means of productivity gains as a result of the separation of labour, the increased costs – 'yet his abilities are still more augmented' when compared to the solitary state.

This whole passage qualifies as a very precise and, indeed, rigorous economic statement, based around changing wants and changing capacity for purposeful activity and a trade-off of relative costs and benefits involved in combining together. His points are subtle, almost marginalistic in nature, and the sophisticated suggestions, often packed into one long sentence, could be easily missed. Hume in the *Treatise* is already thinking about economic life, its scarcities and incentives, in a relatively sophisticated way. Deleule sums up Hume's understating of the human condition neatly: '… l'individue se trouverait dans une situation d'instabilité perpétuelle' (Deluele, 1979, 42). In later work, such as 'Of Refinement in the Arts', Hume explores the way in which the dynamic of improvement, based on 'wants' rather than 'needs' is sustained in sociable society. This dynamic is explored by Berry through the concept of 'superfluous value' (Berry, 2008, 49–64).

Hume's overall approach is one of historical evolution based on the capacity to learn and adjust as evidenced by his notion, later in the section, of '*uncultivated nature*' and of the subsequent development of 'judgement and understanding'. But unlike the work of members of the Scottish Historical School, Hume leaves, here at least, the notion of stages of social and economic development more or less implicit. He does articulate contrasting notions of simple and developed society in some of his essays and resorts to notions of the 'savage' in some of his other writing. Smith's concern about different kinds of economic society in the *Wealth of Nations* could be seen, to some extent at least, as a historicization of Hume's thinly drawn account. Both men saw the possibility of social progress, Hume through the development of the 'understanding' based on 'reflection' and experience, Smith through the learning associated with the division of labour. Both were also aware that in offering any explanation of economic activity, 'needs' were very quickly left behind (for Smith see, for example, *TMS*, I.iii.2.1). This is an insight that Hume later exploits in relation to his evaluation of 'luxury'.

In sentence eleven a series of simple propositions are put to the reader and these require specific comparisons and contrasts. Sentence twelve analyses the deficits found in the solitary state: low 'brute' labour inputs, low productivity (because of low levels of skill), and high risks. Notice that the labourer is described by the singular pronoun 'he'. When society is introduced, the pronoun changes to 'our'. The exemplification and justification –

we can now see as a recurrent feature of Hume's approach to his texts – and implied by both his empiricism and the related notion of a chain of reasoning – is the business conducted in the final and closing sentences of the paragraph from sentence twelve to the end (sentence fifteen).

The final sentences are also interestingly constructed. The textual patterning is based upon disadvantage/advantage. This is a reversal, perhaps of the expected order of advantages/disadvantages: Hume is building up the case for society and has chosen this pattern, which goes from negative to positive, with care. The pattern matches that of the ascending order in sentence ten. Sentence twelve is constructed in three parts separated by semi-colons. The parts cover the reduced force found in working apart; the lack of skill that results from trying to work to supply all 'necessities' and the risks of failure involved in the variable application and results of his 'force'. Sentence thirteen numbers the list of disadvantages after their initial presentation and claims that society provides 'a remedy'. By now we can see that by Hume's method of proceeding, such a claim requires exemplification. The next sentence is composed of a list of the three ways in which society overcomes the inconveniences of solitary life. The concluding sentence reorders the elements by replacing the developed attributes with a simple set of nouns (without the article) that refer to the main operating ideas: *'force, ability* and *security'*. This is a lively, summative statement of the benefits of cooperation in economic life, as striking in fact as any produced by Adam Smith. Indeed, in *LJ*(A) it is clear that Smith knew this passage and made use of it in his lectures on 'Police' though there are no simple, direct traces of it in Book one, Chapter one, of the *WN* as there is in the record of his lectures. Smith's choice of the division of labour and of the associated propensities as fundamental to socioeconomic development, and its analysis, is his own.[5]

What is also of interest is the sheer quantity of fertile economic ideas Hume has managed to pack into a relatively small amount of space. Hume's writing, especially in this section, exhibits what early twentieth-century literary critics would come to call 'economical'. This textual richness contradicts Kruse's now outmoded notion that the later essays on political economy 'have no internal connexion whatever with the Treatise' (Kruse, 1939, 2). The whole passage has exhibits a unity of form and function that is remarkable and attests to the notion that there are passages of great clarity and well-worked composition in the *Treatise*. When Hume came to write his essays, especially his economic essays, he had pre-existing writing and analytical skills to call upon.

Hume here is talking throughout about cooperation in 'society': the market may be implied, perhaps strongly by the sense of exchange implicit in the notion of the division of labour, but to jump directly from social cooperation to competitive commercial society, as Stewart (1992, 154) seems to imply, is not justifiable. It would be better to think of the passage as outlining all forms of cooperative economic society leading by a process of experimentation to a fully commercial society based on commercial contract and the keeping of promises. Hume is focusing on 'society' and cooperation (the word is used in both sentence four and sentence six), even if the concept ultimately, after a process of largely unspecified historical change, behind 'this society' – and as we shall see, below, the associated concept of 'justice' – is essentially that of a network of impersonal economic relations.

Hume has now established the economic benefits that come through social development. He has already developed a preliminary theory of social formation (analysed in extract one above). His task is now to bring the two together and this is undertaken in the paragraph that follows the one that has just been analysed. This is basically a rewrite, in context, of what came earlier in Part II and will not be subject to close analysis here.[6] However it, is useful to look at Hume's characteristic opening sentence of the new paragraph: 'But in order to form society, 'tis requisite not only that it be advantageous, but also that men be sensible of its advantages; and 'tis impossible, in their wild uncultivated state, that by study and reflection alone, they should ever be able to attain this knowledge' (*T*, 3.2.2.4). 'Passions' are one thing and the 'understanding' is another. Human nature conjoins the two parts. The 'natural appetite between the sexes' becomes the 'first and original principle of human society' and this is aided, over time, by 'custom and habit', aspects of human nature that play an important role in Hume's approach to society (as they were later to Adam Smith). According to Hume it is habit plain and simple that informs obedience to government and not any kind of contract. For Hume, as it was for Cantillon, political society originates in conquest (Cantillon, [circa 1730], [1755]: in Brewer 2001, 17). Hobbes is Hume's target throughout.

'Conjunction' is a powerful possibility. Hume however must consider all aspects of human nature and not just sex and procreation 'yet there are other particulars in our *natural temper*, and in our *outward circumstances*, which are very incommodious, and even contrary to the requisite conjunction' (*T*, 3.2.2.5). Selfishness is one issue and another is 'a peculiarity in our *outward circumstances*', i.e. the existence of 'such possessions as we have acquir'd by our industry and good fortune' (property). In the initial passage on the benefits of society, no direct mention is made of possessions though it is implied that as output increases, so goods and possessions are also likely to increase.[7] This is made specific in sentence two below. Hume focuses on the potential instability of the ownership of possessions:

The last only are both expos'd to the violence of others, and may be transferr'd without suffering any loss or alteration; while at the same time, there is not a sufficient quantity of them to supply every one's desires and necessities. [sentence one] As the improvement, therefore, of these goods is the chief advantage of society, so the *instability* of their possession, along with their *scarcity*, is the chief impediment. [sentence two]

(*T*, 3.2.2.7)

The two parts of sentence one are required for a full understanding of the problem. The taking of life and limbs are of no use to others in any positive sense. Possessions can be stolen with relative ease and put to use. The motivation for theft is described in what we would recognize as economic terms: there are not enough goods to go round. Hume's insights are essentially economic and rooted in the idea that relative scarcity and allocation are at the heart of a modern, commercial economic system. Sentence two is the problematic implication of Hume's analysis. Sentence two draws its force from the earlier analysis of the benefits of society. For society to be beneficial, security in production (through risk-sharing) must be backed by security (stability) in the possession of the increased output. The link between individual effort and stability of individual reward must be a strong and maintained. In '*uncultivated nature*' there are dispositions towards and against society. Engaging the 'understanding' is necessary for progress. Society, for Hume, is a historical fact so there must be a means, related in some way to human nature that makes society possible. To put the problem this way is to have already understood Hume's methodology. The solution to the problems posed by the 'partiality of our affections' is '*artifice*'. In this, the 'natural' is contrasted with the 'artificial' rather than with the 'unnatural'. Although Hume chose his term with care, it was not careful enough and he was subjected to (unwarranted) criticism for the suggestion that 'justice' was 'artificial'. The point is that people need to make an agreement (in the first instance this is conditional) to desist from making off with the possessions of others. Hume makes the analysis of this idea in various interconnected paragraphs. Only one of these will be examined in textual detail. It needs to be made clear (as Hume does later in the text) that Hume regards 'interest' as a powerful and potentially destructive motivating force:

This avidity alone, of acquiring goods and possessions for ourselves and our nearest friends, is insatiable, perpetual, universal, and directly destructive of society. [sentence one] There scarce is any one, who is not actuated by it; and there is no one, who has not reason to fear from it, when it acts without any restraint, and gives way to its first and most natural movements. [sentence two] So that upon the whole, we are to esteem the difficulties in the establishment of society, to be greater or less, according to those we encounter in regulating and restraining this passion. [sentence three].

(*T*, 3.2.2.12)

Sentence one is dramatically composed and cumulative in its impact – not unlike in its construction the lengthy and emotive sentences strategically used by Smith for dramatic purposes in the *Wealth of Nations*. Smith's aphorisms have caught the modern imagination and Hume's tend to be, in popular discourse, ignored. Smith's ideas, often in reduced accounts, are frequently mentioned in the press at times of economic stress. Hume is rarely called upon and yet, given his account of social formation and justice, he is relevant in analytical terms at least to discussions of governance and the maintenance of the rule of law particularly in certain parts of the developing world. It is an assumption about human psychology, as Rotwein recognized, significant for much of the insight into human economic behaviour that developed in subsequent economic thought. Hume's essays on government stress the need for rules to constrain avidity and self-interest.

The idea of the accumulation of possessions could suggest stability and growth but underneath is a selfish passion that, according to sentence two, can reassert itself. An important consideration is how to regulate and restrain and the time that it takes to secure regulation. Note the use of the phrase 'greater or less' in sentence three. Also recall that Hume thinks that it is not reason that restrains a passion, only the operation of some other passion. Given the way in which Hume approaches the question of inferences and evaluation, this sentence is a textual hint that the time period needed to overcome the difficulties will be discussed at some stage. It is in fact discussed in the next but one paragraph. There Hume holds that the 'establishment' of the rule could be 'the effect of many ages' (a notion of social evolution found in Mandeville) though Hume, conveniently impressed by the natural affection of parenthood and with its associated duties, is more inclined to feel that parents would quickly establish 'that rule' (to restrain from taking the property of others) within families. Hume's naturalism is pervasive. This move allows Hume (in a later passage in which he reflects on his own methodology and on that of those who support the notion of a 'state of nature') to conclude that the *'state of nature'*, which he also depicts as a 'solitary and forlorn condition', is largely a 'philosophical fiction' similar to the *'golden age'* of the 'poets', and not, in common with the views of subsequent writers such as Smith and Adam Ferguson, a historical fact.[8] There is nothing practical about utopian thinking. Hume remained critical in his later work on economics of utopian projects, preferring to base his economics on his view of human nature (Velk and Riggs, 1985, 155). Hume is prepared, however, to make use of both fictions to justify his point of view. 'Justice' operates in a society that is just above the 'necessitous' and falls short of universal abundance as envisaged in a golden age.

These are some of the conclusions towards which Hume is driving. Selfishness is the source of the convention that gives rise to justice, property and finally government. Note that for Hume, the idea of justice is prior to the formation of government. Even in the details he differs from Hobbes. By 'property' Hume is exploring the relationship between an individual and the right of control over an object.[9] By 'justice', Hume is concerned with what Cohon (2006, 259) calls 'honesty with respect to property' and hence what she sees as a very restricted view. This may well be a restricted notion but it is one that when broken, as it has been in recent history in many 'kleptocratic' sub-Saharan African states, leads to sustained economic decline and social disintegration. Hume's suggestion of sudden societal collapse when agreements are broken is perhaps exaggerated with respect to societies in slow economic decline but may be not so in the initial process of social formation. The stability and predictability that is inspired by not stealing is what counts if the benefits of cooperation are to be realized. Smith clearly reflected upon this problem in the *TMS* when looking at a society of thieves.

Justice is an 'artificial virtue' only because it is based on a set of rules, the result of the self-regulation of a passion, rather than on the direct operation of natural moral instinct. These rules have to be socialized by habit and education and have to be recognized for their 'utility' (see Chapter 5). For an action to be judged virtuous, it must arise from some motivation located in human nature and independent of the judgment (*T*, 3.2.1.2.). This is an idea that Hume may have developed from Hutcheson. The action is produced by human nature from motives that are 'distinct for its sense of morality' (*T*, 3.2.1.7). Hume holds that it would be circular to take the virtue of the action as the motive for the action. Motivation must be founded directly on human nature. Hume also holds that there is 'no such passion in human minds as the love of mankind, merely as such, independent of ... relation to ourself' (*T*, 3.2.1.12). The notion of public benevolence is limited by the same considerations as apply to private benevolence. Adam Smith's suspicion of public benevolence is partly rooted in Hume.

Justice is founded upon convention and rules and is not concerned so much with judging individual moral actions but with rights and with system-wide benefits or the public good. Indeed application of the rules of justice could lead in some cases to an outcome that some would find emotionally challenging (such as, using Hume's example, a result of judicial process, the returning of a fortune to a miser). Of course, this puts institutional development – Hume refers to 'conventions' – the result of 'artifice and contrivance' that are 'purposefully contrived and directed', by a process of reflection and evaluation, at the heart of economic life. The rules are designed with some public and hence impersonal good in mind in comparison to the direct interpersonal and often reciprocated good associated with acts of benevolence (see also Cohon, 2006, 259–260). The motive for keeping to the rules, once these have been established, is based upon habit or education or a culturally created sense of duty. Morality, jurisprudence and economics are drawn together in ways that are suggestive of Smith's concerns in his *Lectures on Jurisprudence*.

All the relevant text cannot be analysed here. It is sufficient, given Hume's capacity to repeat the analysis in a variety of ways, for present purposes that the passage immediately following the above quote be analysed as a representative sample.

'Tis certain, that no affection of the human mind has both a sufficient force, and a proper direction to counter-ballance the love of gain, and render men fit members of society, by making them abstain from the possessions of others. [sentence one] Benevolence to strangers is too weak for this purpose; and as to the other passions, they rather inflame this avidity, when we observe, that the larger our possession are, the more ability we have in gratifying, all our appetites. [sentence two] There is no passion, therefore, capable of controuling the interested affection, but the very affection itself, by an alteration of its direction. [sentence three] Now this alteration must necessarily take place upon the least reflection; since 'tis evident, that the passion is much better satisfy'd by its restraint, than by its liberty, and that by preserving society, we make much greater advances in the acquiring possessions, than by running into the solitary and forlorn condition, which must follow upon violence and an universal licence. '[sentence four] The question, therefore, concerning the wickedness or goodness of human nature, enters not in the least into that other question concerning the origin of society; nor is there anything to be consider'd but the degrees of men's sagacity or folly. [sentence five] For whether the passion of self-interest be esteem'd vicious or virtuous, 'tis all a case; since itself alone restrains it: So if it be virtuous, men become social by their virtue; if vicious, their vice has the same effect. [sentence six][10]

(*T*, 3.2.2.13)

Hume's first sentence has a double role. It recapitulates the main ideas introduced in the development of the section thus far. The restatement of principles, of conclusions and implications are needed to sustain the long chain of reasoning that the *Treatise* aims at. The sentence is also, given its position within the paragraph, an introduction to a new set of ideas. The paragraph starts then on a negative note but ends on a positive note, in sentence six, however paradoxical. Hume's introductory sentence is very carefully constructed: 'no affection of the human mind has both a sufficient force, and a proper direction to counter-balance the love of gain ...'. The phrase, 'a proper direction' is significant and finds its counterpart in sentence three in the phrase 'by an alteration of direction'. Recall that Hume's view is that reason is unlikely to subvert a passion; only a countervailing passion will restore balance. Hume views human nature as composed of the 'affections' and of the 'understanding' but here he is concentrating, largely for reasons of analysis, on the 'affections'.

Sentence two identifies a specific and significant 'affection', that of benevolence. This general–specific text pattern is commonly found in Hume, as it is, no doubt, in other systematic discourses. Hume has already demonstrated that 'benevolence' weakens as it moves away from family and friends towards the wider society. In this he reflects to some extent the ideas of Hutcheson (Stewart, 1992, 88).[11] Like Smith, Hume recognized 'benevolence' but did not see it as enough in itself to motivate economic life. Hume sees, as does Smith later, that what governs economic life are 'interests'. However, Hume's idea of 'benevolence' is complex, even if not in view within this section, for it is not 'love' but the desire to help the person loved and hence limited in its social scope. Further, any economic system that involves unseen exchanges over space and even over time is essentially impersonal. There is therefore no agent present in the mind or in the environment capable of becoming the subject of benevolence. By 'other passions', he intends potentially destructive passions such as those of 'vanity', 'envy' and 'revenge' (taken up in his notion of 'jealousy' in his future economic writing).

Sentence three is the turning point within the paragraph and has as its fulcrum the idea of the 'passion' regulating itself 'by an alteration of its direction'. This is a new way of stating the idea but by this stage, given previous developments in the section (not analysed here), the idea is not likely to be as paradoxical as it is when the paragraph is read out of context. We are experiencing one of Hume's altered but nonetheless conceptually consistent recapitulations.

Sentence four is complex but the key idea is that 'this alteration must necessarily take place upon the least reflection'. The conditions that are required to be reflected upon are then set out, culminating in the phrase 'violence and an universal licence'. The need for 'reflection' admits the 'understanding' and hence the possibility of experience, experimentation and reflection. Hume tells us this in the middle of the next paragraph, in an episode that justifies the methodology used in considering one principal at a time, when he states: 'Human nature being compos'd of two principal parts, which are requisite in all its actions, the affections and the understanding; 'tis certain, that the blind motions of the former, without the direction of the latter, incapacitate men for society'. '[S]ociety' here is not to be taken as the foundational familial units but rather the sense of participating within an economic network capable of increasing want satisfaction, in other words a socioeconomic system.

The end of sentence five, a sentence that directs attention to the question 'concerning the origins of society', Hume's main theme in the whole of this section, reinforces the notion that the understanding comes into play: 'nor is there anything to be consider'd but the degrees of men's sagacity or folly'. Human conventions are located in the understanding. People bent on accumulation need to consider, on balance, where their true economic interests lie and hence must create conventions and institutions (customs, habits, rules of justice, contracts, promises, other conventions) to govern economic life.[12]

Once the institutions are in place and functioning, there are additional reasons for lending them moral support. So impressed is Hume by this aspect of social organization that he holds that once the 'conventions for the distinction of property' are settled, 'there remains little or nothing to be done towards settling a perfect harmony and accord'. The question of the distribution of wealth and its acceptability on other terms is not fully discussed. This shows, at sentence level, Hume's admiration for commercial society as he knew it. Hume's point about justice and property has enduring significance. Extreme libertarian thinkers such as Rothbard ([1982] 1998) insist that the relationship between a person and property is the sole human right (the integrity of the person and of the property, as in Hume, being essential). However, there are other considerations. People, contrary to Hume's assertion, can under certain circumstances miss what they have never had (when expectations are rising for example). Present day advocates of 'governance', in the context (say) of the economic development of sub-Saharan Africa, would stress the need for the rule of law to counteract 'kleptocracy' but they would add 'democracy' as well. Hume was of the opinion that good government could flourish under a variety of constitutional arrangements, provided 'justice' was observed.

Sentence six is to be understood as a comment on the discussion that arose out of Mandeville's views on 'private vice' giving rise to 'public virtue'. For Hume the issue is that the passion is in need of restraint and either way the outcome of the self-regulation is socially beneficial. Berry (1986, 96) sees this Hume as operating with given human nature and the human response to it. The artifice however precedes the formation of government and relatively poor societies can exist, according to Hume, for long periods of time through the 'conjunction of many families' without 'government' though not without the rules of justice (*T*, 3.2.8.1). It is increased wealth and riches, and hence increased temptation, and competition and disputes between societies, which produces 'government' and hence the production of groups of persons for whom 'justice' is their immediate interest.

Hume is however aware of the need for farsighted government to counterbalance the short sightedness of 'interest'. His comments on the potential economic role of government are economically interesting.[13] They point to the need for collective action to overcome the problems of what we would call 'free riders' and of such market failures that are due to the human preference for that which is close to that which is distant, both in time and in space (*T*, 3.2.7.8). He argues: 'But 'tis very difficult, and indeed impossible, that a thousand persons shou'd agree in any such action; it being difficult for them to concert so complicated a design, and still more difficult for them to execute it; while each seeks a pretext to free himself of the trouble and expence, and wou'd lay the whole burden on others' (*T*, 3.2.7.8). It is 'political society' and governments, interested in what interests 'any considerable part of their subjects' that carry such works forward. This is, of course, in as much as the role of government is concerned with the wisdom of taking the long view, the classical role of prudence (Hume does not use the term in this context but see Chapter 5). Taking the long view, thinking through present implications and working practically to achieve a due and good end are all wrapped up in this notion of prudence (Nelson, 1991, 81). The discourse of prudence stresses the role of experience and habit. Government in this sense is also cooperative rather than dictatorial. For Hume, 'interest' generates action and is significant in motivating all practical human action, political as well as economic. In his later writing Hume is concerned with balancing individual interest and party interest with the needs of the polity (see Soule, 2000, 144).

Later and by consideration of the 'natural affections' of parenthood, Hume thinks that the rule would be quickly established as families are linked one with another through marriage, by family leaders in the ordinary business of life. The issues here are in practice historical and methodological rather than simply moral. Hume makes, in concluding the paragraph, no further moral judgments on the 'passion of self-interest'. Either way, its self-restraining nature, the product of reflection, or perhaps, as we would put it, of rational calculation, leads, in conjunction with 'natural appetites', to the formation of society. However, for cooperation to be maintained government and other institutions need to be able to continue to direct economic action by the maintenance, composition and development of general rules of behaviour. Such general rules inform also relations between political societies: 'the three fundamental rules of justice, the stability of possession, its transference by consent, and the performance of promises, are duties of princes as well as of subjects. The same interest produces the same effect in both cases. Where possession has no stability, there must be perpetual war. Where property is not transferr'd by consent, there can be no commerce. Where promises are not observ'd, there can be no leagues nor alliances' (*T*, 3.2.11.3).

Outcomes

Hume's approach to the urge to society is based firmly in the two principal components of human nature as he sees it, i.e. on the 'affections' and on the 'understanding'. The close analysis has revealed the consistency with which Hume approaches the topic of social formation and of the fundamental economic nature of the societies constructed as a result of the actions of human nature. In the details of the writing Hume reveals an interest in and a sensitive awareness of economic motivation (including in passages not analysed here, miserly attributes and deferred gratification); the advantages of specialization and the division of labour; the emotional and needful drive to activity; the trade-offs of 'wants' and 'means' to be expected in society; society as a source of new wants and hence the possibility of development and change (in passages not analysed here, the psychological desire for and necessity of 'external objects'); the potential destructive strength of 'interests'; 'interests' coupled with 'justice' as the foundation of economic life; the link between pride/vanity and property; the significance of scarcity in both absolute and, more significantly, relative terms; the free-rider problem;

the individual human failure to take the long-term view and the significance of conventions and of contracts and other issues and, in passages not analysed, the manner, by means of 'a general sense of common interest', in which 'gold and silver become the common measures of exchange' (*T*, 3.2.2.10) (see Chapter 7).[14] Hume's future contribution to the development of economic thinking has a secure foundation in the economic subject matter, methodology, textual method and in the psychological details of the *Treatise*. Hume's insights in the *Treatise* go considerably beyond the emphasis placed in the literature on Hume's economics on his monetary ideas. This does not preclude other influences, including new thoughts. This is merely pointing to the extensiveness of what is actually or potentially available.

The close reading also reveals the consistency, conceptual clarity and, indeed, elegance with which he pursues his economic ideas in written format. Kemp Smith holds that taken singly Hume's arguments are 'admirably lucid' – the problem comes in his judgment with the structure. For example, from Chapter 3, the lack of advanced signalling of the arguments – an important aspect of making structure cohere whilst maintaining transparency for the reader. Close reading supports the judgment as far as textual and conceptual episodes are concerned (Kemp Smith, 1941, 79; see also Stewart, 1992, 110). The passage dealing with the division of labour illustrates a tight style of writing and shows that even in the *Treatise* Hume's writing is not all of one piece. His 'political economy' essays if anything are slightly more elaborated.

Economic advantage is the idea that drives people towards society, commercial or pre-commercial, and this advantage lends stability to social organization, once society has learned to control the potentially destructive force of rampant self-interest. Sexual drive and parental affection are not enough, in themselves, to secure social stability beyond the family and its immediate connections. Society beyond the family is based upon conventions. Hume's approach in methodological terms is to work first though one principal and set of associated conditions and appetites (sexual conduct and its consequences; 'interest' and familial partiality) and then through the other (a precarious self-regulation, located in complex societies within justice and political life, and based on a reciprocal agreement to desist from the property of others as a result of reflection and the operation of the understanding).

His method of analysis, and its realization in text, is derived from that of natural philosophy.[15] He tells us this in the overall introduction to the *Treatise* and in various parts earlier in the work. He tells us again in the middle of the passages dealing with his views on the fictitious nature of the '*state of nature*', referred to, and partly quoted, but not fully analysed, above:

And it may be allow'd us to consider separately the effects, that result from the separate operations of these two component parts of the mind.

The same liberty may be permitted to moral, which is allowed to natural philosophers; and 'tis very usual with the latter to consider any motion as compounded and consisting of two parts separate from each other, tho' at the same time they acknowledge it to be in itself uncompounded and inseparable.

(*T*, 3.2.2.14)

Hume is aware that he is conducting his business – much in the manner of a modern day economist though based upon induction – by building a model of social formation under certain operating assumptions (each component principal part of human nature examined in turn) and then by alteration (both together) changing the outcomes and the associated predictions. His model is natural philosophy and his aim is to reach settled and predictable conclusions. Such an approach is an implication of his view of the procedures that would take place in natural philosophy. If we consider this passage in this light we have a further instance of his experimental method applied to moral subject matter. He is prepared to make use of, as we have seen, the notion of the 'forlorn and solitary state' as a means of making comparison between a solitary man and a given animal (ignoring the social life of animals) and then as a means of comparing society and its attendant advantages and disadvantages with that of the 'solitary state' in order to demonstrate, by comparison, the value of social life.

The comparative method is, at least in the extracts examined, also fundamental to his analytical method (see *T*, 1.3.2.2). Reasoned passages constructed around a series of comparisons, unsurprisingly for statistical methods were not developed, are also basic to the opening chapters of Smith's *Wealth of Nations*. Hume is again using an approach based on modelling, but unlike society (which is not, in his view, a model but something that has existed through long periods of historical time) Hume holds that the '*state of nature*' is, like the notion of a '*golden age*', essentially a 'philosophical fiction' without any meaningful historical existence. Such 'fictions' serve some limited analytical purposes – Hume uses the imagined abundance of a '*golden age*' to illustrate analytical issues about property and justice – but they must not be confused with historical events or seen as a basis from which to construct economic policy. Isolation is neither an economic ideal, nor a practical proposition. Humans are by nature interdependent and interactive.

Society and its rules are formed (partly) in the context of the selfish urge, limited general benevolence, comparative scarcity and the mobility of 'external objects'.[16] Hume, in a textual recapitulation, puts the 'proposition' thus: 'that 'tis only from the selfishness and confin'd generosity of man, along with the scanty provision that nature has made for his wants, that justice derives its origins' (*T*. 3.2.2.18). Hume asks us to reflect on what would happen with respect to the development of conventions if human nature were more generous or if nature were more bountiful and in doing this he activates the 'fiction' of a *'golden age'*. The point is that justice, property and scarcity are bound up together. If property were universal and all wants could be satisfied equally there would be no need for Hume's view of justice. Living in society suggests that wants themselves are dynamic. Hume does at least with respect to the *'golden age'* acknowledge the question of distribution.[17] This alternative look, testing his ideas from different vantage points, is basic to Hume's methodology, set within the 'compleat chain of reasoning', founded upon 'experimentation', observation and example.

Hume uses a few key principles and applies them. He regularly recapitulates his arguments in ways that add to the development of the ideas. He reaches conclusions about society on the basis of key examples. He tests the implications out against other data or against modified assumptions e.g. 'I can imagine only one way of eluding this argument, which is by denying the uniformity of human actions', the sentence used to open the counter-argument, found deficient, and mentioned, here, in reviewing the first extract. He appeals to 'common experience'. In writing he makes very finely honed and carefully constructed, cumulative and progressive comparative arguments and analyses. In short he models his ideas with respect to society, develops them systematically and tests them, and has his readers test them, in a variety of ways – ways that sometimes threaten to overwhelm. He is intent on demonstrating the power of his method. He does so with professionalism seemingly beyond the capacity of most of his initial readers. His notion of a 'compleat chain of reasoning' is his writing strategy for the textual realization of his Newtonianism and awareness of his sense of a 'chain' assists in understanding the unity of the *Treatise*.

Hume starts with social and universal human nature in the round, rather, and moves from there to 'rules', expectations and intentions and institutional development. As Commons (1931) says in a foundational paper on 'Institutional Economics', Hume found the unity of 'economics, jurisprudence and ethics' to be built on 'the principle of scarcity and the resultant conflict of interest'. Commons claimed Hume for the institutional cause and certainly in contrasting 'artificial' with 'natural' Hume is putting constraints on the spontaneous nature of economic life – though he is careful to make sure that the reader understands that 'artificial' is not to be equated either with 'arbitrary' or indeed with 'unnatural' – and on the ever-present danger of removing direct and predictable reward from productive activity. He follows this though by stressing that Hume's discovery of the '"rights" of property in law are working rules in economics'. Hume's method and his understanding of the importance of general rules for the good order of economic and social life should recommend his work to social scientists, as well as to economists. With respect to the development of his later economic thinking, and indeed in some of its details, that of Adam Smith, the *Treatise* is likely to have content, methodological as psychological, significance.

5 Hume's social and moral economy

Hume is, in the same sense as Smith, a social philosopher. Finlay (2007) has argued that the extent of Hume's interest in the social context of human-kind has been underestimated with respect to the *Treatise*. It has been already shown through the analysis of selected passages from the *Treatise* that Hume sees humankind inherently in need of cooperation for survival, for self-definition, moral action and for fulfilment. This chapter focuses on the account given in the *Enquiries* of the means of realizing economic and social cooperation.

Hume's economic thinking is based, in the *Treatise*, on the notion of cooperation, once the selfish principle has been altered by the artificial notion of justice. It is also, however, based on the notion of cause and effect and this is articulated very early in the *Treatise*, much earlier than the treatment of justice and property. The fact that cause also entails the power of producing action and is then 'the source of all the relations of interest and duty, by which men influence each other in society, and are plac'd in the ties of government and subordination' (*T*, 1.1.4.5). Hume is not blind to the fact that power and subordination are entailed in cooperation.

The task here is not to so much to secure a fundamental repositioning of the significance of the *Enquiries* but less ambitiously to continue the exploration of Hume's social economy to establish how it is constructed in that work and whether or not such a construction reinforces the social economy of the *Treatise*. In this sense it is accepted that its messages are mixed. The method of textual analysis (here involving ultimately comparisons between the *Treatise* and the *Enquiries*) will continue but summarization and synthesis (contrived by looking across Hume's writing) will also be in evidence.

It has to be kept in mind that the *Enquiries* are part of the essay genre in the sense that each section is more or less self-contained and the writing is informed by Hume's decision to avoid long chains of reasoning. Some sections are surprisingly short and although the opening and closing moves not nearly as dramatic as in his *Political Discourses*, it is best to keep in mind that Hume is also striving for communicative and literary effect. *ECHU* ends with a dramatic flourish and one that has often given rise to adverse comment, as Hume seems to be recommending a frenzy of book burning:

> When we run over libraries, persuaded of these principles, what havoc we must make? If we take in our hand any volume; of divinity or school metaphysics, for instance; let us ask, *Does it contain any abstract reasoning concerning quantity and number?* No. *Does it contain any experimental reasoning concerning matter of fact and existence?* No. Commit it then to the flames: for it can contain nothing but sophistry and illusion.
>
> (*ECHU*, 12.3.34)

Hume writes this at the end of a chapter in which he is attempting to evaluate two questions: 'What is meant by a sceptic? And how far it is possible to push these philosophical principles of doubt and uncertainty?' It is a play on similar sentiments expressed in the 'Conclusion of this book' where he says: 'I still feel such remains of my former disposition, that I am ready to throw all my books and papers into the fire, and resolve never more to renounce the pleasures of life for the sake of reasoning or philosophy' (*T*, 1.4.7.10). The context (of both) is that of Cartesian doubt, a doubt which Hume holds to be impossible to be attained and useless if it were to be obtained for 'no reasoning could ever bring us to a state of assurance and conviction upon any subject' (*ECHU*, 12.1.3). In this sense he starts with Descartes. In the rest of the section, Hume suggests a mitigated scepticism, and recommends a (Ciceronian?) degree of 'doubt, caution and modesty' as aspects of just reasoning. What undermines 'the excessive principles of scepticism' are 'action, and employment, and the occupations of common life' (*ECHU*, 12.2.27). He ends with a dramatic flourish which not only sets out, in a number of lists, the agenda for the 'proper subjects of science and enquiry' but which playfully makes implicit reference to Descartes and his views on the significance of book-learning and of the content of libraries. Hume focuses his sceptical concerns on 'divinity or school metaphysics'. He is also stressing his naturalism and his commitment to experience (see Ayer, 2000, 117). Some books will survive the Humean modified sceptical purge, including if his list is adhered to, some few books on divinity. Would any survive Descartes? The passage represents Hume at his most playful and ironic. He shortly afterwards became Librarian to the College of Advocates.

Economic content: indirect

There was, as shown in Chapter 4, very little direct economic content in Book I of the *Treatise*, though the importance of causal analysis for the development of the subject should not be overlooked. With respect to direct economic subject matter, the same is the case with the *ECHU*. Both works have other targets in mind, though it should be clear that the specification of appropriate causal links has significance for all forms of social investigation, including Hume's economics.

There are methodological issues that are significant but the methodology does not, at first sight, occupy such a prominent position in the *ECHU* as it does in the *Treatise*. Hume does however seem to modify his approach to the Newtonian notion of simplicity of principles or explanation that he is strongly committed to in the *Treatise*. Buckle draws attention to Hume's notion that in the search for 'some common principle' (causal principle) theorists 'have sometimes carried the matter too far' (Hume, *ECHU*, Section I.9; Buckle, 1991, 238). Buckle gives other examples and rightly concludes, however, after some discussion, that Hume did not essentially back away from the ideal of simplicity (Buckle, 1991, 239). Hume, however, already says as much in the text immediately surrounding – and essential to its full meaning – the initial quote that Buckle provides. Selectivity even at paragraph level (see Chapter 2) is an activity that needs to be handled with caution:

> Moralists have hitherto been accustomed, when they consider the vast multitude and diversity of those actions that excite our approbation or dislike, to search for some common principle, on which this variety of sentiments might depend. And though they have sometimes carried this matter too far, by their passion for some one general principle; it must, however, be confessed, that they are excusable in expecting to find some general principles, into which all the vices and virtues were justly to be resolved.
>
> (*ECHU*, 1.15)

Although this does not seem to have an equivalent passage in the *Treatise*, Hume's stance in the *ECHU* is not entirely unrelated to his 'Rules by which to judge of causes and effects' particularly to rule five, which sets out the need for a careful investigation 'where several different objects produce the same effect' (*T*, 1.3.15.7). This analytical requirement is applied at *T*, 2.1.12.1 and *T* 2.2.4.5 (Annotations, Norton and Norton, 2000, 468). It is also implicit in item two of Hume's consideration of one man's capacity to reason in relation to another's where there is, for example, 'a complication of causes' (*ECHU*, 9.5 footnote). The 'caveats' that Buckle finds in the *Enquiries* are also found, though buried, in the *Treatise*. The *ECHU* is in this and in other respects much more helpful to the novice reader.

The methodological issues are integral to the development of the first section of the *ECHU* as well as other locations within the work. Hume starts with a division of moral philosophy between virtue ethics (a 'practical' morality) and enquiries that examine human nature to establish 'those original principles, by which, all human curiosity must be bounded' (*ECHU*, Section I. 2). His concerns are with 'speculative' philosophy.

The methodological stance, underlying his approach to the subject matter, is less forceful than in the *Treatise*, and gently interwoven with the development of the writing. Hume's method, given the self-contained nature of the sections, is mentioned in various places and context. Indeed if anything, the *ECPM* makes clearer reference to the experimental method than does the *ECHU*, though even in that work the points are not laboured.

Hume accepts in the *ECHU* that humans are 'born for action' but his aim is to explore human understanding rather than paint a portrait of virtuous action. However, his notion of 'Man' is far from one-dimensional:

> Man is a sociable, no less than a reasonable being: But neither can he always enjoy company agreeable and amusing or preserve the proper relish for them. Man is also an active being; and from that disposition, as well as from the various necessities of human life, must submit to business and occupation: But the mind requires some relaxation, and cannot always support this bent to care and industry. It seems, then, that nature has pointed out a mixed kind of life as most suitable to human race, and secretly admonished them to allow none of these biases to *draw* too much, so as to incapacitate them for further occupations and entertainments. ...
>
> (*ECHU*, I, 6)

Hume has a rounded sense of human nature and human life as dictated by nature – the balance anticipated at the end of Book One of the *Treatise* – and he has, therefore, a complex notion of activity and motivation. Hume is not to be seen as a mere hedonist. His agents are, if they act in line with their nature as he depicts it, seeking a variety of ends necessary for their well-being. Work, provided it fits within the well-balanced life, is not necessarily a burden, though it can be so and he does sometimes refer to it as such, but a source of fulfilment as well as of survival. Humankind craves for purposeful activity, 'exercise and employment'. Hume is often accused of constructing notions of the good life in terms of his own ambitions and middle-class aspirations. Hume has something in common with John Ruskin, who in the middle of the nineteenth century saw creativity in work as part of what it was to be human. Thorstein Veblen later speculated in evolutionary terms on why the human animal was the only animal thought not to enjoy the prospect of pursuing its means of livelihood/survival. Hume, in this respect, has less in common with John Stuart Mill and the classical economists with their strongly held notion of the 'disutility' of work.

This rounded view is also found in his arguments in support of the incentive effects of 'luxury' (variously defined and certainly not necessarily associated with sumptuousness) on, for example, agricultural workers. It would seem likely that in the notion of what constitutes the good life or human well-being, there is no one simple and absolute end. It would be difficult for

Hume, as it was for lesser political economists such as Ganilh, to readily accept a distinction between productive and unproductive labour. Those that help us relax, and to restore balance, also help us to return to directly productive work. Hume is consistent about balance in life and about the constructive nature of *divertimenti*. He returns to the notion of what constitutes the 'good life' in the closing paragraphs on the *ECPM*.

Hume does not have a radically reductionist notion of human nature such as that of economic man as defined by the neoclassical school of economics towards the end of the nineteenth century, nor does he have any simple division between the economic and non-economic spheres or even between productive and unproductive activities. Motivation is not reducible only to self-interest is significant, even if not universal in scope. Hutcheson also argued against the idea that 'benevolence is based on self-love' (Rogers, 1997, 132). Hume's target here is Mandeville and his notion that 'morality' was the product of 'Skilful Politicians' just as it was for Hutcheson (Hundert, 1994, 78–79). For Hutcheson, Hume, and indeed also for Smith, natural sociability is, in a sense, inherently democratic in that it is available to all.

The classical school, conventionally seen as starting with Smith worked with income-related or revenue-related socially located categories (landlord, capitalist, labourer). Hume's social agents are located in time and in society as well as in universal principles (abstract) of human nature. Activity is key to all life and not just to economic life. But human activity is complex and based upon needs – social and psychological as well as corporeal – and, as society rapidly evolves in economic sophistication, wants and desires or preferences then customs and manner change. Human economic activity shares the same weaknesses and limitations of human knowledge and near-sighted motivation as other human activities. The sustained and fulfilled human life is a varied one and that variety ought to be available to everyone, as he more than hints in the essay 'Of Commerce'. Hume is also aware of the tendency of philosophy to draw 'too much' to self-indulgence:

> While we study with attention the vanity of human life, and turn all out thoughts towards the empty and transitory nature of riches and honours, we are, perhaps, all the while flattering our natural indolence, which hating the bustle of the world, and the drudgery of business, seeks a pretence of reason to give itself a full and uncontrolled indulgence.
>
> *(ECHU, 5.1.1)*

Although the biographical tone of the *Treatise* is largely absent from the *ECHU*, there are feint shadows of Hume's own experience of the 'drudgery' of unfulfilling business (it is a matter of choice) and of his lack of personal balance before then in the above paragraphs. This is not the only passage in which Hume subjects both the notion of 'riches' and the notion of 'philosophy' to irony. Smith made a thorough examination of wealth, the parade of wealth and associated vanities in the *TMS*. In the *ECPM*, Hume's own lived life and the sociable and 'polite' society that he inhabited and appreciated is rarely far from view even if it is never overtly and directly referred to. Of course he is concerned with building a case for sceptical philosophy (mitigated as it turns out), which according to Hume is because it 'strikes in with no disorderly passion of the human mind'. Hume's problem is that while humankind must make inferences the inferences are probabilistic rather than certainties: the future may not be like the past even in the ordering of events in physical nature. There are limits to human knowledge, induction might just let us down if the course of nature varies, but we simply have to get on with living. Hume also holds that there is nothing to fear from sceptical philosophy as 'Nature will always maintain her rights, and prevail in the end over any abstract reasoning whatsoever'. Hume's naturalism in this respect goes beyond Mandeville's and is a basis for balancing Mandeville's extreme scepticism (Hundert, 1994, 84). The 'bustle of the world', what Marshall was later to call 'the ordinary business of life', and the active principle of human nature, necessary for human survival, will prevail.

Economic content: direct

Economic matters enter into the *ECHU* in a direct way even if the development of economic thinking (even in Book one of the *Treatise* there are minor, passing comments that can be interpreted as economic) as such is not overtly a central or even a significant theme. In the *Treatise* and the *Enquiries* economic ideas are intermixed with the philosophy, sometimes occupying the foreground, sometimes merely implicit in the text. This is a point identified early in the critical literature on Hume (Schatz, 1902). The notion of men united in society, Hume's definition of politics, derived from the *Treatise*, underpins the discussion in both *Enquiries*. Hume's economics are enmeshed in political life, in morality and in the historical condition of the nation. In the *ECHU*, Hume is occupied with thinking through the implications of his ideas of causality and of the uniformity of human action, to the 'actions and volitions of intelligent agents' (*ECHU*, 8.1.15). There is no providential economic or social order – Hume is no Physiocrat – and in offering explanations of social change, any number of causal factors must be sifted. Indeed in recognizing the fact of scarcity, the artificiality of justice and the need for whole sets of rules, necessary for continuous social formation, Hume links economics, law and moral opinion together in a way that appealed to one of the founders of American institutionalism, J. R. Commons (1931, 650). It may also have hints of Sophism. Given the overlap of the generations, Hume is likewise concerned with what Commons calls 'futurity'. Commons' judgment is even more plausible when evidence of the way in which institutional rules can contain human behaviour is admitted, from the essays.

Hume illustrates his ideas in a manner that will be familiar to those who teach predictive modelling to novice students. General expectations of behaviour may be unfulfilled because of a particular circumstance just as 'in the same manner as the winds, rain, clouds, and other variations of the weather are supposed to be governed by steady principles; though not easily discoverable by human sagacity and enquiry'. He goes on in passage 8.1.16 to show how his philosophical principles relate to everyday human experiences. His extended example, the only direct and *sustained* economic example in the *ECHU*, is set out, and then analysed, below.[1]

> Thus, it appears, not only that the conjunction between motives and voluntary actions is as regular and uniform as that between the cause and effect in any part of nature; but also that this regular conjunction has been universally acknowledged among mankind, and has never been the subject of dispute, either in philosophy or common life. [sentence one] Now, as it is from past experience, that we draw all inferences concerning the future, and as we conclude, that objects will always be conjoined together which we find to have always be conjoined; it may seem superfluous to prove that this experienced uniformity in human actions is a source whence we draw *inferences* concerning them. [sentence two] But in order to throw the argument into a greater variety of lights we shall also insist, though briefly, on this later topic. [sentence three]
>
> The mutual dependence of men is so great, in all societies, that scarce any human action is entirely complete in itself, or is performed without some reference to the actions of others, which are requisite to make it answer fully the intention of the agent. [sentence four] The poorest artificer, who labours alone, expects at least the protection of the magistrate, to ensure him the enjoyment of the fruits of his labour. [sentence five] He also expects that, when he carries his goods to market, and offers them at a reasonable price, he shall find purchasers, and shall be able, by the money he acquires, to engage others to supply him with those commodities which are requisite for his subsistence. [sentence six] In proportion as men extend their dealings, and render their intercourse with others more complicated, they always comprehend, in their schemes of life, a greater variety of voluntary actions, which they expect, from the proper motives, to co-operate with their own. [sentence seven] In all of these conclusions they take their measures from past experience, in the same manner as in their reasonings concerning external objects; and firmly believe that men, as well as all the elements, are to continue in their operations, the same that they have ever found them. [sentence eight] A manufacturer reckons upon the labour of his servants, for the execution of any work as much as upon the tools which he employs, and would be equally surprised, were his expectations disappointed. [sentence nine] In short, this experimental inference and reasoning

concerning the actions of others enters so much into human life, that no man, while awake, is ever a moment without employing it. [sentence ten] Have we not reason, therefore, to affirm that all mankind have always agreed in the doctrine of necessity, according to the foregoing definition and explication of it? [sentence eleven]

(*ECHU*, 8.1.16–8.1.17)

Hume's first sentence ('Thus') is an outcome of an earlier stage in the argument. Volitions give rise to actions and have an analogous relationship with cause and effect. Belief is causal. It gives rise to a potential for action that a mere figment of the imagination (fiction) does not. The concern is with both 'philosophy' and with 'common-life', key to his philosophical project. Experience suggests that there is regularity and such a notion is in common-life essential to the development of the social economy. Here the concern is with volitions, passions and hence with the consequences for action that the passion gives rise to. Hume is concerned, if sentences ten and eleven can be anticipated at this point, with tracing out the links (by analogy) between events in physical nature and their consequences and events in human nature and their consequences. But the inferences are probabilistic rather than certainties and custom and habit suggest a course of action that it is then believed that the inferences will be fulfilled. The *Abstract* also makes this clear.

Hume takes the example of economic activity to show how the expectations of regularity arise out of and lead to action. Sentence four insists on the social dimensions of human society and action. The 'agent' does not necessarily reflect deeply upon the actions of others: past behaviour or habit leads to an expectation that the required subsequent action will be available. Notice that this is a general statement concerning all human action. What follows from sentence five up to and including sentence nine constitutes a specific example from the economic domain. Hume starts with the simplest situation (sentences five and six) the 'artificer, who labours alone'. There is no complication of the division of labour and multiple stages in production or any other complexity in this stage of the example. Even such an 'artificer' expects the protection of the law in a cooperative relationship. His property is expected to be secure and the link between effort and reward is expected to be maintained. He is working even in embodying his labour in production within a set of social institutions and expectations. The 'protection of the magistrate' is needed because of the pervasive nature of scarcity. This is here in anticipation of Hume's arguments (later in the *ECPM* and derived from the *Treatise*) about the link between effort and security of product and hence about the nature of 'justice'. Maintenance of the link between effort and reward is necessary for a sustained production and hence for the possibility of growth.

The artificer's other expectations are that he will sell his goods and with the money acquired will therefore be able to purchase other items. Hume is not considering that such expectations will be disappointed (because some other casual factor comes into play: this is a consideration that comes later in the argument and which does not get reworked into the economics example) or that the price anticipated will be 'unreasonable'. The artificer will know from experience what a 'reasonable' set of price expectations are. For all that, Hume's story is not static for the fairly straightforward set of exchanges of the 'artificer' is replaced by the extended 'dealings' of more robust economic agents (more roundabout economic methods based upon the division of labour) and this in turn extends further the range of 'voluntary actions' which are expected to support the extended dealings.

The assumption is that 'men, as well as all the elements, are to continue, in their operations, the same as they have ever found them'. Hume does not in this passage consider what happens when such connections need to be revised nor is there any reflection on competition. He is clear in sentence three that he is focusing on the practical significance, or rather the necessity, of making 'inferences'. The mode of interaction is cooperative. Hume is not making an analysis of the competitive economy so much as he is making a point about his methodology. He is looking at 'the people' and showing how 'this experimental inference and reasoning concerning the actions of others enters so much into human life that no man, while awake, is ever a moment without employing it'. It is only when the 'bustle of the world' ceases that 'experimental inference' ceases. Hume moves his methodology in a sense away from the philosopher towards everyday human experience and chooses the regularity and predictability of economic life to illustrate the point. This is part of his developing strategy of socializing 'mitigated scepticism' in the sense that 'nature is stronger than principle'. Hume is in a sense consistent about 'the people' and its judgment, as this is a theme that he initiated in the *Abstract*. He uses a very similar kind of passage in 'Of Money' to show how an increase in the quantity of gold will impact on an economy experiencing less than full employment and where the question of price expectations is at least indirectly considered.

The structure of the sequence of sentences from four to eleven goes: generalization (sentence four); economic exemplification (sentences five–nine); generalized summary and implication (ten–eleven). Of course there is a commitment throughout to link expectations with respect to the course of nature to expectations in economic life, particularly well-drawn out in sentence eight. Humankind has desires and the desires initiate purposeful action, with reasoning, habits, passions and beliefs mediating the links between the two. There is regularity overall even if this is conditional and sometimes disrupted and even where there are individual exceptions to the general trend. In the middle of the next passage he asks 'How could *politics* be a science, if laws and forms of government had not a uniform influence upon society?' Predictability, regularity in an established social context is significant. For economic life – a significant and visible part of 'common life that it is the duty of philosophy to examine' – the causal links are beliefs/motives leading to voluntary action based upon *inferred* predictability and reciprocity. However, the knowledge is probable rather than certain. Hume's *Treatise*, of course, presents 'experimental' data drawn from behaviour 'in the common course of the world'. Unlike 'experiments' in physics, the data derived are historically laden.

Both 'science and action' require the acknowledgement of 'the doctrine of necessity, and this *inference* from motives to voluntary action, from characters to conduct' (*ECHU*, 8.1.18). If the expected results do not obtain, that is if the 'conduct of mankind in such particular situations' turns out to be different from what is normally expected, differences need to be accounted for. Such differences will be accounted for by an unforeseen change in events or circumstances as new causes give rise to new effects.

Methodological elements relevant to Hume's later economics writing

For Hume's political economy, the methodological statements in the *ECHU* are significant largely because of their clarity but also because of the added detail with respect to analogy. Reasoning concerning matters of fact are 'founded on a species of analogy'. The steps in an analogy, observation, habit, are not necessary lengthy and a formal analogy is constrained, the formal steps in a chain of reasoning are short. It is interesting that Cicero, in *De Officiis*, stresses the human capacity to relate cause to effect and to draw analogies and link present and future (*De Officiis*, I. 11).

There does not seem to be a formal equivalent in the *ECHU* of the with respect to rules for judging cause and effect (*T*, 1. 3.15). In those rules Hume clarifies what is required for proceeding in circumstances in which 'several different objects produce the same effect' and where it is necessary to search for a common quality. Hume realizes that where a number of causes are possible contenders for an effect, it is necessary to fix on the predominant cause. Hume sees that 'Where there is a complication of causes to produce any effect, one mind may be much larger than another, and better able to comprehend the whole system of objects, and to infer their just consequences' (*ECHU*, 9.5 footnote1). Such understanding is the role of the socially engaged philosopher. He adds that 'The circumstances, on which the effect depends, is frequently involved in other circumstances, which are foreign and extrinsic. The separation of it often requires great attention, accuracy and stability'. The *ECHU* advances the discussion in terms that are more readily understood.

Hume faces just such a problem when he comes, in his *Political Discourses*, to the analysis of monetary phenomena. It is difficult to see how Hume (see Chapter 7) would have sorted out linkages in his monetary essays without his skills in the analysis of cause and effect.

What Hume has to say about the significant use of analogy is interesting. Analogy is discussed in three places in the *Treatise* but the concept is better spelled out in the *ECHU*. The Logic in the *Treatise* with respect to causality is not suspended, rather enhanced (clarified) by the additions in the *ECHU*. In his eight rules in the *Treatise*, Hume sets out a clearly defined approach to establishing causes based on experience. Hume claims in rule three that the 'cause and effect must be contiguous in space and time'. This has been claimed to be anti-Newtonian. It is a useful guide to Hume for avoiding error in social analysis. Events relating to the Magna Carta might (to take an fictitious example) have had an impact on the events leading to the Glorious Revolution but maybe the Protestant Reformation is more relevant, but in either case some significant subsidiary causal arguments would be needed. These seem different from observations about the moon and the tides, though there is contiguity of observation in time with respect to the moon and tides, rather than in space. Even if this is left aside, Copleston (1964, 83) argues that Hume adjusts this element of contiguity later in the *Treatise*.

Analogy more widely is key to the progress of the understanding. Analogy is a vehicle in which the idea is to look for similarities ('resemblances'), stress the connections and to suggest implications or outcomes. It is important to differentiate operations in the mind (natural or instinctive operations as part of Hume's associative psychology) from thinking through social or scientific problems and understanding, i.e. analogy as a source of causal reasoning with respect to matters of fact. So Hume states that '... where the objects have not so exact a similarity, the analogy is less perfect, and the inference is less conclusive; though still has in it some force, in proportion to the degree of similarity and resemblance' (*ECHU*, 9.1). The circulation of the blood in one animal, Hume argues, suggests a similar process in another species of animal as a guide. In the *ECPM*, his notion of extension by analogy, a process widely accepted in modern-day economic analysis, is clearly stated and the end of Section III:

> It is entirely agreeable to the rules of philosophy, and even of common reason; where any principle has been found to have a great force and energy in one instance, to ascribe to it a like energy in all similar instances. This is indeed Newton's chief rule of philosophizing.
>
> (*ECPM*, 3.2.48)

Hume compares animal understanding with human understanding in this respect and then one human's capacity with another. Hume is concerned with intellectual capacity and locates it in the capacity to work from the known to the unknown, from the present to the future. There is the question of observation, consequence and memory, or what could be called attentive behaviour. There is the capacity to see a 'whole system of objects' and not just focus on a small range as well as the need for attention to be supplemented by 'accuracy, and subtilty', not to be taken in by the first sight of things. And so 'When we reason from analogies, the man, who has the greater experience or the greater promptitude of suggesting analogies, will be the better reasoner' (*ECHU*, 9.5. footnote 20). Such a well-read and thoughtful person is more able to generate relevant analogies. Experience and reading expand the relevant capacities. It is Hume's analogies and capacity to generate analogies that are of significance for the development of his essays in political economy.

Economy and *ECPM*

Hume was very fond of the *Principle of Morals* and described it in *My Own Life* (1776) as 'of all my writings, historical, philosophical, or literary incomparably the best'. For Hume, moral subjects were essential to his science of man. *ECPM* is sometimes referred to as the *second* Enquiry as it was written and published later than the *ECHU*. Certainly it is much easier to read that the *Treatise* and Hume in writing it was much more concerned with helping the reader understand and follow the argument. It is also sometimes described as a rewrite (rewrite rather than a summary or abstract) of Book Three of the *Treatise*. Finlay describes the *Enquiries* as 'discrete' and (implicitly) contrasts them with the reasoning of the *Treatise* as a whole which he sees as 'an account of reason and reasoning in an ever-broadening series of contexts' (Finlay, 2007, 2).[2] The notion of a 'long chain of reasoning', which is a significant feature of all of the Books of the *Treatise*, is absent from the *ECPM*, as is, largely, the formal language of impression and ideas. Indeed, both *Enquiries* are to be seen a series of self-contained essays and hence as being structured through a textual strategy that is fundamentally different from that which informed the *Treatise*. The location of moral judgment in 'sentiments' is to locate it in 'impressions of reflection' but the formal logic/methodology is largely absent. Such changes are in keeping with the insight Hume achieved in the writing of the *Abstract*.

ECPM is concerned with the development of what Hume sees as an empirical and modified naturalistic theory of morals. The search is for 'universal principles' using, since he is dealing with 'questions of fact', the experimental method of 'comparison of particular instances' (*ECPM*, 1.10). It is naturalistic because benevolence operates by a 'direct tendency or instinct' (*ECPM*, Appendix III, 2). It is modified because society requires conventions and contrived means of engendering trust. It is not *primarily* concerned, or rather overtly concerned, with economic life but as in the Books Two and Three of the *Treatise*, the framework of property, justice, and instinctive or contrived moral behaviour is the basis for the development of a warm commercial society.

Benevolence and self-interest

Hume treats again of the issues of benevolence and justice – hence with motivations to judge and to act – and it is on these two topics and the treatment of utility that will be the main focus for examining the work. Indeed it is in his selection of utility as the central focus of the whole of his argument that marks a difference in communicative emphasis between Book III of the *Treatise* and the clearer statements in *ECHU*. Utility in Hume, however, is a feeling rather than a rational calculation.

Sentiment rather than reason is the basis of morality and the key sentiment in this respect is that of benevolence. Copleston puts Hume's general view thus: 'if the moral sentiments are due to the original composition of men's minds, it is only natural that there should be some fundamental agreement' (Copleston, 1965, 135) or sympathy. In reflecting on 'Personal Merit' (through the observation of actual persons), Hume argues that benevolence is admired and recommended because it leads to outcomes that are positively evaluated in society (*ECPM*, 1.10). There is mention of other societies and other times – 'Pericles' when he 'was on his death-bed' – though much of Hume's direct observation of such 'Personal Merit' is, perforce, in context of contemporary eighteenth-century society. Hume claims the universality of his argument, the 'epithets' for benevolence 'are known in all languages', and universally express the highest merit that human nature is capable of attaining but the focus is his own society in his own time. The conclusion is 'So true is it, that this virtue derives its existence entirely from its necessary *use* to the intercourse and social state of mankind'. Good morals are socially useful: 'may it not thence be concluded, that the utility resulting from the social virtues, forms at least, a *part* of their merit, and is one source of that approbation and regard so universally paid to them?' (*ECPM*, 3.2.6). (Hume follows through the investigation into such merit in Section VI, where he treats 'Of Qualities Useful to Ourselves'.) It should be clear as Copleston points out that 'utility' carries the implication of 'a tendency to produce some further or ulterior good' (Copleston, 1965, 137). It is interesting that Cicero in *De Officiis* comes to see that there is no conflict between '*honestum*' (moral good) and '*utile*' (Jones, 1982, 33). 'Utility' indirectly results in concern not just for the stability of a developed but static society but for one experiencing economic growth.

Hume, in introducing the intercourse and 'good offices' of the benevolent man is clear that such a person promotes 'happiness and satisfaction'. Although he resorts several times to the use of the term 'happiness' with respect to the direct ends promoted by benevolence, he is clear that observation and reflection upon the consequences of acts of benevolence are beheld 'with complacency and pleasure'(*ECPM*, 2.2.22). The footnote to 5.2.17 states: 'No man is absolutely indifferent to the happiness and misery of others. The first has a natural tendency to give pleasure; the second pain. This every one may find in himself'. At *ECPM* 5.2.23 is found: 'In general, it is certain, that, wherever we may go, whatever we reflect upon or converse about, everything still presents us with the view of human happiness or misery, and excites in our breast a sympathetic movement of pleasure or uneasiness'. There is an observer capable of feeling and making judgments. This is seen in the definition of virtue that Hume offers in Appendix I: 'It defines virtue to be *whatever mental action or quality gives to a spectator the pleasing sentiment of approbation*' *(ECPM*, Appendix 1, 9). Elsewhere in the text, Hume's 'spectator' *tends* to be ideal or at least someone with Hume's sensibilities.

Adam Smith's innovation in the *TMS* is to place the impartial spectator 'within the breast'. Smith also accepts that a society without benevolence, motivated only be self-interest, would be cold and uncomfortable but one without 'justice' – in Hume's sense, that the 'general peace and order are the attendants of justice or a general abstinence from the possession of others' resulting from a general system of justice (*ECPM*, Appendix 3) – would be impossible. Smith talks, as does Hume and Locke, of the need for honour among thieves. Such talk goes back as far as Cicero. There does not seem to be any direct treatment of the different senses of the notion of 'pleasure' as found in the *Treatise* at 3.1.2.4.

Hume is interested in increasing the happiness and diminishing misery (keep the sense of economic well-being) even if it is only by implication but does not seem to formulate his ideas about this in the *ECPM*, though the *Treatise* is more developed in this respect, in the manner later achieved by Bentham. Hume does not accept that benevolence is merely a disguised form of self-interest. Hume's interests are certainly consequentialist even though he also works in the *ECPM*, in keeping with the *Treatise,* with a character-based virtue ethics.[3] The notion of 'character' leads to the anticipation of behavioural regularities. The two systems are sometimes seen as conflicting but part of Hume's concerns is that certain virtues should be encouraged – economically relevant character traits, privileged by Xenophon in *Oeconomicus* and by early capitalist society, such as 'art, care and industry'. Frugality, which was destined to play such a big part in Smith's theory of economic growth, is for Hume the mean between '*Prodigality*' and '*avarice*' (*ECPM*, 6.1.10). These virtues, associated in later Hume with an active middle-class of merchants – Routh criticizes Hume's view of this class as too comfortable – carry with them the possibility of social transformation over time. As Hume stipulates the significance of a natural and balanced life for human flourishing, then Hume's potential for a balanced set of consequentialist judgments would need to be explored. Hume's notion of natural balance as essential to the good life, and is a sense a restatement of the closing moves in Book One of the *Treatise*, is how he chooses to end the *ECPM* (9.2.25).[4]

The benefits the benevolent person brings in his account are in the first instance material in the sense of relief from economic uncertainty, from poverty in old age and so on. Indeed in the *ECPM*, strength of character, and hence also personal merit, consists in rejecting immediacy – 'pleasure' – and opting for the deferred gratification of mixed ends – 'happiness', in the sense of domestic felicity or, over time, a prosperous and sustainable family and 'honour':

> And however poets may employ their wit and eloquence, in celebrating present pleasure, and rejecting all distant views to fame, health of fortune; it is obvious, that this practice is the source of all dissoluteness and disorder, repentance and misery. A man of a strong and determined temper adheres tenaciously to his general resolutions, and is neither seduced by the allurements of pleasure, nor terrified by the menaces of pain; but keeps still in view those distant pursuits, by which he at once, ensures his happiness and his honour.
>
> (*ECPM*, 6.1.15)

Happiness is the achievement of longer-term goals, including economic security, and pleasure is associated with instant gratification.[5] Hume is advocating the classical virtue of prudence. There is more than a hint of Epicurus in this passage. It could be argued that, as the pursuit of longer-term objectives is an ends–means relationship, behaviours leading to deferred gratification are based upon '*reason*'. Hume contests this and allocates the motivation to 'our calm passions and propensities' (one set of passion versus another set) often overlooked because they do not lead to a disturbed state of mind. The pleasure of an observer when contemplating moral action – the positive outcome of a struggle (say) between 'happiness' and 'pleasure' – by another is instant but this is of a different order, as it were, for it is the primary ways in which approval is felt.

Natural and artificial virtue

The exclusion of the notion of 'artificial virtue' from the *ECPM* is a puzzle. Hume does not abandon the idea of conventions. It is this concern for conventions that allows Commons to claim Hume for the institutionalist cause. In Appendix III he restates the case for the notion of justice arising from 'conventions' ('a sense of common interest') as distinct from 'promises'. Promises are necessary, and the social disapprobation applied to breaking promises, because there is a gap between benevolence and self-interest. Natural behaviour and the behaviour necessary to keep promises may be at odds. But with respect to conventions, he starts in a curious way, 'It has been asserted by some, that justice arises from Human Conventions...' (*ECPM*, App. III, 7). Who is this if not primarily Hume himself? The example given of a convention, of two men pulling the 'oars of a boat', is also found in the *Treatise*. The point is that it does not require the manipulation of politicians in the final stages of commercial social formation, in the manner of Mandeville, to produce conventions. Hume goes on to reflect on the word 'natural':

The word *natural* is commonly taken in so many senses and is of so loose a signification, that it seems vain to dispute whether justice be natural or not. If self-love, if benevolence be natural to man; if reason and forethought be also natural; then may the same epithet be applied to justice, order, fidelity, property, society.

And later at the end of the paragraph:

In so sagacious an animal, what necessarily arises from the exertion of his intellectual faculties may justly be esteemed natural.

(*ECPM*, Appendix. III, 9).

This is not his last word on the issue for he adds a footnote at this point in the text and the footnote looks both ways. It is worthwhile stating it in full:

Natural may be opposed, either to what is *unusual, miraculous,* or *artificial.* In the two former senses, justice and property are undoubtedly natural. But as they suppose reason, forethought, design, and a social union and confederacy among men, perhaps that epithet cannot strictly in the last sense be applied to them. Had men lived without society, property had never been known, and neither justice nor injustice had ever existed. But society among human creatures had been impossible, without reason and forethought. Inferior animals, that unite, are guided by instinct, which supplies the place of reason. But all these disputes are merely verbal.

This is disconcerting, as Hume seems to point in two directions (consider the force of 'perhaps' and of the 'but all these disputes are merely verbal'). It is clear that in the *Treatise*, Hume is committed, as part of his 'Logic', to the notion 'that those impressions, which give rise to the sense of justice, are not natural to the mind of man, but arise from artifice and human conventions'. It would seem that in the *ECPM* he has shifted his ground slightly in that, given the problems his division created for some readers, he is showing that 'reason' and the 'understanding' are natural. Indeed the harnessing of 'reason' and 'instinct' is a feature of the introductory sections of the *ECPM*. Hume is more willing to work with the capacity in the evolution of experience, of reason and understanding to refine judgments based on experience and reflection, in society, even although he continues to see 'sentiments' as primary.

Hume, however, did not originally conceive as 'artificial' meaning 'un-natural' as in the contrast of 'natural/unnatural', rather as Hume also puts it in the *Treatise*, his stress is on 'artificial' (*T*, 3.1.2.8–3.1.2.10; *T*, 3.2.1.19)). This stress carries different connotations from natural/unnatural. As Schatz argues, Hume, is anxious to distance himself from 'natural law' arguments in so far as he wishes to remain isolated from considerations of 'God'. Hume, in Schatz account, 'reste loin de la notion de droits naturels' (Schatz, 1902, 70). This is however now seen as too bold an assessment as Hume's relationship to natural law theory is a disputed one (Westerman, 1994). 'Natural law' or 'natural rights' would be too fixed for Hume's philosophical taste. He feels the split between 'nature' and 'convention', a dispute which also has classical origins. As Westerman points out, Hume sees humankind as inventive (Westerman, 1994, 93). He uses 'natural' in many ways and in many places in the *ECPM* but the distinctions made in the *Treatise* are still relevant. 'Natural' often carries the notion of 'usual'. What Hume is sometimes getting at is the difference between responses that are innate and those that are contrived through experience, historical reflection, education (an influence that Hume is concerned to isolate) and so on.

In the *ECPM* Hume illustrates how experience can alter 'natural' judgments concerning the 'utility' of an action:

> Giving alms to common beggars is naturally praised; because it seems to carry relief to the distressed and indigent: but when we observe the encouragement thence arising to idleness and debauchery, we regard that species of charity rather as a weakness than a virtue.
>
> (*ECPM*, 2.2.18)[6]

Moral judgments are modifiable by reconsideration of the consequences based upon experience and reflection. An implication is that any judging agent (or should this rather be any *feeling* agent?) needs to be well-informed about the situation that is subject to a consequentialist judgment. Reasoning is necessary. But in the ordinary business of life when I am approached by a person seemingly in distress and asking for money, it may feel right that I ought to 'help' and deal with the request as it confronts me rather than refuse on the more distant possibility that others may at some stage in the future be added to the list of the indigent.

Another implication might be one of time-period. How far in the future do we need to trace out the consequences? This is not simply a philosophical problem. The impact of a change in economic policy, for example, requires an analysis of a series of implied 'rounds' of adjustments before any judgment can be made on the usefulness of a policy change. Some policy consequences may be 'unseen' or at least 'unforeseen'. Smith's 'unintended consequences' are about outcomes concerning social benefits that are not part of the decision-making process as considered by the (self-)interested economic agent and these need to be traced out or recognized by a philosophical observer. The indigent savage who, in Book one, Chapter two of the *WN*, first starts exchanging arrows based on his 'natural ability' does not foresee the future development of a whole system of society and production based on, largely mutually unseen, agents and exchanges.

Hume, by the same principle, refers to attempts to reverse the conventional mercantilistic judgment about the corruptive force of 'luxury' (and its tendency to frustrate the policy 'rule' of exporting more than importing). The stress is on how its refinements 'rather tend to the encrease of industry, civility and arts' (*ECPM*, 2.2.21). In his treatment of Luxury, Hume states the connections as follows: 'Thus *industry*, *knowledge* and *humanity*, are linked together by an indissoluble chain, and are found, from experience as well as reason, to be peculiar to the polished, and, what are commonly denominated, the more luxurious ages' (II, Essay II, 271). Hume did not publish 'On Luxury' (later republished under the title 'Of Refinement in the Arts') until 1752, so this short passage (only just) anticipates the argument in that work. In both, Hume shifts attention for production to consumption.

Even in the *Treatise* where the distinction must be considered in the context of before and after the formation of society – in the process of social formation the 'original motive' relevant in the rude state of society (and Hume is concerned that such motives be clearly established) is (instinctive) self-interest and after (i.e. in the 'civiliz'd state') the motive is '*sympathy* with *public* interest' – Hume equivocates on the nature of the distinction. This equivocation in the *Treatise* is the motivation for the footnote in the *ECPM*:

> To avoid giving offence, I must here observe, that when I deny justice to be a natural virtue, I make use of the word, *natural*, only as oppos'd to *artificial*. In another sense of the word; as no principle of the human mind is more natural than a sense of virtue; so no virtue is more natural than justice. Mankind is an inventive species; and where an invention is obvious and absolutely necessary, it may as properly be said to be natural as any thing that proceeds immediately from original principles, without the intervention of thought or reflection. Tho' the rules of justice be *artificial*, they are not *arbitrary*. Nor is the expression improper to call them *laws of nature*, if by *natural* we understand what is common to any species, or even if we confine it to mean what is inseparable from the species.
>
> (*T*, 3.2.1.19)

Hume's omission becomes less puzzling in this context. The potential for dropping the terminology already exists in the *Treatise*. Resolving terminological ambiguity and removing redundancies is a theme that has been shown to be significant for his approach to the writing of the *ECHU*. Either way, in both works, Hume insists that with respect to property *(mine/yours)*, 'uninstructed nature ... never made such a distinction' (*ECPM*, 3.2.30) and, with respect to 'occupancy' and 'inheritance' and so on, 'Can we think that nature by an original instinct, instructs us in all these methods of acquisition?' (*ECPM*, 3.2.41). Hume even resorts to the notion of 'artificial': 'Volumes of law' necessary for the definition of 'inheritance and contract' are 'complicated and artificial objects' (*ECPM*, 161). In the *Treatise* Hume sees such laws as arising out of the imagination through argument by analogies and refers to the 'slightest *analogies*' here. Thus the eldest son of the eldest son who predeceases his father stands in place of the father and hence inherits his own father's share of his grandfather's estate.

Hume's concern with respect to the investigation of the origins and nature of 'justice' in the *ECPM* is clearly stated: 'That public utility is the *sole* origin of justice, and that reflections on the beneficial consequences of this virtue are the *sole* foundation of its merit' (*ECPM*, 3.1. 1). The *Treatise* in comparable sections, makes little explicit use of the word 'utility' in quite the same way as it is expounded and used in the *ECHU* (as far as I can establish), nor, indeed, is there any *directly* equivalent proposition set up for investigation. The proposition for investigation in the *Treatise* is as follows:

> We now proceed to examine two questions, viz. *concerning the manner, in which the rules of justice are established by the artifice of men*; and *concerning the reasons, which determine us to attribute to the observance or neglect of these rules a moral beauty or deformity.*
>
> (*T*, 3.2.2.1)

In the comparable sections of the *Treatise* Hume is trying to do a number of different things – account by a chain of reasoning for the origins of society, locate the rules of justice in self-interest, being of considerable significance. In context Hume is arguing that 'In general, it may be affirm'd, that there is no such passion in human minds, as the love of mankind, merely as such, independent of personal qualities, of services, or relations to ourself' (*T*, 3.2.1. 12). Hume clearly founds 'justice' on what Norton refers to as 'our deeply rooted self-interest, and then on our tendency to approve actions that contribute to the common good' (*T*, Annotations, 563–564). In *ECPM*, Hume could be seen as restating the second questions as the main question and translating into a general consideration of 'utility' while changing the point of view from that of origins to that of continuation. In the *ECPM* with respect to justice he is intent on locating the origins of justice in 'utility' even if this draws him into a simplified account of the social origins and shifts the balance of the account away for self-interest towards 'humanity' or through 'fellow-felling' or 'views of general usefulness' (*ECPM*, 9.1.8). Such sentiments are in the *ECPM* reinforced by social concerns for 'Personal Merit', in the human search for acceptance, approval and the avoidance of blame (see also Selby-Bigge, 1975, xxvi; Westerman, 1999, 98–99). Hume is careful to set up his proposition as something to be investigated and something to be hedged but the shift is clear enough. Westerman says that Hume 'did not consider his theory of justice [in the *Treatise*] as his lasting achievement' (Westerman, 1999, 96). Hume tells us as much in the *Abstract* where he singles out causality. It is nonetheless a significant achievement.

Scarcity and limitations

Hume starts by examining a society experiencing '*abundance* of all *external* conveniences'. Where everyone has more than enough there is no need for the division of property and hence no need for justice to be introduced into the 'catalogue of virtues'. The arguments are familiar from the *Treatise*. They are nicely and tellingly executed in the *ECPM*. Hume considers universal abundance, universal poverty and what would be the case if humankind exhibited greater benevolence so that trust were to become universal. Hume's capacity to consider alternative possibilities is exhibited again, later, in 'Of Public Credit'.

It is only where wants and means are expanded and there is no universal abundance that there is potential conflict between negative emotions and the demonstration of relative affluence.

The account of the condition of abundance is followed by the example of unalienated land and water drawn from 'the present necessitous condition of mankind'. This is an expansion of an example in the *Treatise* 'as when there is such a plenty of any thing as satisfies all the desires of men: in which case the distinction of property is entirely lost, and everything remains in common' (*T*, 3.2.2.17) with the example given of air and water. Once again Hume demonstrates his understanding of the role of scarcity and abundance with respect to social conditions and the development of social institutions. Although the *ECPM* here is to some extent a summarization, the balance of elements differs from that of the source text (e.g. the discussion about natural and artificial virtues is absent from the main text, as has been noted). The 'alteration of circumstances', including the internal as well as external circumstances – the intensity and scope of benevolence – and its effect on property and on justice made explicit in the *Treatise* is treated unannounced (in advance) in the *ECPM*, where the exemplification of a variety of alternating circumstances is sustained, simple and effective.

Benevolence is an innate, emotive prompt to action rather than a reasoned one. The notion of property and of the private ownership of property is not innate in this sense.

Hume's later summarization makes what has gone before formally evident:

> Thus, the rules of equity or justice depend entirely on the particular state and condition in which men are placed, and owe their origin and existence to that utility, which results to the public from their strict and regular observance. Reverse, in any considerable circumstance, the condition of men: Produce extreme abundance or extreme necessity: Implant in the human breast perfect moderation and humanity, or

perfect rapaciousness and malice: By rendering justice totally useless, you thereby totally destroy its essence, and suspend its obligation upon mankind.

(*ECPM*, 3.1.12)

This would seem to be the formal (and summative) equivalent of the proposition in the *Treatise*:

that 'tis only from the selfishness and confin'd generosity of man, along with the scanty provision that nature has made for his wants, that justice derives its origin.

(*T*, 3.2.2. 19)

Hume is in the *ECPM* more concerned with illustrating the origins of the esteem for justice, in utility, by which he means in the *ECPM* something objective and functional that can give rise to pleasurable sensations when contemplated, and with making an analysis, either theoretical or historical of the consequences of judgments made on the basis of utility in different context (e.g. war with barbarians) but mainly with respect to normal conditions of peace and progress.

Hume's judgment is of course historically accurate about such consequences in his time and, even in ours, but this relativism brings with it a sense of unease. It may not be hard to justify in this respect the notion that the *ECPM* is an intellectually reduced version of the *Treatise* but caution is required. The relative shift to 'utility' is a significant shift for it is understanding utility that makes the judgment on the significance of virtue and vice possible. Views on what is morally good and morally evil can be adjusted in the light of new information concerning consequences: 'if any false opinion, embraced from appearances, has been found to prevail; as soon as farther experience and sounder reasoning have given us juster notions of human affairs, we retract our first sentiment, and adjust anew the boundaries of moral good and evil' (*ECPM*, 2.2.17). His example of alms to beggars – an act that is 'naturally praised' – articulates a classical economic dilemma as to whether alms-giving alleviates need in the short-run or increases need in the long-run through labour disincentive effects. In general terms Hume is following through, with simple but precise examples, his challenge to the notion that moral judgment is 'eternal and immutable' (*T*, 3.1.1.22).

Hume is consistent with his notion of the link between economic actions and incentives. Thus, when discussing rules for the allocation of property rights, 'perfect equality' may seem like a good idea but it is '*impracticable*' or at the least 'extremely *pernicious*': 'Render possessions ever so equal, men's different degrees of art, care, and industry, will immediately break the equality. Or if you check these virtues, you reduce society to the most extreme indigence; and instead of preventing want and beggary in a few, render it unavoidable to the whole community' (*ECPM*, 3.2.26).[7] By 'art' Hume intends practical knowledge with respect to production. He is dealing with a classic dilemma – and a continuation of concerns in the *Treatise* – concerning the links between effort and reward, but a fuller analysis requires of this example a distinction between the short and long run. Hume must have been aware of the need to consider tendencies over time but here if he did have such an awareness it is suppressed for rhetorical effect (immediacy). The changes would take place 'immediately'. He does not thereof consider that such a redistribution could release the energies of a different set of people who were unable to act prior to the redistribution. Neither does he consider possible beneficial consequences in increased output that may accrue in the short to middle term from such a redistribution of land. No doubt the forces that he sees would lead to a reallocation would start quickly enough but still take considerable time to re-assert themselves as a profoundly unequal division of property. Repressing the forces would be necessary to maintain the equality but such repression would, according to Hume, lead to a new tyranny. It is interesting that Cicero argues, against 'Phillipus', that an equal distribution of property would be 'ruinous' as the 'chief purpose of constitutional state and municipal government was that individual property rights may be secured' (*De Officiis*, II 73).

Hume follows up the argument and makes the link explicit: 'Who sees not, for instance, that whatever is produced or improved by a man's art or industry ought, for ever, to be secured to him, in order to give encouragement to such *useful* habits and accomplishments?' (*ECPM*, 3.2.28). This is a labour productivity argument that goes back as least as far as Aristotle and which was brought to a fuller development by Locke. Indeed Hume's quick test for the validity of his views on the utility of justice has a strong family resemblance to Aristotle's empirical, and utilitarian, views on property: 'Were the distinction or separation of possessions entirely useless, can anyone conceive that it ever should have obtained in society?' (*ECPM*, 3.2.47). Hume's focus is not directly on property but on the institutional arrangements necessary to sustaining possession, though the one implies the other.

The argument is a general one, lacks contextualization (though it must be read in the context of the sweep of paragraphs that come before it) and telescoped into a small space. It justifies initial possession but can it really be used to justify inheritance? Here it lacks any significant contextualization or moral limits on accumulation (as is found in Aristotle's notion of friendship and assistance or in Locke in terms of what can be legitimately taken from the commons). It is clear that Hume is concerned with guaranteeing the supply of 'art, care and industry' essential to the progress of mercantile/commercial society. The search is for 'those rules which are, on the whole, most *useful* and *beneficial*' in that respect. Justice will stabilize the link and hence encourage generally such useful social practices and will avoid the mere recirculation of the existing stock (land or material objects) within a developed but nonetheless static society. In a later section he will examine at the level of the individual such positive attributes ('Of Qualities Useful to Ourselves'). Hume is concerned primarily with the 'general interest of society'. In particular cases, 'lawyers' may reason, for the purposes of avoiding disputes, based only 'on very slight connexions of the imagination' (*ECPM*, 3.2.31). With respect to the general interest of society, 'The safety of the people is the supreme law' (*ECPM*, 3.2.32) and this may override, though not 'commonly', particular sectional interests. Aquinas also held that, *in extremis*, theft of the means of subsistence was not properly speaking theft. Such concerns surface again in 'Of Public Credit'.

Given what Hume says about war with barbarians, and what he says about the 'virtuous man' who falls into a 'society of ruffians', it would seem that individual survival is significant in altered circumstances. One who falls into such a society 'must consult the dictates of self-preservation alone, without concern for those who no longer merit his care and attention' (*ECPM*, 3.1.9). The question here is that of what we owe to ourselves in relation to what we owe to others. Hume in following his positive social science is himself a little uneasy: 'The great superiority of civilized Europeans above barbarous Indians, tempted us to imagine ourselves on the same footing with regard to them, and made us throw off all restraints of justice, and even of humanity, in our treatment of them' (*ECPM*, 3.1.19.). 'Tempted' suggests, as does 'imagine', disapproval of the set of actions Hume refers to. The mirroring of atrocities in such circumstances would seem to become inevitable. Hume is aware of the notion of duty but his experimentalist/ empiricist focus is on actions in the world. Of course, Hume is concerned normally with the 'common situation of society' but the relativistic implications of his thinking are, nonetheless, present.

Hume follows the proposition just quoted with a 'backward' look at other propositions that are then rearticulated as not being the origin of justice. There is little of this in the *ECPM*. The extensive argument through the benefits of economic cooperation is telescoped into a very few lines in the *ECHU* and the chain of reasoning presented without any significant support. The productivity argument is basic to Locke's notion of the origins of property and the significance of labour:

> Few enjoyments are given to us from the open and liberal hand of nature; but by art, labour and industry, we can extract them in great abundance. Hence the ideas of property become necessary in all civil society: Hence justice derives its usefulness to the public: And hence alone arises its merit and moral obligation.
>
> (*ECPM*, 3.1.13)

In the *Treatise* Hume needed to build a bridge between the limited nature of benevolence as set out in the *Treatise* and the development of justice as he defined it. His development of the notion of historical evolution feels clumsy. Given the more positive role for the social approval of benevolence, through utility, as set out on the *ECPM,* Hume still needs to build the bridge enabling the development of justice. As he holds that there is no innate universal love of humankind (though sympathy can be activated in particular instances), there is a need to secure the general good through some mechanism located in affective human nature. Hume is aware of individual self-interest and the problem that this can create for cooperation yet he views society in cooperative terms. To complete his logic he supplied a reflection on 'Why Utility Pleases'.

The social and moral economy

The *ECPM* is saying similar things to Book III of the *Treatise* but it is constructed differently. Its rhetorical strategy is concise. It avoids explicit 'egotisms' and paradox; it lacks, in comparative terms, the detailed technical apparatus of 'impressions' and 'ideas'; 'the chain of reasoning' (related to the technical apparatus) is restricted in scope and duration; its developed in line with the rhetorical insight set out in the *Abstract.* The analysis focuses on benevolence (given more significance, especially when compared to the role of self-interest, than in the *Treatise*)[8] and justice and 'utility' and 'love of utility' – present in the *Treatise*, largely through synonym. It is 'love of utility' – a propensity which Hume demonstrates in terms that are more sociological than philosophical – that is given central stage in the account of why justice is a 'virtue'.

Hume's *ECPM* is constructed around the notion of social approbation and its concomitant notions of character, happiness and honour. The analysis is pursued within a gentler, less laboured, notion of experimental philosophy than that developed in the *Treatise.* Indeed, in rejecting the selfish hypothesis as the basis of all morals, he also rejects placing unquestioning faith in an unexamined 'love of simplicity', a significant feature of this Newtonianism as expressed in the *Treatise* (*ECPM*, appendix 2, 6). In the *ECPM* Hume shifted the balance between benevolence and self-interest. Justice and conventions and their significance for the creation, acquisition and settlement of property, and hence for a well-regulated and predictable economic life, is not, however, diminished.

The economy and the actions of economic agents are predictable (argued in the *ECHU*) but the expectations are provisional and liable to change. Hume does not contemplate, in the *ECPM*, what happens when the social balance itself goes wrong and society tends to an extreme or takes a distorted view of moral or economic action. Hume's experiential philosophy reflects Hume's own experience of the 'good life'. The social balance seems to be maintained by consideration of what looks like an Aristotelian or Epicurean learned mean or balance between different types of possible behaviours and the evaluation of such behaviours by agents and spectators attuned to their natural sentiments as refined by social habit or custom and manners in polite society.

Hume's economic agents have a social and emotional life. In this context there are, by implication, social approbation benefits and social disapprobation costs. Trust is significant as it is in the *Treatise* with respect to social commerce (both the self-interested and the benevolent). With respect to economic agency, frugality is a mean between the vice of avarice on the one hand and of prodigality on the other. Economic success is a struggle between worthwhile long-term goals and present and often desultory pleasures. A full and successful human life is one that charts a careful path between minimal economic security, on the one hand, and the temptations of 'useless toys and gewgaws' (*ECPM*, 9.2.25) and the 'feverish, empty amusement of luxury and expense', on the other. Luxury is not to be condemned out of hand as in its 'refinement of the pleasures and conveniences of life' it is to be welcomed but, it is also to be treated with discernment, as a potentially empty trap.[9]

This balanced and prudent life encompasses economic action as well as the appropriate use of leisure.[10] Personal merit and the institutional framework provided by law and government ensure stability and the supply of the socially necessary attributes (art, industry, frugality and so on) that ensure continued economic wellbeing and expansion over time. Such a life envisages an almost Aristotelian notion of friendship as well as the peaceful contemplation of nature and character: 'conversation, society, study' as well as 'health' (itself achieved by pursuit of a mean between self-indulgence and self-neglect), 'the common beauties of nature' and, 'above all the peaceful reflection on one's own conduct'.[11] Hume puts these joys, somewhat curiously, beyond the market, resisting in a sense their commodification, with everything else merely building toward them. Again there are significant traces of classical thinking in this moral stand. In his own life, he nevertheless expended considerable energy and acquired considerable sums of money, in which he took more than a little pride, to ensure just that kind of enlightened sociability. Hume's economy, and the actions of economic agents, and the judgments made on them, as it emerges from the *ECHU* and the *ECPM,* is one that is enmeshed in the sociable and cooperative (rather than competitive) nature of humankind, in the potential predictability of economic life and within the context of purposeful lives exhibiting longer-term, and essentially moral, objectives. Hume's notion of economic wellbeing ('happiness' as well as 'virtue') goes beyond the mere accumulation of material resources. The opening moves of Hume's work on 'economics' carry forward elements of his social and moral economy as set forth in the *ECPM.*

6 Hume's essays

From popular to political economy

Introduction

The extreme judgment of Kruse, who expressed disappointment with Hume's popularizations and who sees 'no internal connexion' between 'the essays on political economy' and the *Treatise* (Kruse, 1939, 2) – Schumpeter has essentially a similar view – has given way to a gentler, more appreciative understanding of Hume's 'connexions' and to the potential unity of Hume's approach to social analyses. This does not mean however that the mapping of the content/concepts of political economy on to the economic content of the *Treatise* results in a perfect match. Mankin (2005, 62) points out, though this may be over-generalized, that '... the *Essays* [1752] make no attempt to reflect on the role of pride and vanity, or that traditional economic passion, avarice'. There is also little in the way of specific monetary analysis in the *Treatise*.

Rotwein (1955, 1976), challenging the notion that there is no connection, from the mid-1950s onwards, points to the link between Hume's view of the 'science of human nature' and his exercises in economic thought, particularly the psychology of motivation. Whereas Hume's general stance is analytical, his point of view is that of the balanced, prudent and essentially liberal, policy-maker, a role in which the political and the economic come together. A full scholarship with respect to the evolution of the essays would have to take into account, as Box does, the fact that they were written, edited and re-edited with the passage of time (Box, 1990, 112; see also Mankin, 2005).

The essays, then, arose out of Hume's disappointment with the reception of the *Treatise*. The role of the *Abstract* in helping Hume identify the problem of the *Treatise* from a reader's point of view has already been explored. In writing the *Abstract* Hume is exploring his own understanding of why the *Treatise* failed to find an audience. Long chains of reasoning, essential to the fullest textual development of the experimental/inductive method, were part of the problem. Obviously, in making these reflections, the empirically minded, and hence practically minded, Hume wondered about what sort of writing could serve as a model for serious, but not overdemanding writing.

He wanted literary fame, albeit virtuous fame – fame, perhaps, as a modern day orator, given his discovery of audience, and concern with virtue – and recognition by his peers. Hume wished to shape an understanding among the people who counted of the proper requirements of a liberal, commercial society and its associated policies.

A developing *genre*

In the early years of the eighteenth century, the most popular forms of writing, suitable to the pursuit of Hume's aims with respect to political stability and the construction of a philosophically informed 'polite society', were either essays or some form of history or the emerging novel. There was a growing market for literary output – one that was to become so big that a writer such as Smollett could live directly on it proceeds while incorporating into his novels moral comment and 'customs and manners' satirized in line with Scottish thinking. Hume was in need of a market to satisfy his desire for literary fame but also to supplement his income. The essay as a developing mid-eighteenth-century *genre* was available, as was its identifiable market niche. It had its limitations. It was largely developed by writers who were essentially journalistic. Its existing use was primarily for some form of absorbing entertainment. In Book Three of the *Treatise*, Hume was aware of the tendency of his age to 'convert reading into an amusement, and to reject every thing that requires any considerable degree of attention to be comprehended' (*T*, 3.1.1.1). As he wished for a wider audience, he needed to find a vehicle that would bring together his social and moral concerns with a suitable middle-class readership (see Phillipson, 1983, 180). Some working compromise was required.

It remained to be seen as Hume was writing the *Abstract* whether or not an established *genre* could be used to push more consistent and more demanding material to the public. We must imagine that he was reworking all sorts of literary ideas and possibilities, including simultaneously finishing Book III of the *Treatise* – a book that, according to the Advertisement, he still hoped 'may be understood by ordinary readers'. Hume consistently saw himself as a 'man of letters' rather than as a remote academic locked up in a university. He wanted his ideas to be engaged through public discussion but nonetheless to retain intellectual validity. It was intellectually necessary that this be so for his philosophy that human nature and hence human phenomena be studied in its entirety (*T*, 1.4.7.13; *T*, 1.4.7.14). He readily uses/explores existing models and popular topics in his earliest essays (such as 'Of Impudence and Modesty' and 'Of Love and Marriage'). These are highly 'journalistic' pieces and some of them were quietly dropped by Hume (Box, 1990, 112, 147–48). It is not surprising that Hume looked, initially, to those already well established in the *genre* for guidance. In his 'Of the Standard of Taste', Hume argues that 'none of the rules of composition are fixed by reasonings *a priori*...' (I, Essay XXIII, 231). Hume is clear that 'experience' is needed and 'rules of art' can be established either by 'genius' or 'observation', including 'observation of the common sentiments of human nature'.

Hume tells us of his concerns in his initial essays themselves. Although these essays are remote from those that are conventionally classified as economics, without the success of the earlier essays, where he developed his command of the *genre* – essentially understanding the strengths and limitations of the stand alone essay – the later ones would have been an unlikely prospect both with respect to their business-like style as well as to their subject matter.

There are several essays in which Hume reflects on the nature of audience and of context. They differ in length and in complexity but all of them are concerned, to some extent at least, with the 'what', 'how' and 'why' of communication. In this respect Hume is searching for a set of ideas that will help him communicate his technical expertise in the context of both readership and the associated concept of persuasion. Hume has the model of the popular essay, but Hume himself had an understanding of classical rhetoric – Cicero and Demosthenes in particular.[1] Rhetoric in Scotland was to be subjected to revision in the context of the need for Scottish students, as part of way in which the modernization process was interpreted, to be exposed to the most modern and successful of contemporary writers rather than simply being exposed to classical models. Nonetheless, Hume, and his fellows, looked to classical sources and hence also to Cicero. *De Officiis* is an important source, not just for rhetorical devices but for Hume's ethical understanding at least as far as the notion of 'duty' is concerned (Desjardin, 1967, 238; Baier, 1988, 767; see also Buckle, 1991, 247 for a related point and especially Jones, 1982)[2] *De Officiis* is also significant, in economic and political terms, for it is there that Cicero stresses the significance of property rights in state formation (Radford, 2001, 30).

Finding the right approach: 'Of Essay Writing'

Hume, for example, in 'Of Essay Writing', first published in 1742 and then excised from later editions, identifies the audience as essentially the '*conversable*' rather than the 'learned', though both are part of 'elegant' society. The *Treatise*, by implication, was addressed, the hope for Book Three notwithstanding, to the 'learned' (a significantly smaller market) but even they could not grasp its meaning in a way that was satisfactory to Hume.

Grose (1898) argues that 'Of Essay Writing' was intended as an opening essay in a sequence of essays (Box, 1990, 116). The 'learned' concentrate on difficult subject matter requiring 'long Preparation and severe Labour' contemplated in solitude whereas the '*conversable*' seek out topics suitable for exploration in the company of others. This is in effect 'polite society', a complex, cultural aspiration of the early eighteenth century, saturated with status concerns and consumerism.[3] Hume, in the essay, complains of the separation of the learned from regular society, though lessened in recent times, and claims 'History, Politics and the more obvious Principles, at least of Philosophy' as part of the informal curriculum that ought to be available to the '*conversable*'. The restrictions that he seems to find in existing patterns of 'polite' conversation are his targets to overthrow:

> Must the Mind never rise higher, but be perpetually:
> Stun'd and worn with endless Chat
> Of Will did this, and Nan did that
> (Essays withdrawn, Essay I, 534)

Something more demanding for sustained sociability than gossip is what Hume seeks to establish.[4] Even this we can link, without too much straining to Hume's view's in the *Treatise* as to what is likely to 'fix our thought' and be 'contemplated with satisfaction': 'the histories of kingdoms are more interesting than domestic stories' (*T*, 3.3.5.14) and so on in a hierarchy of intellectual complexity. Hume incorporates the 'history of kingdoms' into his more demanding essays. He enjoys idle conversation provided it is not the sole aspect of social discourse. Hume's ideal human life is balanced: reason, action, indolence.

'Of Essay Writing' is a light piece, as Box argues, but the point made here is significant for the development of the idea of, or possibilities for, 'polite society'. Hume, in his significant *Dialogues Concerning Natural Religion*, stresses, as does Cicero,[5] that dialogue is essential in areas where final conclusions are likely to prove elusive. Hume states, 'And if the subject be curious and interesting, the book carries us in a manner into company; and unites the two greatest and purest pleasures of human life, study and society' (Hume, *DCNR*, 158). For Hume, intellectually informed social life is dialogical, stimulating and, in the end, challenging. Battersby, commenting on 'Of Essay Writing' writes: 'Hume sees experience and conversation to be closely connected ...' (Battersby, 1976, 246). Pleasing conversation is exchange-based (social 'commerce') as points of view are shared and new points of view become possible through the sympathetic response. His model he is trying to promote is that of the 'conversazione' (an evening's discussion of significant topics in a social context),[6] which is why he later found salon society in France so very engaging. Hume is of course aware that critical discussion could, given the manners of the early eighteenth century, end as a fight. This disagreeable outcome had to be avoided and conversational etiquette was required. Disagreement, for Hume, was 'natural'. If disagreements were properly conducted, then outcomes could be beneficial. Even in this there are Ciceronian overtones: liberty must not be confused with license and conversation should promote civic accord (Burke, 1969; Miller, 2006, 47). Hume's agenda as demonstrated in his essays reflect to some extent Cicero's criteria for conversational subject matter (*De Officiis*, I, 134).

An implication of 'elegant' society is the potential to stress the calm and reflective passions. Hume's essays tend to demonstrate the engaged (because the topics call for thinking through contemporary issues) detachment (because Hume demonstrates the distance required for useful thought) needed to avoid eristic voices. By building a discursive audience for popular but also for more demanding political discussion, Hume was able, in due course, to make political economy, at least with respect to the conceptual underpinnings of 'police' (policy), a suitable subject for drawing-room discussion and so, inadvertently, helping to create a market, in the fullness of time for Adam Smith's *Wealth of Nations*.[7]

Hume, based upon his views in the *Treatise*, makes it clear that philosophical thinking ('learned' thinking) and philosophers would find in (improved) everyday conversation an antidote to 'chimerical' conclusions through interaction with ordinary 'Experience'. Hume constructs himself, rather grandly, as an 'Ambassador from the Dominions of Learning to those of Conversation' and he sees in his position the possibility of a genuine and significant intellectual exchange between the two groups: 'The Balance of Trade we need not be jealous of, nor will there be any Difficulty to preserve it on both sides' (Essays withdrawn, Essay 1, 535). Hume was working, as was Cicero, to bring philosophical understanding together with virtuous rhetoric. Trade in a sense is dialogical. In *De Oratore*, Cicero talks in terms of bringing the would-be orator 'out of this sheltered training ground at home, right into action, into the dust and uproar of the camp, into the camp and the fighting-line of public debate' (*De Oratore*, 157). This is a restatement of Cicero's views as set out in the *Tusculan Disputations* (Jones, 1982, 33). Cicero's reputation ('easy philosophy') for bringing philosophy and rhetoric together impressed Hume. Blair, writing in 1783, stresses Cicero's commitment in case preparation to examining his preparation from his own point of view, from that of the 'Judge' and of the opposing 'Advocate' (Blair, 2005, [1783] 304). Dialogue is in this sense fundamental to the rhetorical project. An Ambassador's role it perhaps more sedate, and 'polite conversation' less heated, but nonetheless the role is a persuasive one. In playing the role, Hume is secure in his philosophical knowledge. His oratory has good Ciceronian credentials. Hume in his self-estimation was extending his role of philosopher, and challenging it at the same time.

Hume constructs the relationship as one of exchanges but in the full quotation he sees one area that lacks symmetry: 'The materials of this Commerce must chiefly be furnish'd by Conversation and common life: The manufacturing of them belongs to Learning' (Essays withdrawn, Essay 1, 535). Topics for philosophical consideration are to be generated in social contexts. If this really were the case then Hume, given his sociability, had direct access to the demand side. This statement is noticed by Box, who, like Moore before him, stresses the 'empirical presuppositions' (Box, 1990, ft.11, 119). The sentence consists in a very distinctive, and carefully elaborated, economic metaphor, in keeping with the kind of sensitivity to economic cooperation that Hume first displays in the *Treatise*. It is not accidental for something similar is to be found in the opening essay of the *ECHU*. It is significant that Hume, well aware of the economic significance of success in publishing, sees the writer–reader relationship as a set of transactions and exchanges: an economy of the text, an idea not fully developed until recently. This sophisticated use of an economic metaphor also suggests that Hume's economic interests in the *Treatise* were still active at this time.

Hume is careful to add that discerning women, though he takes pains to gently ridicule their reading of 'Books of Gallantry and Devotion',[8] constitute a significant part of the audience for his version of polite literature. Women are, in the improving spirit of the essay, called upon to 'concur heartily in that Union I have projected betwixt the learned and conversable Worlds'. Hume was to find just such women, later, in the salons of Paris and engaged them as intellectual co-discussants. Jonathan Swift felt, as Hume does here, that the presence of women in a conversation improved its tone (Miller, 2006, 6; see also I, Essay XIV, 134). Women later became a significant part of the audience for philosophically informed history.

The same sort of themes ('the entertainment, instruction, and reformation of mankind') are taken up in an essay that latterly became the introduction to *ECHU*. These are, if considered as teaching, pleasing and emotionally engaging the audience, a direct reference to the purposes of Ciceronian rhetoric. 'Of Essay Writing' is a piece that cannot have taken long to write, a few days at the most, though there is more in it than meets the casual eye. 'Of the Different Species of Philosophy' is, despite its popular elements, a much more substantial piece and is likely to have taken much longer to compose.

'Of the Different Species of Philosophy'

This is an essay that although not nearly so 'popular' in its expression, nonetheless attempts to find a way between 'the accurate and abstruse' philosophy and the 'easy and obvious'. It is written much later than 'Of Essay Writing' and hence is more sophisticated intellectually. The relationship between the two essays considered here stems from the understanding that Hume achieves concerning his role as potential essayist. It became the first section of the *ECHU*.

Hume, again, outlines a set of acceptable cultural attributes that, in his view, moderate both extremes: the philosopher is too 'remote' and the 'mere ignorant is still more despised':

> The most perfect character is supposed to lie between those extremes; retaining an equal ability and taste for books, company and business; preserving in conversation that discernment and delicacy which arise from polite letters; and in business, that probity and accuracy which are the natural result of a just philosophy.
>
> (*ECHU*, 1.1.7)

Mediating between the two extremes produces Hume's ideal cultural life in society: 'By means of such compositions, virtue becomes amiable, science agreeable, company instructive, and retirement entertaining'. From the outset, the essay format, as developed by Montaigne, was intended to be entertaining as well as thoughtful.[9] Hume is not capitulating to vulgar taste and mere popularization. He is attempting to create a taste for his kind of philosophy and philosophical discussion, albeit in humanized terms: 'let your science be human and such as may have a direct reference to action and society'; 'Be a philosopher; but, amidst all your philosophy, be still a man' (*ECHU*, 1.1.6 as anticipated in the closing moves of Book One of the *Treatise*). All of this is in keeping with Hume's desire in the conclusion of Book One for 'founders of systems' to add to their notions, a 'gross earthy mixture' of everyday concerns (*Treatise*, 1.4.7.14). Hume hopes to avoid metaphysical speculation through this focus on how people actually are. This is not a mere capitulation to popular taste so much as an attempt to construct an audience, an audience in which his actual readers seek to take on the characteristics of his intended readers.

Hume's next move is to make a case for abstract philosophies. He pleads 'in their behalf' but does so in a spirit of compromise. Abstract philosophy assists the development of the easy philosophy just as the anatomist serves the artist. All 'polite letters' encompass moral qualities. Abstract philosophy encourages 'accuracy' and such accuracy helps achieve 'perfection' or helps improve society. There are practical benefits that flow from the diffusion through society of 'the genius of philosophy'. Hume's oscillation between the negatives and positives in abstract philosophy is really a negotiation with the readership, a negotiation in the spirit of the balance of trade metaphor that is specified in 'Of Essay Writing'. Careful reasoning can challenge abstruse philosophy only when it itself is 'accurate' and 'just'. Hume's targets remains the same in this essay as it does in the *Treatise*. His commitment remains to undertake an 'accurate scrutiny into the powers and facilities of human nature' and to set out the 'mental geography'. He is helped in this task by his knowledge of society and of what Merrill calls 'his attention to how people actually live, think, feel and judge' (Merrill, 2008, 3). This sustained concern for an accurate discussion informs his 'political' essays.

Hume stresses that many distinctions to be made such as between the 'will and understanding' (action and understanding) and between 'the imagination and the passions' can be understood at some level by 'every human creature'. The distinctions make in Hume's philosophy 'are no less certain and real, though more difficult to comprehend'. Hume is saying to his readers that it is worth making the effort. The pay-off in this *trade* in philosophical ideas is clear: 'And whatever pains these researches may cost us, we may think ourselves sufficiently rewarded, not only in point of profit but of pleasure, if, by that means, he can make an addition to the stock of knowledge, in subjects of such unspeakable importance'. There are costs and benefits. The benefits are in material terms, as it were, 'profits' (this is part of the practical benefits that Hume earlier suggested comes from abstract philosophy percolating through society) and emotional, 'pleasure'. Hume, here, is not so much an ambassador as a trade attaché. The textual strategy for engaging readers in his text is that of 'avoiding all unnecessary detail' (with respect, though this is unsaid, to his main ideas). Selection from the curriculum established by the *Treatise* is to be expected. This is a matter of Hume's judgment – as it is in all forms of summarization leading to the development of new work – concerning the aims of the *Enquiries* rather than a matter of ambivalence about his commitment to the intellectual content of the *Treatise*. In trade both parties give up something in order to move towards a beneficial outcome. Hume is looking for a improving conversation with the reader, a conversation that has useful outcomes such as the 'stability of modern governments above the ancient' (*ECHU*, 9.10) and settles, in the *Enquiries* for a simplified curriculum.

It is clear that in these two essays Hume tackles the question of what type(s) of material is appropriate to be treated in the essay format and sets out to ensure that it is something more than mere gossip. Progressively, as he becomes more certain of the market by experience, he is able to extend the curriculum, as it were and create opportunities (as in the essay 'Of Commerce' and the set that it introduces) of applying general principles to more practical policy problems. His intention is not to extinguish his philosophical role but adapt it to his new and enhanced concept of his intended readership, readership that is potentially influential. This move is in keeping with the 'Conclusion' that he reaches at the end of Book One of the *Treatise*. He creates the 'how' (already established from the ideas set out in the *Abstract,* i.e. the avoidance of long-chains of reasoning) in terms of shorter and free-standing pieces. He had experience of tightly written episodes in the *Treatise* to drawn upon, as illustrated, for example, by his economic passages, analysed in an earlier chapter. He still needed to find a popular topic that would make it possible to write in a self-contained way while increasing the significance of that which was written. The 'what', in terms of topics for consideration, if his trade analogy was in fact indicative of his practice, he derived directly from talk and conversation though focused by his concerns to support the development of liberal society. Political questions, and the constitution, gave him his way in.

Answering 'why' is slightly more complex. Informed discussion is good for society: the arguments based on utility are exercised in both of the articles examined above. The domain of action ought to be informed through the dissemination of the products of critical thinking. It is good for philosophy by grounding its discourse in every day experiences. It is good for the philosopher as virtuous rhetorician for just persuasion is helped by detailed knowledge of the intended audience, a point made by Cicero (*De Oratore*, 219). Hume made a case against 'eloquence' in the *Treatise* by which he must have meant something like 'mere' eloquence, elegant but devoid of significant content. It is good for readers as it brings careful thought to play in current topics of concern. Hume brings to bear, in the sweep of the essays, valid ideas from philosophy, as it was broadly defined and understood in the mid-eighteenth century, to the world of social discourse and social action. It is good, too, for Hume: it satisfies his desire to find a profitable market for his philosophical ideas (this combination of profit and amusement is in a sense also Ciceronian) while grounding his approach to the 'science of man'.

From the political to the economic

The subject matter that was seen to have the most obvious connection to the *Treatise* in an immediate and direct way is developed in his political essays. The essays conventionally classified as economic came later. This classification or identification of a fixed set is not based on Rotwein's work of 1955, as Kruse refers to the 'essays on political economy', distinguished from the 'political' essays in 1939. Gide and Rist refer to Hume's 'essays on economic questions, the most important among them dealing with money, foreign trade, the rate of interest etc.' (Gide and Rist, [1909] 1960, 71). By focusing on title Hume becomes an economist interested in money and trade. His economic and political concerns are much wider. Although a hard and fast line can be drawn between the publications by date and even, for the most part, by title, there is no hard and fast line dividing the content. 'Of the Jealousies of Trade' is a political essay (in both active and passive senses as Hume is declaring a political/economic position) as much as it is an essay in political economy. At the same time, for example, 'Of the First Principles of Government' (a relatively lightweight piece), while it is primarily concerned with government, also verges, inevitably, in the distinction made between interest and right and power and property into economic themes, at least as in so far as these would be recognized in the mid-eighteenth century or by latter-day institutionalists. Mankin makes the point that Hume could have in the *Political Discourses* signalled that he was opening up 'a new space of reflection that we call economy' and that he did not do so, (Mankin, 2005, 60).

Even Smith's *Wealth of Nations* is more than a mere economic text and some of Hume's insights and topics in the political essays are also to be found in the *WN*. Smith is acutely aware of the fact that wealth is the product of the annual application of labour. Hume is clear that 'men and commodities are the real strength of any community' rather than money ('Of Money'). The origin of chiefly government growing out of warfare and the organization of savage society (I, Essay V, 40), and other reflections on the savage condition, are elaborated in the stadial theory that Smith develops both in the *Lectures on Jurisprudence* and also in the *Wealth of Nations*.[10] Both Hume and Smith no doubt were drawing upon the same sources in European natural law but Smith was also drawing directly upon Hume.

The interface with the *Treatise* is in both cases through the passions as well as through the tendency in human nature to prefer the present to the future. With Hume, as with Smith, we are often not dealing with one discipline at a time. Even a topic such as 'Of Civil Liberty' (I, Essay XII) becomes, in its second paragraph, in part, an economic essay: 'Trade was never esteemed an affair of the state till the last century ....' (I, Essay XII, 88). Hume's liberal concerns with respect to 'commerce', weave in and out of the discussion thereafter. Hume himself was, in addition, in much of his writing concerned with sustaining the development not only of 'polite' society but of a very specific form of such a society. He was interested in the possibility of a benign liberal society in which the beneficial influence of commerce could be experienced and shared. The risky capacity of 'free governments' to 'contract debt' becomes the subject matter of the final paragraph of this essay, anticipating future concerns. It is usually a question of more or less. Hume, as was Smith, was working for the realization of a liberal, commercial society that did not at the time fully exist – Smith in the *WN* draws attention to numerous feudal remnants, such as over-long apprenticeships that restricted economic choice – and the political and economic policy requirements of which were also not fully understood (Henderson, 2006). Hume lived in an age of transition and was concerned with the achievement of a beneficial transition in terms of human welfare or as he would say, happiness. There is not much point in being an Ambassador from the world of ideas unless the ideas as a result engage positively with social and political concerns.

The series of three essays on personifications of the Stoic, Platonic and Sceptical philosophy are clearly primarily philosophical essays. But the Stoic is defined as 'the man of action and of virtue' in the essay's alternative title. It rehearses in a highly reductionist form the situation of mankind in nature, first worked up in economic passages in the *Treatise*, and identifies happiness 'as the great end of all human industry', physical, economic or intellectual (I, Essay XVI, 148). The set taken together, as Rotwein (1955, xciv) himself points out, relates easily to Hume's concerns with 'pleasure, action, liveliness and indolence' and hence to human motivations in the natural pursuit of the rounded life.[11] Hume's essay 'Of the Populousness of Ancient Nations' make use of this notion of ends, i.e. happiness, to undertake the comparison between the ancient and modern worlds. It contrasts 'domestic oeconomy', a potential location of happiness, in the relevant time-periods (see Chapter 8). Yet, the essays are more or less characterized by their titles and part of this chapter, and all of the next, will be devoted to those conventionally classified as 'economic'.

Perhaps the most significant essay for the development of the works on political economy is 'That Politics May Be Reduced to a Science'. As Hume defines politics in the *Treatise* as 'men untied in society', then this clearly covers many aspects of what would now be called 'social science' and, hence, political economy. This is, of the face of it, is a practical example, in the sense of establishing potential patterns of cause and effect consequent on the rules and structures of constitutions, of the 'science of man'. Hume offers a discussion and a search for evidence that will show the utility of treating politics as a science.

But the essay can be interpreted in another, and essentially, deeply ironic way. Hume in his essays on political economy is usually writing against some proposition or set of propositions. James Conniff (1976) reads the essay as an ironic attack on Harringtonian ideas and that Hume's intention is rather to show that generalizations about political life are not easy to arrive at and hence the need, as with other aspects of Hume's thought, of proceeding with caution. This does not, of course, reduce its scientific content as establishing valid knowledge claims is, according to Hume more generally, a problematic exercise. Letwin (1998, 83) makes a similar point when she argues that Hume was more concerned, ultimately, with the classical virtue of 'prudence' that he was with the 'laws of social science'. The essay is therefore essentially, according to Conniff, about the need for moderation in the light of uncertainty, a topic that closes the discussion. Hume's standpoint is philosophical or may be also in terms drawn from 'Of Essay Writing' ambassadorial. It is possible to cautiously produce maxims about (say) political stability but it terms of the day-to-day processes of politics as an activity, the uncertainties are such that 'moderation' and all that it implies is the better course of action.

Details of Hume's language reflect the need for accuracy in abstract philosophy stated in the opening essay of the *ECHU*: Hume is involved in making a 'distinction'; in making 'a yet more accurate inspection'; and, with a large hint of the *Treatise*, he argues that 'Effects will always correspond to causes'. He observes the fray, comments upon it the topic and it simplifications for institutional development and individual behaviour from a neutral point of observation. Hume demonstrates from the outset that he is expanding upon a topic that is already part of the curriculum of the 'conversant' members of society. The opening move is an indirect reference to Pope's views that 'Whate'er is best administered is best'. Hume starts, again in a manner characteristic of some sections of the *Treatise*, with a question (a kind of proposition), for evaluation, presented as a pair.[12] He seems to contest Pope's view but this may be more superficial than real. He is not concerned with the character of individual men but with general principles and institutions conducive to stability. The text then provides example and counter-example within each of the two following paragraphs and these led to his first significant proposition:

> So great is the force of laws, and of particular forms of government, and so little dependence have they on the humours and tempers of men, that consequences almost as general and certain may sometimes be deduced from them, as any which the mathematical sciences afford us.
>
> (I, Essay III, 16).

This is exaggeration for effect and it is an argument against individual merit and demerit, perhaps, as Letwin (1998, 86) suggests, as made by Bolingbroke. It is possible to point to a passage in the *Treatise* where, with respect to natural philosophy, the science of man many even have an advantage. Notice that the second part of the sentence is hedged, not once but twice. This is a very specific example of Hume's caution with respect to the formulation of knowledge claims.

Stable institutional arrangements make for consistent outcomes and hence normally predictable behaviour even if this behaviour is itself likely to lead to instability. This is a claim and once the evidence is presented to support this claim, then the process of investigation becomes inductive and cumulative. Hume then demonstrates the evidence that he has for such a claim. He considers the constitution of the Roman republic, and its negative consequences, when citizenship was expanded in Italy to those well beyond Rome itself. He moves from the Roman republic at the opening of the paragraph and closes with the generalization that 'Such are the effects of democracy without a representation' (I, Essay III, 16).

Hume considers two different types of government by nobles (Venice and Poland) and, by evidence, shows how that of Venice was preferable to that of Poland.[13] According to Conniff there is a sleight of hand here as Venice in Harringtonian views was rather a commercial meritocracy and hence republican. He examines kingly government (either elected or hereditary) and reflecting on these in much the same way as Adam Smith was to do later in the *WN* when reflecting upon primogeniture (Henderson, 2006). The most stable arrangement in a monarchy is the hereditary principle. Hume supplies no evidence for this and this fact has led to the suggestion that he is using deduction (Conniff, 1976, 93). Hume could easily have supplied evidence and indeed had partly done so with the respect to the case of Poland. He does not need to supply evidence for a chain of reasoning that could be exemplified by his readership. From this emerges his next significant 'scientific' claim:

> It may therefore be pronounced as a universal axiom in politics, *That an hereditary prince, a nobility without out vassals, and a people voting by their representatives, form the best* MONARCHY, ARISTOCRACY, *and* DEMOCRACY.
>
> (I, Essay III, 18)

Hume's concerns for the good and bad aspects of given constitutional forms reflect to some extent Cicero's concerns for pure forms and what Radford (2001, 31) calls 'their evil twins'. This is only the start. Hume is anxious 'to observe other principles of this science'. With the Roman model in mind, Hume observes that free governments benefit those who directly participate in the freedom but are 'ruinous and oppressive to their provinces'. He then makes a very clear point about the nature of Roman political economy – he has already considered the negative political economy of an elected system of monarchy – even though he is dealing with the issue in general terms: 'The conquerors, in such a government, are all legislators, and will be sure to contrive matters, by restrictions on trade, and by taxes, so as to draw some private, as well as public advantages, from their conquests' (I, Essay III, 19). Later he cites the case of Ireland to support this example of the abuses of provinces by a free people and the constraint shown in France, where an absolute monarch remains indifferent with respect to all his subjects. What Hume is doing is following a general textual pattern: situation, cause (evidence supplied), consequences (evidence supplied and evaluated). This type of pattern and these types of examples, counter-examples, have already been shown to be part of the rhetorical structure of smaller-scale passages in the *Treatise*. He is using analogy, working from the case in Rome to the case in Ireland. In addition, he is consistently arguing against the idealization of republican views as expounded by Harringtonians (Conniff, 1976, 94).

Institutional arrangements, not just whole constitutions but the details of 'the smallest courts or offices', provide in their 'stated forms and methods' a significant 'check on the natural depravity of mankind' (I, Essay III, 24). He then elevates the focus (moving from the particular to the more general) and suggests that the stability through time of the Venetian republic (a stable nobility without vassals evidence of the superiority of which having already been presented) to its 'form of government' while using the Roman republican constitution as an example of a defective constitution creating instability through time. His really telling example (and his acute observation) is shown in the case of Genoa, where the 'same men' generally governed poorly except with respect to 'the bank of St. George', whose rules were sound. Hume's interest in the evolution of institutions is developed in the *Treatise* in the context of the development of justice as an artificial virtue. Conniff sees Hume's declaration that governments 'ought to provide a system of laws to regulate the administration of public affairs to the latest posterity' as 'unwarranted' optimism and the evidence supplied earlier by Hume as leading to 'defective' judgment. In the end, this is to misunderstand Hume or, at least, overstate the irony. The view expressed concerning rules is in tune with Hume's views of rules about property in the *Treatise* and the *Enquiries*. He is committed to his proposition. Humans make rules as a matter of social practice, based upon conventions and supported by notions of 'utility' (set out very clearly in the *ECMU*).[14] At a personal level, individuals live within their own historical experience that sanctions, through habit, their beliefs. Societies exist over time even if in the end they fail. Sustained constitutional practice and historical experiences provide instruction in rules and their consequences.

But to leave it at that is not enough, for Hume's intention is to work for the best with what is already in place: 'Here, then is sufficient inducement to maintain, with the utmost ZEAL, in every free state, those forms and institutions, by which liberty is secured, the public consulted, and the avarice or ambition of particular men restrained and punished' (I, Essay III, 26) rather than socially recommend utopian, theoretical constructs (see 'Of Parties in General' and the passage on parties 'from principle', religious or otherwise (I, Essay VIII, 60). The significant word is 'maintain': evolution rather than revolution. There are many forms of good government, and to maintain those forms in the case of Britain that actually promote good administration requires a degree of moderation. The implication is, again consistent with the *Treatise*, that these forms have not emerged easily and that good practices are essential. Taking things to extremes in terms of the (unwholesome) personality of a minister (the 'casual humours and characters of individual men' of the initial exordium) distorts the constitutional and, indeed, the practical policy questions to be asked. Hume attacked Harrington and his followers by using the Ciceronian tactic of subverting their arguments for radical change and by recommending the calmer passions. It is significant for his argument that his principle generalization on the best forms of government holds water.

Hume is fulfilling his ambassadorial role. He is also adapting his Newtonian sense of 'induction' and the power of correctly specifying causal links to suit a general audience. This concern for working through example is as much in line with Ciceronian advice with respect to rhetoric as it is with Hume's more extensive demands for reasoning by induction found in the long chains set up in the *Treatise*. By treating from instances, arguing counter-cases with flair, Hume is dealing with argument from example, a sub-set of what is required for a fully scientific induction. That he intends a certain outcome is an implication of his Ciceronian approach. And setting out a position that he maintained in other contexts: the significance of government by laws for progress and well-being over governments by personality and, by implication, by fractious and splenetic party. Institutional and constitutional constraints are more significant than individual merit or demerit. Stick to the rules and take human nature as you find it.

The dialogical nature of the exiting moves is a display not just of even-handedness but of Hume's commitment to discussion and hence moderation. He also, towards the end of the essay, uses his historical examples not simply scientifically but morally. Although indulging in an application of the 'science of man' Hume is also concerned with 'virtue' and presents the carefully hedged proposition: 'Let us therefore try, if it be possible, from the foregoing doctrine, to draw a lesson of moderation with regard to the parties, into which the country is at present divided; at the same time that we allow not this moderation to abate the industry and passion, with which every individual is bound to pursue the good of his country' (I, Essay III, 27). Hume's stance here, for 'moderation' (a form of balance) in the evaluation of political actions, is another of the positions that he maintains over time.

A political economy essay (traditionally defined)

It is useful to look at an economics essay in the context of what has just been developed above. The essay to be examined here, 'Of Commerce', has as its main topic the interdependency of the 'greatness of a state, and the happiness of its subjects'. Its theme is the value of liberal policies in the political and economic sphere and the need to resolve sovereign interest with that of the wider society. 'Of Commerce' is constructed as an introductory essay to a set of 'discourses on commerce, money, interest, balance of trade, &' (II, Essay I, 255) and as such must modify, even if only slightly, the sense in which Hume's approach to essay writing is primarily the construction of free-standing material. This set, from which 'Of the Populousness of Ancient Nations' is not to be excluded, is concerned with, broadly speaking, policy issues concerning the relationship between commerce and the state and hence with challenging the assumptions, as well as the relevance of mercantilist thought. The essay 'Of the Balance of Trade' and 'Of the Jealousies of Trade' could relatively easily be combined into one but for the fact that they were produced widely apart.

Hume sees as the unifying purpose of the essays taken together as the introduction of 'some principles which are uncommon, and which may seem too refined for such vulgar subjects' (II, Essay I, 255). The wider philosophical context is derived from the notion of '*shallow*' and of '*abstruse*' thinking, notions derived from the *Treatise* (see for example *Treatise*, 1.3.12.20) and refined in the introduction to *ECHU*. Hume maintains the notion of a distinct contribution to be discovered by careful analysis: 'An author is little to be valued, who tells us nothing but what we can learn from every coffee-house conversation' (II, Essay I, 253). International policy, often at that time the prerogative of kings or a few individualized actors, is more prone to 'accidents and chances, and the caprices of a few persons' (II, Essay I, 255). Hume also warns of too great a sophistication in other practical activities: 'When a man deliberates concerning his conduct in any particular affair, and forms schemes in politics, trade, oeconomy, or any business in life, he never ought to draw his arguments too fine, or connect too long a chain of consequences together. Something is sure to happen, that will disconcert his reasoning, and produce an event different from what he expected' (II, Essay I, 254). General reasoning needs the right subject matter and the appropriate attitude of mind.

It should also be said that although not every topic in the essays which follow is raised in 'Of Commerce', a surprising number are: national power (an important policy consideration for governments, for Hume and for Cantillon);[15] luxury and refinement; taxation, taxable capacity and the distribution of the tax burden; economic incentives for peasants and farmers; the changing balance of production over time; the inter-related nature of economic well-being; a rejection of the notion of the usefulness of low wages. There are, in addition, links to be made, even where the topic is new, such as 'Of Money', through the contextualization or implied backward references to earlier discussion, as in the following short paragraph: 'The greater the number of people and their greater industry are serviceable in all cases; at home and abroad, in private and in public. But the greater plenty of money, is very limited in its use, and may sometimes be a loss to a nation in its commerce with foreigners' (II, Essay III, 283). The first half of this paragraph looks backwards to 'Of Commerce' and the second part is predictive of some of the content in 'Of Money'. While there is usually no overt internal cross-referencing – though there is linking either through the opening paragraph on the closing paragraph in at least two of the essays[16] and a direct link through a footnote from Essay V to Essay III – there are numerous examples of anticipation from one topic to another. It seems clear that they were conceived as a set united both by general principles and topic areas.

Schemes in everyday life are normally, Hume argues, concerned with particulars. The philosopher's business is with '[g]eneral reasonings' provided these are 'just and sound' (again the language and the sentiment are both consistent with the opening essay of the *ECHU*). In working on 'general' topics, refinement of thought is essential. Hume is maintaining his chosen ambassadorial role, and, indeed extending the range of applicability of the notion of regularity, particularly in economic matters, as already demonstrated for the content of *ECHU*. The general principles that Hume is taking about are to be argued for and not assumed: the reasoning is not 'merely chimerical' but founded on history and 'experience' (II, Essay I, 257). Hume is consistent in his rejection of *a priori* speculation. His sources of evidence, here as elsewhere, will be ancient and recent history and contemporary experience, viewed either directly or through the lens of his established principles of human nature. He is careful to argue that the 'general principles' founded on human nature and experience 'must always prevail in the general course of things, though they may fail in particular cases' (II, Essay I, 254): again drawing upon ideas already stated in the *Treatise*. Hume is careful to draw a parallel between the context and interests of philosophers and of those 'politicians' concerned with domestic policy which also results from events that share characteristics with the 'general course of things'. There is something to say and a target audience to whom it can be said.

In the first key paragraph that relates directly to his topic, Hume establishes the accepted proposition that as far commerce is concerned the power or a state and the capacity to generate welfare ('happiness') of the populace are related. He does this however in a very interestingly constructed paragraph that underlines his empiricist credentials: 'This maxim is true in general; though I cannot forebear thinking, that it may possibly admit of exception, and that we often establish it with too little reserve and limitation' (II, Essay I, 255). It is possible to cast this statement as a statement of mercantilist political policy, in the first part, and of its economic policy aim in the second.[17] Hume's basic approach in the *Treatise* is that no proposition should go unexamined. The case to be investigated is in fact whether or not 'luxury' – this is to be seen as a short hand for improvement in the arts and hence expansion in the nature and type of commodities produced and consumed, or, in other words, economic progress – adds to or detracts from the strength of the public domain. This is fundamentally a question about a state's capacity to raise an army. The mercantilist notion of power is the power to wage war or defend the state's interest. Hume and Smith were both in agreement that the first duty of the state is to defend its interests against foreign aggression (*WN*, V. i. 1). Indeed, in the *Treatise* Hume sees the origin of formal government in a community's need to defend itself against outsiders not held by the same convention not to steal.

Hume then sets out a very brief outline of human socioeconomic progress. In a mere eight lines Hume sets out a simple theory of development. Hume (see Chapter 8) does not have an explicit stadial theory (Adam Smith was to make a very elaborate version of stadial theory the concomitant in the *WN* of his notion of the division of labour) but nonetheless some of the elements are there: from savage society, agriculture develops and henceforth population in a state is divided between husbandmen and manufacturers. This balance is destined to play a significant role in the development of Hume's argument. Specific reference to the division of labour is absent in Hume's account here but, as has been shown, it is clear that Hume understood the concept. Here he is concerned with progress merely through the accumulation of experiences over time. Subsistence needs are passed by and the 'arts of *luxury*' both supply new wants and absorb labour released from agriculture as a result of increased productivity.

Characteristically Hume then poses paired questions: 'But may not another scheme be proposed for the employment of these superfluous hands? May not the sovereign lay claim to them in fleets and armies, to increase the dominations of the state abroad, and spread its fame over distant nations?' (II, Essay I, 256). These questions make more sense within the notion of allocation as conceived in a traditional, less liberal form of mercantilism where some managing agency is directly in charge of economic life. Such questions are not likely to be raised so readily in the context of an established system of market resource allocation – 'so readily' because Adam Smith does in fact raise them, though in a modified form. But Hume has contrived his potential source of conflict, employment in luxury versus employment by the state in war-making capacity, carefully hinted at in the opening paragraph. Hume draws attention to the opportunity costs involved in the choices: 'The one can never be satisfied, but at the expence of the other. As the ambition of the sovereign must entrench on the luxury of individuals, so the luxury of individuals must diminish the force, and check the ambitions of the sovereign' (II, Essay I, 257). This is Hume's first major proposition and, in the manner of the *Treatise*, it has to be defended (not 'merely chimerical') and evaluated. Hume's definition of luxury is very broad and, here at least, imprecise. Any consumption beyond the subsistence level in agriculture, beyond as it were the Aristotelian notion of the natural needs of the household, would seem to qualify.

Sparta and Rome ('in early times': Hume is careful to contrast such times with the time of Livy and so uses Rome's evidence both for and against his proposition) are drawn into the argument and Hume is drawing upon material from the 'natural law' tradition. Both could raise large armies from the populace as the luxuries were few and the farmers were soldiers during the campaign season. Evidence is then made more general: 'And indeed, throughout all ancient history, it is observable, that the smallest republics raised and maintained greater armies, than states consisting of triple the numbers of inhabitants, are able to support at present' (II, Essay I, 257). Smith uses similar evidence to draw similar conclusions. Plunder as a source of sustenance is cancelled out (both sides plundered). The conclusion is unavoidable: 'In short, no probably reasoning can be assigned for the greater power of the more ancient states above the modern, but their want of commerce and luxury' (II, Essay I, 258). Here Hume is simply dealing with power in terms of numbers and not power in terms of (say) specialist technology, though he deals with just that elsewhere.

Hume raises another policy question: 'whether sovereigns may not return to the to the maxims of ancient policy, and consult their own interests in this respect, more than the happiness of their subjects?' (II, Essay I, 258–259). The ancient policy of Sparta was 'violent' and contrary to 'human nature'. Special, and non-reproducible, circumstances explain both Sparta and early Rome.[18] Hume then states his next significant proposition: 'But though the want of trade and manufactures, among a free and very martial people, may *sometimes* have no certain effect than to render the public more powerful, it is certain that, in the common course of human affairs, it will have a quite contrary tendency' (II, Essay I, 260). Hume's hedging here is strategic. Such reversals would be difficult to accomplish as 'Sovereigns must take mankind as they find them' II, Essay I, 260). Leaders have to work with the 'common bent of mankind'. Take the common bent of mankind to mean enduring aspects of human nature and think of the law making capacity of sovereigns. In this there is a hint of Cicero's notion of nature, reason and justice and law (*De Officiis*, i. iv)? Hume's view here is consistent with his view of the limitations of politicians in the face of nature (*T*, 3.2.2.25). Such working makes possible, by implication, a slow improvement over time in the 'arts'.[19] As these improve so does the state.

Hume develops a scenario of what happens if the 'mechanical arts are not cultivated' (II, Essay I, 260). The focus on agriculture will lead to a situation in which there is little incentive to increase production as there is no stimulation to internal trade in luxurious commodities ('which may serve either to their pleasure or vanity'). The argument is logical – a story of cause and effect – rather than empirically evidenced. The result is 'indolence' and tracts of uncultivated land: this picture of relative underdevelopment, and uncultivated land, is one that is familiar from the writings of early mercantilists and one that early mercantilists were anxious to avoid. This is further testimony to the way in which mercantilist ideas permeate the text. A national emergency and a sudden demand for military capacity could not be met 'for want of subsistence'.

The next significant knowledge claim is that 'every thing in the world is purchased by labour, and our passions are the only causes of labour'. Labour is the source of all good things and labour is the effect of which the passions are the cause. Hume's notion of the passion covers many different emotions or conditions and it must be understood to include wants and desires as well as emotional states and even predispositions or what Smith called 'propensities'. Reason helps us understand the world and passion motivates us to act upon the understanding. There can be conflicts involved, e.g. between our short-term and longer-term interests, balancing our selfish needs with reflection though the activation of gentler passions. This statement is a very direct link to the psychology of the *Treatise* and its focus on the passions and its downgrading of reason, though care has to be taken in interpreting this. Both are needed for action but it is Hume's sense of passion that motivates either to avoid or change or promote the object or event contemplated.

Hume is not explicit in this passage about the passions that are in play – a certain amount of shorthand is inevitable in the condensation of ideas – though elsewhere in the text he writes of the link between effort and reward and on luxury satisfying 'vanity'. Individual desire for more or less will regulate the quantity of work. In this sense individuals are the best judges of their own happiness and best able to direct their own effort. Want satisfaction in one area will create opportunities in another. There is an implicit sense of the ambition to better one's condition as being natural to human kind, something explicitly recognized in Smith, part of the dynamic encountered in 'the natural course of things'. Smith appropriates the idea of passion over reason in the opening paragraphs of Book One, Chapter two, of the *WN*, a chapter that has given rise to many confused interpretations (Henderson and Samuels, 2004). Smith also appropriates the idea that with respect to sustained economic action, people soon leave the satisfaction of subsistence needs behind, driven by the propensity to continue to improve their condition and to be deluded by the false promises of wealth. In this essay it is not 'necessaries' that are driving increased output but 'luxuries'. In this sense Hume is reversing the argument that expenditure on 'luxuries' is wasteful by the notion that it stimulates production and pays for itself in general opulence. Indirectly he also extends, in contra-distinction to Mandeville, economic rationality to the poor. Bishop Berkley, 'implacable foe of extravagance and licentiousness' also thought that want creation encouraged industry (Hundert, 1994, 193).

The first part of Hume's paragraph deals with the interaction between the agricultural surplus and the produce of industry (Hume takes up this issue elsewhere). This theme is found in a highly expanded from in Smith's general opulence chapter (*WN*, III, i). In times of peace the system continues to grow but in times of war or the threat of war, the sovereign needs an army and obtains the resources necessary by imposing taxation. This will cause some entrenchment and the resulting unemployment will generate a supply of potential recruits for the army. Hume has justified his proposition about the relationship between advances in commerce and advances in state authority.

As for incentives, agricultural output will automatically increase if manufactured commodities are available to the labourer: 'Furnish him with manufactures and commodities and he will do it himself. Afterwards you will find it easy to seize some part of his superfluous labour, and employ it in the public service, without giving him his wonted return' (II, Essay I, 262). The incentive is maintained, only some is 'seized' and taxation is better than the alternative, which is forced labour.

The notion of a market or market system is not specifically mentioned and the language is rather that of administrative action. Hume does not say who or what does the furnishing. The challenge to the notion of what Soule (2000, 148) refers to as 'universal poverty' is strong and Hume, in challenging this aspect of mercantilist thought, is doing so within mercantilist-type talk, even if the incentives are psychological and implying an individual bent towards self-improvement. This notion of economic life as something 'governed' continues in the next paragraph, where Hume argues for governing 'men by their passions, and animate them with a spirit of avarice and industry, art and luxury' (II, Essay I, 263). There is more than a hint of Mandeville in this phrase.

The argument with respect to foreign trade is informed by 'the same method of reasoning', again a form of argument by analogy. Hume maintains his empiricist stance but without exhausting the reader: 'if we consult history, we shall find that, in most nations, foreign trade has preceded any refinement in home manufactures, and given birth to domestic luxury' (II, Essay I, 263). This gives rise to a beneficial impact, through the incentives of pleasure and profit, to further improvements in lifestyles and marketable commodities and the banishment of 'indolence'.

Although Hume is attacking various kinds of ideas, roughly labelled mercantilist, it is Hume's predisposition, as has been established from the consideration of 'Of Essay Writing', to draw his topics from conversations taking place in his own orbit. Hume tends to deal with general ideas but his targets are not general. Robert Wallace had already publicly, at a meeting of the Philosophical Society of Edinburgh sometime around 1744, made population as issue (see the next chapter). Given that Wallace answers Hume on population in a very long Appendix rather than amend his text, it can be assumed that the content of the Dissertation is accurate with respect to what he delivered publicly several years earlier. In the printed version of his Dissertation, published much later, the following passage can be found:

> Hence it follows likewise, contrary perhaps to what many apprehend, that trade and commerce, instead of increasing, may often tend to diminish the number of mankind; and while they enrich a particular nation, and entice great numbers of people into one place, may be not a little detrimental on the whole as they promote luxury, and prevent many useful hands form being employed in agriculture. The exchange of commodities, and what by carrying them from one country to another by sea or by land, does not multiply food; and if such as are employed in this exchange, were employed in agriculture at home, a greater quantity of food would be provided, and a greater number of people might be maintained.
>
> (Wallace, [1753] (1809), 22)

It would seem that this is Hume's specific target, though the response is, characteristically, constructed in general terms in the light of Hume's principles. Hume saw a draft of the proposed publication in the middle of 1751 (Mossner, 1980, 263; Amoh, 2003, 69). If this passage is 'mercantilism' then it is a very confused and debased version, though it is conceded that in the very long-run high levels of general affluence have, in fact, led to dramatic falls in the birth rate.

Hume considers the case for universal affluence and finds that it has many advantages, not the least being a more equitable distribution of the burden of taxation and an improved political economy for 'where riches are in few hands, these will enjoy all the power, and will readily conspire to lay the whole burthen on the poor, and oppress them still further, to the discouragement of all industry' (II, Essay I, 265). Hume in 'Of the Populousness of Ancient Nations' holds that an extreme imbalance in wealth is detrimental to society. Hume's thinking here is not out of line with late mercantilists such as Defoe, Davenant and Postlethwayt (Grampp, 1952, 476).[20] Poverty only begets poverty, as in the case of France. Where there is an incentive to production and the link between effort and reward promoted, there is progress when people are also free. Arbitrary government and the power of the rich can 'conspire' against labouring people and break the link to the detriment of production. Hume's latter-day reputation as 'no friend of the poor' needs qualification.

Hume's 'Of Commerce' is informed by state power and policy considerations arising out of late mercantilist thinking. The details of the text, the images drawn and the language used illustrate the contextualization. There is no direct investigation of the idea of a market or a market system but the idea of letting artisans and labourers find their own level by the maintenance of what really can only be achieved by market incentives. Much of this is left implicit, without any specification of a market system, a point also made, though much more generally, by Checkland (1956, 387). It is written in terms that his intended audience would understand even if it is intended to shift that audience's point of view. It demonstrates in the approach a Ciceronian understanding of the audience's needs.

The essay, in common with others considered, is also constructed in line with Hume's ideas about the avoidance of *a priori* thinking, the need to question and evaluate evidence for and against key propositions and his general stance in the *Treatise* concerning evidence and the enduring psychological qualities of human nature. Hume understands that cultures differ but that underlying human nature will win out in the end. There is a limit that chief magistrates must face in any attempt to manipulate economic life in their own interest. There is a chain of reasoning and a logic at work (historical evidence is treated analytically) but this is set out in a tightly controlled and well-integrated text that operates over a very short span. The policy conclusions are clear: luxury (meaning the consumption of goods beyond the needs of subsistence) is not detrimental to growth but supportive of it; universal affluence in a free government is better than universal poverty both in itself and in the achievement of state power; that there is no conflict between affluence and state power; that passionate human beings can specify their self-interest (implicit); that the burden of taxation is better shared in an affluent state than in a poor one; and that power relations are also of a more equitable nature. The links with the *Treatise* are to Hume's empirical and inductive methodology – modified by Hume's reflections on the nature of the audience and, in the Ciceronian-type move to fill the gap between (clear and properly grounded) abstruse thought and social action, the consequences for his writing strategy – and his views on the passionate basis for human action. Hume's economic concerns are politically located and policy oriented and need to be read in context.

7 Hume and economic knowledge

Hume's discovery and exploration of the essay format allowed him, once established in the market and in the *genre*, to turn his attention to the application of his philosophical ideas to 'politics' broadly defined to include economics and 'police'. Political economy – Hume is concerned with the relationship between individual motivation, developing commercial society, prudence, state action and power – was a significant location for the application of his philosophical ideas. Setting philosophical speculation within the limits ordained by the ordinary business of life meant that economics topics would be tackled directly sooner or later. Even in the *Treatise* Hume was never really that far from the 'kinds of practical matters that that might arise in the ordinary social transactions and interactions of eighteenth-century civil transactions' (Finlay, 2007, 1). This suggests at least the potential progression from the general logic of the *Treatise* to direct social application. The rhetorical turn was also a shrewd and progressive, marketing strategy. Hume slowly started to get noticed in the review journals, reviews that generally contrasted well with what Hume thought of as the 'somewhat abusive' attack on the *Treatise* that appeared in 1739 (Fieser, 1996, 646).

This chapter will focus on his views on money and related topics. The 'internal' and literary foci will be maintained with only minor references to historical context and other secondary writing. The treatment will be discrete rather than synthetic. Readers interested in issues not dealt with here can consult Wennerlind and Schabas (2008) for more detailed contextual analyses and references to the wider literature.

'Of Money'

The essay 'Of Money' would seem to be unequivocally an economics essay. Such a view is hard to sustain. As with the earlier essays of a political nature, the essay mixes economic, policy, institutional and social considerations together. Economic issues predominate but the same interpenetration that is in evidence in the earlier essays is found here. The economic generalizations that Hume makes – these are best thought of, as he would have thought of them, as 'maxims' – are mixed with concerns of state, historical detail, analogy and institution building of a somewhat speculative kind. Thinking about 'money' has a long intellectual history, going back at least as far as Aristotle, and Hume undoubtedly consulted widely. Locke, the pamphlet by Massie 'On the Natural Rate of Interest' (1750) and the (then) unpublished *Essai* by Cantillon are cited in the secondary literature. Massie's ([1750], 1912, 10) main concern is the same as that of Hume with respect to the rate of interest: '… to find out what the Rate of Interest depends on'. Cantillon's idea of treating 'of Commerce in General' has a similar ambition to Hume's search for theoretical insight, though differently expressed.

In the exposition of this essay, as with those that follow, links will be made between Hume's approach and his other works. Some caution is required. Hume considers barter and the exchange of services on a reciprocal basis over time (*T*, 3.2.5.8) and also briefly mentions money in the *Treatise*. He does this in the context of the development of conventions. Hume says that the use of gold grows out of a convention 'without the imposition of a promise' – it starts on a direct reciprocal basis and is then socialized in wider contexts and social confidence and the necessary 'regularity' is established. He continues:

> In like manner are languages gradually establish'd by human conventions without any promise. In a like manner do gold and silver become the common measures of exchange, and are esteem'd sufficient payment for what is a hundred times their value.
>
> (*T*, 3.2.2.10)

Two systems of exchange have their origins in convention rather than directly in human nature. The process is one of widening acceptability of shinny metal in a series of mutually beneficial exchange relationships.

Promises are somewhat different. Hume treats promises initially in the context of reciprocal relationships. These relationships may or may not involve the exchange of money but for their binding effect promises are based on social disapprobation (the loss of honour for example) experienced in failing to keep a contract. Wennerlind has argued that Hume in taking of such promise is taking about 'fiduciary money'. This is limiting Hume's discussion for he is not taking exclusively about money-directed or interested commerce. A promise to marry in Hume's time, for example, was a serious and 'interested' commitment, the breach of which would bring social criticism. A marriage contract was about the regulation of property, including inheritance, and income but its successful conclusion is founded on a promise. Hume's example of the possibility of bartering services (*T*, 3.2.5.8) involves no money, though it is interested commerce, and the problem can be resolved by the notion that promises should be honoured. This would remain the case even if a promise of money for work done was made.

The example is about the reciprocal exchange of services based on the promise of cooperation. Trust is the significant issue. Money does not enter into the example and even if it did, any supply of labour would be based on the promise to pay. If the promise is not fulfilled, the agent would experience the penalty of 'never being trusted again' (*T*, 3.2.5.10). Where Wennerlind is right is that even if gold is established by convention, the stamping of gold by the state's authority merges an originating convention with the promise of backing by associated aspects of state power such as political stability and authenticated quality. These are '*symbols*' and '*signs*' but the problem for Hume is to give 'each other security of our conduct in any particular incident' (*T*, 3.2.5.10). This is about formal and informal contracting.

Trust is also significant with respect to the value of gold coins and in the case of paper money where that which is circulating has no value in itself ('artificial') then trust is everything. Money is laden with the promises of agents and institutions (see also Schabas, 2008, 130). A problem with money and promises is that of distanciation: the location of the initiating promises is far from the scene of the transaction.

Wennerlind also talks of Hume defining money 'as an artificial virtue that has to be observed in order for justice to be maintained' (Wennerlind, 2008, 124). Even allowing for the fact that this is a quote taken from a final summarization of a chapter – it is also part of the title of the chapter concerned – this again seems to stretch Hume more than can be justified. Justice for Hume was an 'artificial virtue', one of the four cardinal virtues of classical thinking. Virtue in this sense refers to the actions of human agents. Promises are also categorized as an artificial virtue. Of course, in Hume's talk, money could be, like luxury, 'virtuous' or 'vicious' depending on how human agents react. Money can be judged with respect to its 'utility' and human action with respect to paper money, based on conventions and promises, must respect those very conventions and promises on which paper money is founded otherwise there can be disaster. 'Virtue' is a moral concept that implies behaviour; money is utilitarian. Where Wennerlind is right is that in as much as paper money is based on a variety of promises including the trustworthiness of politicians then such promises need to be maintained if the 'wheels of trade' are to keep turning. Hume is sceptical about the capacity to keep such promises and the mechanism of detecting where such promises can be kept.

The essay opens with a provocative set of statements:

> Money is not, properly speaking, one of the subjects of commerce; but only the instrument which men have agreed upon to facilitate the exchange of one commodity for another. It is none of the wheels or trade: it is the oil which renders the motion of the wheels more smooth and easy.
>
> (II, Essay III, 281)

This is another interesting exordium. The first half of the first sentence is a direct challenge to mercantilist ideas, where gold was an object of accumulation as a result of trade, as they were popularly understood. Hume qualifies his views on mercantilistic understanding later as the paragraph develops. The second part of the sentence restores money to its Aristotelian function, even if only temporarily, that of a means of furthering exchange, conventionally arrived at (and hence in keeping with Hume's views on money as established in the *Treatise*).

The next two statements are also interesting. Money is 'none of the wheels of trade'. Hume is normally very careful in his selection and use of analogies. What is this intended to mean? Clearly, he clarifies a purpose or rather function of money in the following statement: 'It is the oil which renders the motion of the wheels ...'. Strictly speaking these are two related metaphors. They work, like all metaphors, through expressed and suppressed comparisons, hence the notion of positive and negative analogies. Money is to trade as oil is to wheels. This does not really tell us very much other than lubrication makes all 'smooth and easy'. But what then are the 'wheels of trade' and what pushes the wheels into motion? This may seem irrelevant, the image may simply be meant to be descriptively interesting rather than to have any substantive content. Perhaps the simple answer is 'exchanges'. Given Hume's notion of action related to the 'passions' this does not seem quite enough. At the same time it is clear from the next sentence that in an *isolated economy*, 'the greater or less plenty of money is of no consequence, since the prices of commodities are always proportioned to the plenty of money ... '. Hume's concern is to explore the quantity theory of money. Oil, one supposes, merely lubricates but the propulsion comes from somewhere else. Hume follows the (now) expected pattern of generalization followed by, in this case, a brief historical example that justifies and illustrates the preceding generalization. This proposition Hume takes as more or less self-evident and he spends little time in examining it.

The second half of the opening paragraph is concerned with establishing a public political benefit from 'the greater plenty of money'. Gold may be used to purchase mercenary armies, in Hume's term, or subsidize the armies of allies. This was a policy pursued by the British in the War of the Austrian Succession and even more importantly, for the policy endured, during the future Napoleonic Wars, when British gold was essential to the war effort. Hume's argument is developed in terms of the cost of labour in a commercial society such as Britain and the cost in less well-developed continental countries. His evidence is drawn from the contemporary and from the classical world. Hume, who also held, as did Smith, that the first duty of the state is defence, understood the strengths as well as the weaknesses of mercantile thinking.

The next paragraph, though short, also carries significant distinctions:

> The greater number of people and their greater industry are serviceable in all cases; at home and abroad, in private and in public. But the

greater plenty of money, is very limited in it use, and may, even
sometimes be a loss to a nation in its commerce with foreigners.

(II, Essay III, 283)

Hume is making the distinction between real and nominal resources as
well as signalling a shift from an economy that is relatively closed to trade
to one that is more open. Looking at an economy's capacity to generate
well-being means looking at the real resources. For Hume it is real rather
than monetary resources that count in determining the level of economic
activity and well-being. Note that Hume is careful to hedge the second
proposition. This is interesting. The knowledge is presented tentatively.
Hume is suggesting that the claim or inference is in need of further careful
exploration.

The next long paragraph though it contains a number of related international themes concerning the mobility of capital and enterprise is to be
understood as an illustration of the manner in which an abundance of gold
and related economic activity in a leading country impacts on the increased
price of labour. Such a situation in turn suggests that 'every nation which
has not an extensive commerce, and does not much abound in gold and
silver', and hence has low wages, can catch up by the migration of enterprise. These differences while expressed in the relative price of labour are
not developed in terms of any theory of comparative advantage. This
passage adds to the sense that Hume sees growth and decline as more likely
that perpetual growth in any given geographical location. He is, though,
careful to observe elsewhere that the Dutch will be able to ward off any
potential economic decline as a result of the imitation of their commercial
expertise. The experience would tend to be cyclical. The outcome of the
discussion is another significant generalization:

> And, in general, we may observe, that the dearness of every thing, from
> plenty of money, is a disadvantage, which attends an established
> commerce, and sets bounds to it in every country, by enabling the
> poorer states to undersell the richer in all foreign markets.
>
> (II, Essay III, 284)

Hume ('in general') is careful to hedge his knowledge claim in line with
his approach in the *Treatise*. Such an insight is in keeping with mercantilistic thinking. This paragraph and its conclusion serve to introduce, though
the link is not made overtly, the first observation on the impact of money
which comes two paragraphs later. The long paragraph on paper money
will be ignored in this analysis.

The bulk of the essay is devoted to exploring two topics: that of money
in a relatively closed and relatively open economy and secondly, an exploration of counter-examples that need to be accommodated, somehow, within
the maxim that 'the quantity of gold and silver is altogether indifferent'.

In setting up the structure of the essay, Hume is following his sense of method in the *Treatise*. Inferences are not certain but merely probable; nothing is to be taken at first sight; counter-examples are to be proposed and investigated. Hume, like any good modern social scientist, works from the simple to the complex. The process is simplified within the constraints of the essay format but the textual structure and method remain familiar.

Hume, calling upon 'Anacharsis the Scythian', an obscure and somewhat acerbic figure mentioned in Plutarch and also in Cicero's *Tusculian Disputations*, adds to the functions of money the notion that it is a unit of account, serving to assist in 'numeration and arithmetic'. But Hume continues: 'It is indeed evident, that money is nothing but the representation of labour and commodities, and serves only as a method of rating them or estimating them'. Hume uses this notion of 'representation' again in 'Of Interest' (see below). What remains important in a closed economy is the quantity of goods however that quantity of goods is represented. In a closed economy then, in latter-day terms, money is neutral or nearly so for a very vast quantity of money adds to the problems of accounting.

Hume then shifts the location of the discussion. As a result of gold from the New World, 'industry has increased in all the nations of EUROPE, except in the possessors of those mines; and this may justly be ascribed, amongst other reasons, to the increase of gold and silver'. This is a proposition to which his readership would readily assent and hence it has no further justification. What is important is to exemplify the relationship between an inflow of money, expectations and the supply of human effort: 'labour and industry gain life; the merchant becomes more enterprising', and 'the manufacturer more diligent and skillful' and eventually, in a decreasing hierarchy of enterprise, with the humble and un-enterprising farmer following along behind: '*even the farmer* follows his plough with greater alacrity and attention' (emphasis added here). The supply responses would be relatively quick to come and significant but given the example of the farmer and the associated seasonality and hence a necessary lengthening of the adjustment period, they could not be immediate. There is no hint here of the farmer as 'entrepreneur' or of the farmer as the first mover of all commercial activity, as there is in Cantillon.

The general illustration is simply an expansion of what Hume means by 'industry'. This is how industry increases: it is the supply of human effort that moves the 'wheels of trade'. Each different category of labour or each different social class has its own contribution to make. How is this increase in industry in Europe to be accounted for? It stands in contrast to the idea that the quantity of money is neutral in a closed economy and potentially disadvantageous in a more open one.

Hume in the next lengthy paragraph, in a manner that is found in various places in Smith's *Wealth of Nations*, tells, after some conceptual generalizations, a plausible story. In fact, the story is told, if we take into account the episode with the merchants in the previous paragraph, three times: once as a generalized and comparatively abstract or analytical story, with its own internal repetition, and then as a human interest story, again in a manner found later In the *Wealth of Nations*. (For the structure and significance of storytelling episodes in the *Wealth of Nations* see Henderson 2006). Storytelling has always been an integral part of economics writing (think of, for example, Cantillon, Smith, De Quincy, Mill, Bastiat, Marcet) and an aspect of the development of the subject that has not been fully explored in the history of economic thought. During the whole storytelling episode – the commencement of which is signalled by a term familiar to modern readers from introductory textbooks, 'we shall suppose' – stretching over one long paragraph, he makes no reference to anything factual or historical.

The details of the internal structure of the paragraph are also revealing when considered against Hume's rhetorical turn and the content of the *ECHU*. Hume starts with a general statement that contains his un-exemplified maxims. Hume sets out the notion of time-lags and the idea of a path to a new equilibrium. This can be thought of as the equivalent of 'abstruse philosophy' (Hume's preferred mode of thinking) now familiar both from the *ECHU*, the opening lines of Book III of the *Treatise* as well as from the essay 'Of Commerce'. This is followed by the sustained storytelling episode that clothes the key ideas with human action and human inferences. This can be thought of as a representation of his 'easy philosophy' and hence helping to fix the understanding of the general maxim and prevent the conclusions from 'vanishing like phantoms in the night' (see *T*, 3.1.1.).

There is another strong link with the *ECHU*. Hume makes inferences/causal links and holds them together in terms of human motivation. This 'scientific' approach and its clear development though questions and evidence considered unemotionally avoids the 'special pleading' often associated with mercantilist writers. For Hume, the interval between the increased inflow of gold and the rise of prices is the period in which the impact of new money is beneficial with respect to output.

The process starts with exporting merchants, compensated in gold for (new or additional) exports to Cadiz, and works its way, in rounds of activity and expenditure, to the 'farmer and gardener'. Hume assumes underemployed resources and this in itself may not have required a detailed statement since the developmental thinking associated with mercantilist writers such as Munn is itself set in an economy that has unemployment (open or disguised) and underexploited agricultural land. Hume's maxim is that: 'It is easy to trace the money in its progress through the whole commonwealth; where we shall find that it must quicken the diligence of every individual, before it increases the price of labour'. Wage rates in the gap between remain constant but in the end wages and prices rise, though the relative relationship or process is not specified (see, for a detailed analysis, Schabas, 2008, 135).

Hume's next move, essential to his general method, is to face the story's outcome with historical fact. This does not cover all aspects but rather gives a significant historical evidence of the phenomenon that is to be explained (the case of the manipulations of the French king where 'the augmenting of the numerary value did not produce a proportional rise of the prices, at least for some time'). Elements of the story are found in other places in Hume's writing but that is irrelevant to the original audience.

Hume goes on to make further generalizations concerning the negative effects of as decrease in the supply of money. Hume argues that there is more to fear from a deflation than from inflation, under certain circumstances. Hume is writing in the context of the consequences of the recoinage debate and the related policy decision, to recoin at the existing standard of silver content, of the end of the seventeenth century. The result was an export of coin as bullion and a debilitating, deflationary economic crisis (Appleby, 2006). On the plus side, there is suggestion of the prospect of the 'good policy of the magistrate' which is taken to consist in keeping the stock of money increasing as a means of keeping alive 'a spirit of industry'. This is of course inconsistent with Hume's general maxim and his given rise to a significant literature on Hume's intention. Is this just a loose end such as exists in the *Treatise* or does Hume really suggest that mild inflation has a benign effect over time? The policy choice faced in 1696 had been to avoid inflation with unfortunate and strong deflationary results. Hume may here be, in his usual manner, using an unidentified specific event or context to general principles or rather deriving general principles from a specific policy act. Emerson puts Hume's normal approach thus: 'Hume preferred to make general statements unrelated to specific social contexts and often cited an ancient example in preference to a modern one' (Emerson, 2008, 10).[1]

Hume shows later in 'Of Public Credit' that he is very aware of the political nature of discussions about money and debt. Hume does not say how the magistrate would do this nor does he say who or what this magistrate would be. Any intervention for Hume overall has to be in keeping with underlying human nature and not violently opposed to it or excessive, hence the inference of a gentle increase. While this may have some relationship with the 'monetary rule' (the idea of a slow and predictable increase in the money to achieve stability and growth) of modern-day monetarists, Hume does not argue any case. Hume adds a footnote, made slightly more complex by referring to paper money, to 'Of the Balance of Trade' that says as much:

> We observed in Essay III that money, when encreasing gives encouragement to industry during the interval between the encrease of money and the rise of prices. A good effect of this nature may follow too from paper-credit; but it is dangerous to precipitate matters, at the risk of losing all by the failing of that credit, as must happen upon any violent shock to public affairs.
>
> (II, Essay V, footnote, 317)

Hume, overall, argues that policy-makers ought to ignore money, both in a closed and open economy (Wennerlind, 2008, 106). Hume tells it directly, pointing to real resources, thus, though at the conclusion of the 'Balance of Trade':

> In short, a government has great reason to preserve with care its people and its manufactures. Its money, it may safely trust to the course of human affairs, without fear or jealousy. Or if it ever give attention to this latter circumstance, it ought only to do so far as it affects the former.
>
> (II, Essay, V, 326)

This does not really dispose of the potential puzzle: the argument is directed to the consequences for real resources, which is also the concern of the original statement. But the puzzle increases. If money can be trusted to the market, why is this not also extended to commerce and industry? Wennerlind, with respect to government, puts it thus: 'It is notoriously difficult to derive a clear answer to this question from Hume's writings' (Wennerlind, 2008, 113). Given Hume's choice of essay as the vehicle for carrying his economic ideas into society, it seems unreasonable to expect everything to be neatly tied up. Further, can the issue be discussed without reference to the long time periods that Hume uses in citing historical evidence? Hume is striking a note of caution and the need for reflection on objectives. However, the 'spirit of industry' (industry being a very broad term for purposeful activity) might suggest further unspecified changes in (say) the industrial arts that would overcome limits imposed by resource availability.

Hume now deals with his 'second observation' and this is essentially a counter-example or rather a potential counter-example to the established maxim, a maxim that he has accepted without significant historical investigation. Hume uses the counter-example to illustrate the strength of his approach and it capacity to integrate a wider set of conditions within the analysis that he offers. It lends the authority of completeness. Citing Germany and Austria, where he sees a degree of prosperity but no 'proportional weight in the balance of Europe' stemming from a 'scarcity of money'. He asks: 'How do all these facts agree with the principle of reason, that the quantity of gold and silver is in itself altogether indifferent?'

Hume's answer is extremely interesting. The gold can be extended by subdivisions and smaller units mixed with base metal to overcome problems of size and the needs of greater circulation. Hume says however, with respect to the integration of the situation with the maxim, that:

> To these difficulties I answer, that the effect, here supposed to flow from the scarcity of money, really flows from the manner and customs of the people; and that we mistake, as is too usual, a collateral effect

for a cause. The contradiction is only apparent; but it requires some thought and reflection to discover the principles, by which we can reconcile *reason* to *experience*.

(II, Essay III, 290)

Hume is concerned with what causes what. He will use this idea again when exploring the topic 'Of Interest'. In terms of matter of reason, Hume restates the basic relationship: 'the proportion between commodities and money'. Hume clarifies the sense: it is not absolute quantities that matter of money and commodities but the quantities of both that enter into exchange. If coins are held 'in chests' and commodities 'hoarded' then such do not enter into the normal market transaction nor do they have any impact on proportions. These respective quantities will be influenced by human behaviour. Hume illustrates his point in terms of a simple, comparative stadial story, divided into the 'uncultivated' (subsistence economy or a stage in which the 'ancient simplicity of manners' prevails) and the improved economy. Hume, interested in progress, states his preference for the more commercialized society.

In the improved society, 'the coin enters into many more contracts, and by that means is much more employed than in the former'. Smith, borrowing from this idea, defines in the *Wealth of Nations*, commercial society as one in which every man becomes to some extent a merchant and hence underscores the radical nature of the change in 'customs and manners'. Merchants for both Hume and Smith are significant carriers of enterprise and initiative. The changes in the structural characteristics of the economy – hence changes in institutional arrangements and human behaviour – consequent upon changes in human aspirations and desires, i.e. the change in the objects of desire, change the speed at which the 'wheels of trade' turn. Desires in this sense motivate action and seek fulfilment or satisfaction. The social order is not fixed by design, as the Physiocrats would have it, but it is adaptive to human nature and changed human circumstances. Hume is careful in tracing out the implications to restate that 'men and commodities are the real strength of any community' and side steps the issue of 'the balance of EUROPE' by the qualification that: 'It appears, that the want of money can never injure any state within itself'.

Whatever the wider context of Hume's economics thinking, the analysis here has shown how the structure of the writing and the development of the content are related to Hume's philosophical thinking both in the *Treatise* and in the *Enquiries*.

'Of Interest'

The method of close textual examination will be continued here. The material will be dealt with on a more selective basis as the textual development has much in common with other economic essays dealing with monetary phenomena. Ample evidence has already been supplied, for example of Hume's use of history for comparative purposes, essential to his method, or testing out his maxims against the 'facts'. The differences will lie in the aspects of his philosophical thinking that Hume activates in the particular context of talking about interest. Hume's principal concern in the essay is to account for high and low rates of interest. He makes it clear from the outset that interest cannot be explained by making reference to the quantity of silver and gold in circulation (essentially Petty's view). This can be taken as a popular mercantilist notion (see Spiegel, 1971, 211) though Locke's work is an advance on Petty's and Massie's an advance on Locke's. Hume does this by using contemporary (and hence likely to be known directly by some at least of his audience) evidence. He argues that money has 'chiefly a fictitious value', though from his related example it is not entirely clear in what sense 'fictitious' is to be interpreted. Fictions, with respect to the *Treatise*, are in the mind (see Caffentziz, 2008, for a thorough investigation of this notion). Here the sense seems to be rather one of social practice and convention.

Hume, given his experience of causality in the *Treatise* and his capacity to think through causal issues where there are a number of possible causes in evidence, quickly puts forward the proposition and its corollary that:

> High interest arises from three circumstances: A great demand for borrowing; little riches to supply that demand; and great profits arising from commerce.
>
> Low interest, on the other hand, proceeds from the three opposite circumstances: A small demand for borrowing; great riches to supply that demand; and small profits arising from commerce.

And the explanation:

> And these circumstances are all connected together, and proceed from the encrease of industry and commerce, not of gold and silver.
>
> (II, Essay IV, 297)

So Hume, in a similar but less obfuscated way to Massie, is basically concerned with three sets of circumstances and with exploration using the comparative method. He deals clearly and directly with each item in turn though there is a strong sense of functionality in his manner of presentation. Ayer, in his analysis of Hume's notion of causation as presented essentially in the *Treatise*, states:

> ... when Hume speaks of the 'relation of cause and effect' he uses the term in a wider and looser sense that is now current. Whereas we are accustomed to distinguish between causal and functional laws, or between causal and statistical laws, or between events which are

directly related as cause and effect and those which are related as the effects of a common cause or though their joint derivation form some overriding theory, Hume's usage in such than any lawlike connection between matters of fact is characterized as causal.

(Ayer, 1980, 68)

Hume, both in 'Of Money' and in 'Of Interest' is concerned with carefully distinguishing casual circumstances even if he does not articulate a formal difference from his position in the *Treatise*.

He does not normally tell a specific story about the influence of *individual* expectations ('They are thereby enabled to employ more workmen than formerly, who never dream of demanding higher wages'). In each case he tells a developmental story. These stories are about increased economic diversity and hence different interests and behaviours on the part of social classes (landlords, merchants, farmers/peasants). The link between human motivation and aspirations and the economic aspects of everyday life is an enduring feature of Hume's analysis overall (from within the *Treatise* onwards) and in this essay it emerges as an interest in the psychological make-up of distinct social classes.

Hume, unlike Adam Smith, who in dealing with the origins of the landlord class tells a long historical story, gets quickly to the point. Landlords are a settled and passive class who benefit by lending out their land for a 'determinate part of the product'. Most have no other occupation and have 'revenue' to spend. This suggests, on the active psychological principle of human nature, the seeking after pleasure (such as they are in a limited economy) without the balancing element and variety implied by work, and hence leading to a degree of prodigality. If there are only two classes, landlords and peasants, then borrowers far outstrip savers (the small proportion of landlords who are frugal in their pursuits: Hume is, as ever, careful to note that there will be some exceptions to the general rule). Interest rates will be high as the demand is high and the supply of loanable funds is low. Smith has a similar view of the passivity and prodigality of the landlord class.

Hume pursues his analysis in terms of the development not of the '*landed* interest' (already accomplished) but this time in terms of the 'monied interest'. It is only with the development of a monied class that the supply of funds offsets the high demand from the landlord sector. The money men are associated with the growth of the merchant class – 'one of the most useful races of men'. Merchants help integrate national economic society by serving as 'agents between those parts of the state, that are wholly unacquainted, and are ignorant of each other's necessities' (II, Essay IV, 300). The merchants' useful arts become more and more complex and eventually full monetized. Here, though he has recontextualized the material, he is close to Massie with respect to the consequences of unequal distribution: 'Much Borrowing and Lending among the Inhabitants of a Country, is not the Effect of any Want or Scarcity of Money, but of the unequal Distribution of it' (Massie, [1750] 1912, 26).

Hume then goes into a statement, familiar from the *Enquiries*, about the 'craving of the human mind' for 'exercise and employment' and serious work removes the 'insatiable thirst for pleasure'. The merchant class sees a link between their employments and the increase of their monetary value in real terms. A merchant develops a passion for accumulation: 'And this is the reason why trade increases frugality, and why, among merchants, there is the same overplus of misers above prodigals, as, among the possessors of land, there is the contrary'. Commerce, through the active middle-class of merchants and their future-oriented psychology (deferred gratification and, familiar from the *ECPM*, prudence), makes it possible to mobilize strategically large quantities of savings, whatever the quantities of gold and silver in an economy.

Smith, in contrast to Hume, suggests that the desire for savings, rather than merely a characteristic of a given social class, is a fundamental drive (as it is a essentially a drive for economic security) felt by everyone though one that is most easily satisfied or realized, for every man, in the material and institutional circumstances of commercial society. Both Hume and Smith put savings and its associated institutional and psychological aspects within the context of economic development. Economic development is seen as encompassing structural and institutional change and bringing also changed subjective behaviours to the traditional context, as well as in terms of decreases in relative costs as a result of more effective human effort. Hume's contextualization of savings has parallels, not only in the work of Adam Smith, but also in the development thinking of the 1950s and 1960s. As has been seen with other essays, particularly the political essays, Hume's title does not indicate the nature of the detailed content and recalls Hume's definition of politics as 'men cooperating in society'.

Hume next considers how the increase in general commerce reduces the profitability attached to the activity. Low profits are the result essentially of competition among many merchants: both '*low interest and low profits*' arise 'from an extensive commerce, and mutually forward each other'. Spiegel argues that here Hume is making a distinction between a causal relationship and what later generations would see as a functional one (Spiegel, 1971, 211). Even if there were no other direct links with the economic content of the *Treatise*, the links through the nature of causal analysis are significant.

'Of the Balance of Trade'

By writing on the balance of trade Hume is placing himself at the strategic weak point of much mercantilist writing and theorizing. The concept goes back to the early seventeenth century and was reinforced by Locke. There were early suspicions of the nature of trade and these were still not laid to rest in popular opinion when Hume was writing. Mun's *England's Treasure by Foreign Trade*, an authoritative statement that was in Adam Smith's sights when he made his own challenge to mercantilism in 1776, was first published in 1664 and last published in 1755. Hume had Joshua Gee's pamphlet of 1729 in his sights.[2] Hume's approach is normally referred to in the literature as the specie flow mechanism based on Hume's understanding of the quantity theory of money outlined earlier.

Hume, like the essayist Lord Bacon long before him, understood the links between trade, politics and power and writes separately, though much later, 'Of the Balance of Power'. The contents of this later essay are largely political and historical in nature and Rotwein correctly excluded it from his list of economic essays. It does, however, also contain interesting comments, touched on in 'Of Money', on the relationship between economic wealth and structure of Austria and of Great Britain in relation to the relative decline in power of the former and to the rise of the latter.

Hume's essays as has now been established open with a simple and striking phrase. 'Of the Balance of Trade' is no exception: 'It is very usual, in nations ignorant of the nature of commerce, to prohibit the exportation of commodities, and to preserve for themselves whatever they think valuable and useful. They do not consider, that, in this prohibition, they act directly contrary to their intention ....' (II, Essay V, 308). Hume's condemnation of the sentiments involved are carried in evaluative and combative language in the paragraphs that immediately follow: 'ridiculous prohibition' (the prohibition of the export of figs from classical Athens); 'the same ignorance of the nature of commerce' (Acts of Parliament during the reign of Edward III); and the contradictory consequences for the French, in keeping with what is outlined in the opening sentences, for refusing the export of corn. Hume, in citing historical experience, is implicitly making the point that uninformed human nature returns to old errors. Hume feels sure of his ground.

Hume exhibits a combative spirit that is sustained over several paragraphs, among which is:

> The same jealous fear, with regard to money, has also prevailed among several nations; and it required both reason and experience to convince any people, that these prohibitions serve to no other purpose than to raise the exchange against them, and produce a still greater exportation.
>
> (II, Essay V, 309)

International trade, and its associated uncertainties, is an ongoing political issue even in the modern world and the target, when economic life turns difficult, for popular resentment. Hume says as much himself and cites emotional states that result in worries about 'the wrong balance of trade'. Hume argues that the consequences of these emotional states can never really be 'refuted by a particular detail of the all the exports' (Gee's method). Money is never likely to disappear from Britain but to illustrate this requires 'a general argument'. Hume is now on his own ground. General arguments are part of his philosophical method. Again, in this detail, that could easily be missed, Hume is consistent with the *Treatise* and the *Enquiries*. Gee's work is not rooted in such an approach but rather crawls through the very details that Hume dismisses. Hume's focus is on monetary dimensions of the trade balance and his approach is theoretical.

Although this present work is an 'internal' study of Hume's writing, it is appropriate to compare, however briefly, Hume's writing with that of Gee. Such a comparison, even a limited one, will help secure an understanding of the advantages of Hume's approach.

Hume says of trade figures:

> It is easy to observe, that all calculations concerning the balance of trade are founded on very uncertain facts and suppositions. The custom-house books are allowed to be an insufficient ground for reasoning; nor is the rate of exchange much better ... .
>
> (II, Essay V, 310)

Gee is mentioned in the head sentence of the next paragraph. Notice that Hume does refer to other writers, 'are allowed to be', i.e. by those who write on such matters. He also treats it an already established general proposition. He economizes on the writing and does not justify the proposition through examples.

Here is how Gee opens Chapter XXXIV:

> It is a matter of great difficulty to know the true balance of trade; some expect the custom-house accounts will set us to Rights, but there are a great many Falacies in those Accounts.
>
> (Gee, [1729] (1755) 118)

These two statements are very similar. Notice too that Gee is not claiming originality either 'some expect' is a reference to the work of others with the implication that others do not hold this view. However, there is a difference in the way in which Hume and Gee set up the problem. Gee's use of 'some expect' leads into a challenge to the proposition by the provision of lengthy examples ('instances'). Hume, always needful of economy in his essay writing, accepts the judgment that there are problems with the figures and sidesteps the whole issue. Evidence is available elsewhere. It is Gee's method of detailed enquiry into specifics, such as the shipment of silver to various nations, that Hume dismisses when he calls for a 'general' approach. Gee's text is burdened with the full range of mercantilist thinking. Hume merely uses his name to grab attention.

Swift is a different matter. Like Gee for the British economy, Swift is concerned with a wide range of issues relating to the poverty and under-developed nature of the Irish economy. Hume simply abstracts, from the lengthy, and in England, though not in Ireland, contentious pamphlet, Swift's views on the draining of money away from Ireland, thanks to English exploitation and the Irish fondness for French wines, and subjects them to mild satire. Hume does, in 'Of the Populousness of Ancient Nations', briefly acknowledge the exploitation of Ireland. What Hume is signalling is the relevance of the subject of trade balance to contemporary discussion. Hume in forming a general argument needs to focus the topic and treat it with the abstract method. The detailed contexts of Gee or Swift simply fall away.

Hume's reasoning proceeds in keeping with the earlier essays. His method is the general or abstract method. He explores two propositions (signalled by 'suppose'): one concerning the reduction of money in 'GREAT BRITAIN' and the other concerning an increase in money. Hume is thus pursuing the comparative method, a sustained element in his analytical method. The propositions themselves are not justified. They are possible but imaginary. Hume explores the consequences. In the first example, he asks a series of questions that imply their own answer. The writing is efficient. It is a story of cyclical trade. The story is of decreases, its impact on the price of labour, the stimulus this gives to exports, the adjustment to the new situation as a result of increased inflows of money and the attainment of a new equilibrium. The paragraph on the increase in money is constructed in the same way, through questions.

His conclusion:

> Now, it is evident, that the same causes, which would correct these exorbitant inequalities, were they to happen miraculously, must prevent their happening in the common course of nature, and must for ever, in all neighbouring nations, preserve money nearly proportionable to the art and industry of each nation. All water, wherever it communicates, remains always at a level. Ask naturalists the reason; they tell you that the superior gravity of that part not being balanced, must press it, till it meets a counterpoise; and that the same cause, which redresses the inequality when it happens, must for ever prevent it, without some violent external operation.
>
> (II, Essay V, 312)

This is a key paragraph and sets out in short order his theory of trade balance. It exhibits a number of features that persist in Hume's writing. It unites both sets of inferences into one explanatory model. It uses a metaphor, and metaphor (like analogy) is based, at least in elementary use, on comparison: the circulation of water and the circulation of money; equilibrium in money flows and water flows. Its use is justified implicitly by its comparative utility. The significance of argument by analogy will be dealt with in greater detail in Chapter 8. The consequences of the comparison are what counts: Hume is not 'deducing general maxims from a comparison of particular instances' (*ECPM*, I, 10) rather he is shaping the comparison made, through the analogy being used. In short, he is approaching the 'other scientific method'. These comparisons are made in the next five paragraphs.

Spain's treasure drains away to France. This is a fact of key historical significance and the topic is neatly disposed of by Hume. He, characteristically, turns the example and the perplexities that it has given rise to over time – the example which prompted Copernicus and later Bodin to explore the quantity theory of money – into an ironic question: 'Can one imagine, that it had ever been possible, by any laws, or even by art and industry, to have kept all the money in SPAIN ... ?' (II, Essay V, 312). Any readers who were in the grip of another way of thinking are likely to have felt the shock of this tactic acutely. The phrase 'by any laws' is a reference to Hume's view that governments must take people as they are and hence in this instance mindful of buying cheap. Cheaper goods from France will be sold in the more expensive and inflated market in Spain and the result will be the 'draining away of that immense treasure' (II, Essay V, 312).

Hume then considers the circumstances under which there would be an exception to the general maxim:

> But as any body of water may be raised above the level of the surrounding element, if the former has no communication with the latter; so in money, if the communication be cut off, by any material or physical impediment (for all laws alone are ineffectual), there in such a case, be a very great inequality of money.
>
> (II, Essay V, 312–313)

Notice Hume's consistency: 'for all laws alone are ineffectual'. Mun, latterly a director of the East Indian Company, had addressed the fears of treasure draining to India and justified Indian trade. China and India are remote. Hume stresses the underlying importance of real factors, 'The skill and ingenuity of Europe in general surpasses that of China' but with trade and without new world gold, 'money would soon sink in EUROPE and rise in CHINA' (II, Essay V, 313). Trade tends to even out exchange rates and economic life more generally.

Hume, at the end of the paragraph, moves away from the physical metaphor towards the moral and does so in terms of the principle of attraction (a Newtonian notion developed initially in the *Treatise*): 'We need not have recourse to a physical attraction, in order to explain the necessity of this operation. There is a moral attraction, arising from the interests and passion of men, which is full as potent and infallibility'. This is a two-sentence manifestation of the tussle between the physical and the moral first encountered in the *Treatise*.

Although Hume continues to use language associated with the water metaphor, he resorts in a series of subsequent paragraphs to the moral, i.e. he moves from a focus on the model to a focus on human action consequent upon mistaken beliefs. However, his language is mixed and Hume wavers between the physical and human explanation: '... any man who travels over Europe ... may see, by the prices of commodities, that money, *inspite of the absurd jealousy* of princes and states, has brought *itself* nearly to a level. ...' (II, Essay V, 314) (italics added). Beliefs, including mistaken beliefs, for Hume are causal. Violent passions, such as jealousy, can induce men even to 'act knowingly against their interest' and forget the good (*T.* 3.3.10). What then follows is a series of examples of mistaken policy. It is easy to see how 'Of the Jealousies of Trade', which focuses on ridiculing ideas based on negative interests and passions, and promotes the idea that it is beneficial for a rich nation to be surrounded by states that are also rich, grows out of the current essay, even if separated in time.

Hume is concerned with the barriers that stand in the way of trade and is consistently critical of 'jealousy' towards France. Here he complains that the barriers against France have resulted in detrimental conditions for British manufacturers and consumers: 'We lost the FRENCH market for our wollen manufactures, and transferred the commerce of wine to SPAIN and PORTUGAL, where we buy worse liquor at a higher price' (II, Essay V, 315). Buying French wine would encourage the French to import English wheat. But note the little mercantilist sting in the tail (of which more later): '... and it is evident, that we should thereby get command of the better commodity'. Hume liked his French wines.

Hume then blows hot and cold on the question of paper money. His personal stance is that he does not like paper money but even if his language is slightly loaded, Hume, in the interest of balance and just rhetoric, acknowledges that paper money has advantages too: 'It must, however, be confessed, that, as all these questions of trade and money are extremely complicated, there are certain lights, in which the subject may be placed, so as to represent the advantages of paper-credit and banks to be superior to their disadvantages' (II, Essay V, 318).

Hume presents evidence of paper money cheapening trade and makes two notes of caution: paper money can lead to the overextension of credit and the banishment of gold and silver. Modern politics according to Hume 'embrace' paper, reject hoarding – Hume here also implies the institution of a war chest since he rejects the notion of building up a national debt – and 'adopt a hundred contrivances which serve no purpose but to check industry, and rob our selves and our neighbours of the common benefits of art and nature' (II, Essay v, 324). 'Nature', because the 'Author' of the world, a deistic concession to his readership no doubt, gave different natural resource endowments to different places. Hume consistently puts real resources before monetary resources. However liberal Hume may be thought of as, he does not support the notion of completely free trade. In the paragraph which follows, he gives support to taxes on 'GERMAN linen' in order encourage the Scottish and Irish linen trade. The taxation of brandy, 'encraeases the sale of rum and, and supports our southern colonies' (II, Essay V, 324). Both ideas would have found favour amongst those inclined to mercantilistic thought. Hume places a constraint – which he attributes to Swift and found, according to Miller in Swift's Irish pamphlet mentioned above – on the customs authorities that the lower the rate of duty, the higher the revenue is likely to be. This, when properly framed, is the notion of an optimum tariff for revenue purposes. A tariff for protectionist purposes is another matter. That taxes should be mild, placed on luxury items, be clear rather than arbitrary, and, where possible, easy to collect is the subject 'Of Taxation'.

'Of Public Credit'

In 1742, nearly a decade before 'Of Public Credit', Hume wrote a biographical note on Sir Robert Walpole. He did not admire Walpole and mocks his 'vices'. Walpole's 'want of enterprise is not attended with frugality' and Walpole's 'fortune greater than his fame'. Hume hints at his disapproval of the public debt that Walpole was responsible for: 'His ministry has been more advantageous to his family than to the public, better for this age than for posterity, and more pernicious by bad precedents than by real grievances' (Essays withdrawn, Essay XIII, 576). Hume's description echoes Cicero's notion of good behaviour in office, which was to avoid any suggestion of 'greed'. Walpole, in Hume's account, lacked the recommended virtues of 'self-restraint and self-denial' (*De Officiis*, II, 77) but his account, in keeping with his notion of constitutional propriety, remains balanced. Cicero is dealing throughout with the cancellation of *private* debts but he is clear that there are questions of property and justice involved. So far as government's role is concerned, he holds that: 'There is nothing that upholds a government more powerfully than its credit; and it cannot have credit unless the payment of debts is enforced by law' (*De Officiis*, II, 84).

After Walpole's death, Hume added, while supporting the notion of 'humane sentiments towards the dead' that 'he cannot forebare observing, that not paying more of our public debts was, as is hinted in this character, a great, and the only great error in that long administration'. The essay was eventually dropped in the edition of 1770 (see Miller, 1987, footnotes 574–575). This is the personal context of Hume's essay just as the wider discussion of the growth of the public debt is the general context. A question suggested by Hume's attitude to Walpole is that of trusting politicians to handle public debt in the national as opposes to party or personal interest. This existence of the essay suggests that 'Of Public Credit' is something more than a mere economics essay.

'Of Public Credit' opens with praise for the policy of the ancient world of securing a war chest against public disasters and the ever-present threat of war. Once again Hume is tackling in general terms a topic that was hotly debated by his peers. A string of Roman Emperors, he tells us, starting with

Augustus, 'always discovered the prudent foresight of saving great sums against any public exigency' (II, Essay IX, 350). Hume, using the method of comparison, in various contexts, throughout, contrasts classical with contemporary experience and condemns the latter: '... our modern expedient, which has become very general, is to mortgage the public revenue ...'. The 'ancient maxims' Hume holds as 'more prudent than the modern'. Prudence, for Hume, as has already been established (see Chapter 5) is an economic virtue and (see Chapter 6) also a political virtue.

He then asks an interesting question, the mercantilistic origins of which need investigating: 'For why should the case be so different between the public and an individual, as to make us establish different maxims of conduct for each?' It is of course in a famous passage in Thomas Mun that the comparison, in terms of the inflow of revenue, is made between a private household and the state. Hume is predisposed to a unifying set of maxims but he was also aware that doubling the funds available to a household is different and has different consequences from the doubling of funds available to a state as a whole. His question seems out of place.

It is clear that Hume's negative attitude towards public debt has no single explanation. It has been argued, and Hume says as much, that he was concerned with the growth of an active middle class of enterprising and professional people. Any massive increase in the public debt, invested in largely by middle-income people, would develop along with it the mentality of a *rentier* class, so strongly satirized in the nineteenth century by Dickens, Ruskin and Balzac. Landlords consumed without producing and lived, often excessively according to Hume, on their rents. A middle class that supported itself through the earning of interest rather than directly earning their living through the exercise of professional skills or by way of enterprising behaviour would not be able to sustain the development of the commercial and industrial arts. These arts were vital to Hume's notion of progress in the context of the development of commercial society. Both would earn money passively, even as they slept. The custom and manners of the former would become similar to the custom and manners of the latter. Their lack of enterprise, in the manner of Walpole, would not be made up for, as it were, by their frugality! Hume and Smith both saw the middling classes in society as a social class that was prudent, industrious and capable of uniting commerce with virtue. Smith held that the upper classes tended to be debauched by their wealth and the poor distracted by their poverty. The rise of *rentier* sentiments could shift the balance away from industriousness towards passivity. This is undoubtedly *one* of Hume's concerns, but it is only one among many that he states. Latterly he supported himself by his writings and invested the proceeds in public funds (Mossner, 1980, 409–10; Caffentzis, 2008, 166).

If the evidence provided by Hume's political and economic essays is considered overall, it would be hard to avoid the conclusion that Hume held essentially to a fundamental aspect of mercantilist thought. Defence and the related activity of warfare is the first duty of the state according to Adam Smith but also according to Hume. Warfare, particularly as pursued by the British at the time, involved financing foreign armies. Foreign armies are paid for, in the language of mercantilism, by treasure, i.e. by gold and silver. Hume concedes this in his 'Of Commerce'. In his concerns about paper money, he seems, despite his notion of proportionality, to be concerned about the fact that paper diminishes gold, which he continues to call 'money', paper money being thought off by implication as a dubious substitute. It is only in this essay that he uses terms such as 'a kind of money' or 'a species of money' to refer to government debt (Essay IX, 353). War is disruptive and at times of public alarm, banks are vulnerable. Paper money has the added disadvantage that it is difficult for the public to assess the risks involved as the institutions and the promises implied are not transparent and open to reasonable evaluation. Hume also holds that people through history fall into the same traps, dangers or potential dangers cannot easily be avoided, financial bubbles recur.

Hume's stress on what can only be called a war chest is recommended not only by classical experience (Hume ignores the comparative lack of institutional development in the classical world) but by prudence in the light of experience. Even though Hume stresses the rules and conventions, he is convinced that a large volume of public debt contracted through warfare is bad. Hoarding a war chest would, other things being equal, cheapen goods at fuller levels of economic activity and its release at time of war would calm public fears of trade disruption and so act almost counter-cyclically. He has a rationale for his views but they seem to remain rooted in a mercantilistic notion of state power. However, Hume is very concerned about the poor specification of property rights in money out of the potential consequences.

However, the problem can be looked at in another light. Hume does make an analysis, as Rotwein points out, of 'deficit finance'. The new financial asset has positive aspects and Hume is too good a philosopher not to point these out and to point these out accurately (see also Caffentzis, 2008, 146). The new species of money makes it possible to invest in funds rather than in land (the mainstay of feudal remnants and conservative attitudes and often, as Smith illustrates in the *WN*, the destination of the newly enriched merchant class) and so help to stimulate commerce, circulation and to reduce profits. However, there are disadvantages to be considered. Hume lists five. These include population movement into London and the threat of instability ('Jacobitish violence'). Public stock raise prices and the consequent taxation raise the cost of labour and oppress the poor. Public debt can be owned by foreigners and this could have political consequences not in the interests of the state. It is only the last argument, that the public stock is 'always in the hands of idle people' that Hume is concerned with the rise of a *rentier* class. His depiction of this class is not without interest: 'These are men who have no connexions with the state, who can enjoy their revenues in any art of the globe … ' (see II, Essay IX, 357–358 for the full attack). The euthanasia of just such a class was to concern Keynes.

However, Hume is not making an argument that is exclusively economic, as his appraisal of Walpole bears witness, nor even mercantilistic. The tenor of Hume's essay is political and moral rather than merely economic and again illustrates the lack of boundaries with respect to subject matter. It is also highly emotive and unusually partisan but it is probably better to think of the essay as a mixed argument for policy change rather than a precise prediction of immanent chaos. The events foretold by Hume could have been understood by the originating participants with 'but a moderate share of prudence'. 'Folly' is the political consequence.

What he says about burdening future generations and about the consequences of stretching of taxation to the limits, and hence disadvantaging the poor, are reasonable moral and political concerns. As it turned out, the later taxation of the American colonies led to a national disaster. The increase in public debt increases the power of the state and this, Hume fretted, would have a detrimental impact on the relationship between the government and the governed through not only changes in the composition of classes but as a result of taxation upon 'possessions'. Taxation of property would lead to a longer-term change in class structure, a kind of revolution. In the short run the *rentier* class will have more influence than the financially oppressed but potentially productive agrarian class. Such are the changes in the balance of internal power that Hume foresees. It is hard not to see the shadow of Cicero lurking behind Hume's concerns about the taxation of property (*De Officiis*, II. 74). Hume's analysis is also a political economy in the sense that would be recognized by followers of Marx.

Such shifts are possibilities but 'it is more probable' that war and emergencies will cause the 'natural death' of public credit ((II, Essay IX, 361). Any funds available will be used to avert military disaster rather than meet the requirements of the debt. An acute emergency 'often forces states into measures, which are, strictly speaking, against their interest' (II, essay IX, 364). Power will increase but a government that has fully 'mortgaged all its revenues' must sink 'into a state of languor, in activity, and impotence' (II, Essay IX, 360). There are of course such examples in today's world from sub-Saharan Africa in the last decades of the twentieth century. A demoralized and burdened polity may simply resort to inaction and ignore international events and the historic concern for the balance of power, till all 'lie at the mercy of the conqueror'. This would be the *'violent death'* of public credit.

Hume also had historical justification for his fears about debt repudiation and its economic and political consequences. In tracing out these consequences Hume is making, by implication, an argument for the virtues of a balanced budget. His stance is the reciprocal of Cicero's concern about private debt and recurrent calls for private debt cancellation, an attack on private property rights, in the late Republic: 'We must, therefore, take measures that there shall be no indebtedness of a nature to endanger public safety' (*De Officiis*, II, 84). This is moral risk and the undermining of prudence. Although Hume agrees with this specific form of ancient wisdom, he nonetheless understands that credit would recover: 'So great dupes are the generality of mankind, that, not withstanding such a violent shock to public credit, as a voluntary bankruptcy in ENGLAND would occasion, it would not probably be long ere credit would again revive in as flourishing a condition as before' (II, Essay IX, 363).

The essay is essentially a cautionary tale, a potential set of scenarios if no limits are imposed on the growth of the public debt. Hume is pointing out what could happen in an extreme case, in a political world without balance, without prudence, notions which are found behind many of his essays. This is not too fanciful a way of viewing the text. Hume in *ECPM* sets out a series of alternative possible states of society signalled by variations of the word 'suppose' (*ECPM*, 3.1.2–13). These can be thought of as 'if/then' predictions, familiar from introductory positive economics. He is careful in examining the notion of state repudiation (brought on by emergencies) and bankruptcy to hedge his predictions. Hume merely points out the possibility of 'the event in general'. Rotwein draws attention to his 'humorously-worded escape-clause' (Rotwein, 1955, lxxxvi) in a footnote to the essay in which he concedes that it is hard to estimate when the collapse will come as public debt has endured for longer than any one in the past could imagine (II, Essay IX, 364 footnote 19). Hume restricts himself, in the footnote, to 'pointing out the event in general'. See also the delightful final paragraph in which he outlines the 'divine fury' required by ancient prophets and contrasts this state with Hume's liberation from 'popular madness and delusion'. Such an event is, if we are mindful of Hume's use of 'general', a theoretical possibility under certain circumstances. It is as it were a prediction rather than a forecast. Hume wants a change in policy and restriction on the expansion of public credit and the picture he paints, with this slight touch of humour, is that of future possible conditions or cases if prudence is not observed. He eventually withdrew the essay on Walpole when critical judgment moved on after Walpole's death, he did not withdraw the essay on debt.

Hume and Cantillon

It is not possible to leave Hume's monetary ideas without making some reference to the alleged direct relationship between Hume's ideas and those of Cantillon.[3] Apart from the question of how Hume would have been aware of Cantillon, taken up by Thornton (the evidence that the manuscript was circulated is described by Schabas 'as spotty'), there is the issue of the implied 'plagiarism' (Thornton, 2007; Schabas, 2008, ft 1, 144). The relationship has been variously described from the notion that there was none, or none proven, to the idea of Hume knew of the *Essai* before it was finally published and that he committed plagiarism by borrowing too freely from it (Blaug, 1991, ix,). Blaug is catholic in his statement. The work was: 'widely quoted and even plagiarised by, among others, Hume, Turgot, Mirabeau, Steuart and Adam Smith'. Blaug's phrasing is unfortunate. It involves the linguistic problem of 'chunking' and, as a result, it is not entirely clear who he designates as merely quoting and who he designates as plagiarizing. No significant evidence is presented concerning the alleged 'plagiarism' nor any means suggested as to how it could be established.

The above analysis of Hume's economic essays has shown that there is a strong link between Hume's writing in the monetary essays and his approach to other essays and to the more philosophical writing (in the conventional sense). Hume's approach with respect to their form and structure, to characteristic intellectual attitudes and concerns, to the use of history and experience and so on is stamped on all of them. The style of writing and the method of analysis in a general sense is Hume's. In this sense the charge of plagiarism in an unlikely charge. Hume did produce a synthesis (and a synthesis from other sources is a higher-order thinking and hence also higher-order writing skill), but it is his synthesis. Plagiarism is strictly a matter of words and not of ideas, even then. In today's world Adam Smith is not referenced every time reference is made to the 'invisible hand' or Marx when 'alienation' or 'surplus-value' is mentioned. Some concepts (phrases as well as words) become part of the everyday language of a discipline.

Cantillon seems to be the first to make an analysis of what today would be called the automatic adjustment mechanism. Hume clearly is working within a set of ideas that Cantillon was the first to develop. This is different. Cantillon's *Essai* is a work significantly over a hundred pages in length. Hume's work on monetary questions is hence shorter, running to tens of pages. Cantillon's stories, of the circulation of money are complex and lengthy and work upwards from the farmer or outwards from the production of gold from domestic mines. Hume's circulation story is short and starts downwards from the merchant. Both share the notion of hoarding, easily detectable by observation, as influencing circulation in general. They both recognize that the circulation will only lead gradually to price increases. Both illustrate the internal balance within a state. Both see migration of enterprise to new locations in foreign countries as a possibility. They have lexical items in common.

Cantillon's work, as was Massie's, is diffuse and also detailed. Hume's essays are concentrated. Hume sees 'luxury' as advantageous, Cantillon sees 'luxury' as potentially ruinous (Cantillon, [1755] 2001, 76). Hume's analogy circulation of money/circulation of water has no direct link with Cantillon save for one sentence that is accompanied by no significant explicit metaphorical development: 'A River which runs and winds about in its bed will not flow with double the speed when the amount of water is doubled' (Cantillon, [1755] (2001), 73). Hume made significant use of analogy elsewhere. Schabas (2001, 412), as does Barfoot, argues that Hume was 'well acquainted with natural philosophy' and hence with 'hydrostatics' and perhaps with 'the so-called electric fluid'. There are alternative possibilities but only *if* he had actually read Cantillon. Cantillon's work, even without the articulation of the metaphor, is judged to be 'on the same level of priority as Harvey's study of the circulation of the blood' (Higgs, [1886] 2001, 182).

A specific illustration of an episode in story telling that seems very close may help though even in this sentence level example, it must be recognized that the surrounding contexts of the story differs. However close they are even within the sentence there are differences in emphasis. *If* Hume's sentence is derived from Cantillon *it is not* derived by copying.

> They [manufacturers or merchants] are thereby enabled to employ more workmen than formerly, who never dream of demanding higher wages, but are glad of employment from such good paymasters.
>
> (II, Essay III, 286)

> They [mine owners etc] will consequently give employment to several Mechanics who had not much to do before and who for the same reason will increase their expenses.
>
> (Cantillon, [1755], in: Brewer 2001, 68)

Even such a comparison is problematic in as much as the version of Cantillon used here is a translation from the French.

This parallel relationship between Hume and Cantillon in terms of ideas has been long recognized in the history of economic thought (see Spiegel, 1971, 183; Hayek, 1991). Wennerlind and Schabas (2008, 117) urge caution, correctly in my view, with respect to claims 'that Hume's analysis was entirely derivative or that he gleaned his analysis from any one specific thinker'.

Hume is in general anti-mercantilist (he is pro-liberal but it is a question of more or less) and anti-Physiocratic in temperament and tone. There are strong Physiocratic and mercantilist elements in Cantillon, including the mercantilist 'rule' as stated by Mun (Brewer, 1988, 453). Thornton (2007) modifies this judgment. Hume holds commerce and the work of the merchant in high esteem, but does not identify the entrepreneurial function central to Cantillon's ideas and is less focused on land as is Cantillon.

Even *if* he did borrow – and although the question of a direct link is still in doubt, Thornton's careful investigation on Hume's *contacts* leads to his conclusion that 'the probability of a link is much higher than previously thought' – then Hume undertook a huge amount of work to transform the ideas which are in Cantillon 'embedded in involved arguments' (Roll, 1956, 112; Spiegel, 1971, 183; Thornton, 2007) and relocate them in a different *genre*. Hume had hit upon a successful form of communicating complex ideas to a more general public. *If* there were adaptations then such radical adaptation involving work of editing, selecting, refining, condensing and casting into Hume's writing method, cannot be plagiarism. This view is similar to, but not identical with, that taken by Thornton (2007, 478). Thornton's use of Hume's notion of 'abstract' philosophy ('Of Commerce') as a means of referring to Cantillon, is as ingenious as it is misguided. It ignores Hume's self-referencing nature. Hume fulfils both roles in the split between abstruse and easy philosophy. It also ignores the fact that Hume makes such statements in the *ECHU,* where no influence from Cantillon could possibly be suspected.

Rothbard (1995, 360) claims that Cantillon's '*Essai* was certainly read and echoed by the eminent Scottish philosopher, David Hume'. This could mean just about anything, 'echoing' suggests something though already heard, repeated, not copied, but distanced and feint. Thornton surely over-interprets this hint as a charge of 'plagiarism'.

Textually, while there are elements in common, there is no copying. Given both texts and considering the notion of 'summarization' (see Chapter 2) it is difficult not to *feel* a sense of direct relationship. Justification for the feeling would point to textual (but weak) evidence such as elements in the storytelling and similarity of examples. But such a *feeling* is *not* evidence, nor would summarization, especially if it leads to a new and independent work, necessarily be plagiarism. Rather it is a causal prompt, in the sense that would be recognized by Hume, for systematic investigation, of the type illustrated above though such an investigation is likely to prove inconclusive. *If* Hume did borrow – he certainly also used other sources – but produced his own words and avoided those of Cantillon, the worst that can be said is that he did not refer to Cantillon's work directly even if he had had access only to an unpublished version. Even this is to make a judgment that is potentially *ahistorical.* Conventions with respect to acknowledgements were not as sensitively developed in the early eighteenth century as they are today.

Charges of plagiarism have been levelled at Adam Smith and have been dismissed on similar grounds (Henderson, 2006). Blaug is said to have regretted his use of the term.[4]

Outcomes

The focus has been on some of the essays normally referred to as Hume's economic essays. These clearly have significant economic content. The policy contexts, often simply implied by Hume rather than stated explicitly, and political and social concerns found in those essays normally taken to be political, remain in evidence. Hume's context is not an economic context clearly specialized and marked off from other social concerns. At the same time, in the fine details of the writing, Hume gently incorporates his ideas of causality, argument through careful comparison of instances, demonstrates modelling by analogy and underlines the primacy of his view of mankind as active and purposeful.

Economics, as was shown in the *ECHU*, is a location where it is possible to trace causal links and make inferences in a relatively restricted domain of human experience. Hume's notions of the political and the moral, and of the psychological propensities of human nature to ignore what may happen in the future (fully developed in 'Of Public Credit') are all at work. Hume the philosopher, even if only tenuously present at times, and Hume the rhetorician, as it were, work well together. The Ciceronian rhetorical turn not only resonated with Hume's first readers, it secured for Hume a place in the history of economic thought well above the volume of his economics writing. The capacity to formulate economic ideas in a constrained structure, emulated by Smith in the opening chapters of the *Wealth of Nations*, served Hume very well. Even when he seriously disapproves of policy, as he does in 'Of Public Credit', he argues both sides of the case, as any good rhetorician, while taking a stand. The concept of balance, political, social, moral, economic, was important to Hume in the search for the elements of a peaceful and prosperous commercial society. Hume was able, thanks to his understanding of the way in which 'general' concerns and theorizing helps clarify issues without straining partisanship to its limits, to maintain this balance even when dealing with contentious issues.

8   Stadial notions and Hume's influence

This chapter will look at Hume's conceptualization of progress and will focus on the significance of his 'Of the Populousness of Ancient Nations' for the development of stadial thinking. It explores the sense or senses in which Hume himself held a four-stage model of social development and its associated implications.

Hume's *History of England* and other notions of early society

Hume's relationship with the notion of stages in the development of society and its subsistence base, a notion usually referred to as stadial theory – the term was introduced into the literature by Meek – is not straightforward. There has been a tendency recently to assume that Hume operated a developed stadial theory. In the past, the view was different. Meek (1973) credits Turgot with introducing the notion of 'progress' and Pascal (1938) hardly mentions Hume in his review of the ideas about property in the Scottish Historical School.

In his *History of England*, Hume starts with the view of the Britons as first recorded by the Romans. Not for him any excursion into myths, legends or other forms of unsubstantiated speculation. History starts for Hume, according to his account of 'The Briton' from that time 'when literary monuments are framed and preserved' (Hume, *History*, Volume one, 3). There is however a curious ambiguity in his opening account. Barbarians and their political actions are 'guided by caprice', having nothing of the way of instruction to offer and 'terminate so often in cruelty that they disgust us by the uniformity of their appearance'. History is meant to both 'entertain' and to instruct; there are 'scientific' lessons to be learned. He then says that nations, should they be interested in their 'remote origins', can 'consider the language, manners and customs of their ancestors, and to compare them with those of neighbouring nations'. In 'Of the Populousness of Ancient Nations' Hume is clear that fables are to be excluded and that classical history begins with 'Thucydides', who does not start with fables.

Hume in the next paragraph of the *History* outlines the difference between the Britons who were agriculturalists and the 'other inhabitants of the island' who 'maintained themselves by pasture'. These others were 'clothed with skins of beasts', 'dwelt in huts' and had the characteristics of simple and largely undifferentiated society that Adam Smith, borrowing freely from Mandeville, works into his account of the first emergence of the division of labour in a 'tribe of hunters' (*WN*, I. ii). 'Barbaric' and other less developed societies exist, even here, at the margins of Hume's account. Hume himself thought that those volumes which became Volumes one and two, of the *History* were devoted to the 'barbarous years'. In this context it is interesting that Hume, in giving an account of the invasion of Britain under Claudius says: 'without seeking any more justifiable reasons of hostility than were employed by the late Europeans in subjecting the African and the Americans, they sent over an army ...' (Hume. *History*, volume 1, 8–9). In this one quick sentence, Hume displays his interest in the similarities in the exercise of power and of behaviour over long stretches of historical time. This is further evidence of argument by analogy.

Hume's *History* starts with written records and founding myths and legends are ignored, but even in the opening moves Hume cannot escape entirely from the notion of the barbaric. Turgot ([1750] 2006) holds that 'Historic times cannot be traced back further than the invention of writing' but in the first writings it is hard to avoid 'myths' (Turgot, [1750], 2006, 176). The same is true, as was shown in Chapter 4, for Hume's analysis of the origins of society. Society is founded on the certain fact of the copulation of two young savages of the opposite sex and hence on the consequences: the need to care for the long-dependent offspring. Hume certainly does not dwell for long periods of time on the conceptualization of, and problems of life under, 'savage' or 'barbaric' conditions. Hume thought, as did Adam Smith, the poor better off economically in commercial society that in the solitary state or under earlier social formations (*T*, 3.2.2.1–3.2. 2.3; *WN*, [I].4). Such 'savage' conditions are rarely, in his social analysis, at the centre of his gaze.

His primary interests, in the *Treatise* and in his essays, are in the development of an economically dynamic, liberal–commercial society, its constitutional requirements and legal framework for order and regularity. But such a society had not at the time fully emerged from the pre-commercial stage. Hume is usually content to work with simple and improved society rather than the full set of stages as found in Smith's version of stadial theory. However, if more attention were paid to Hume's notion of progress, then some of the controversies around Hume's alleged *ahistoric* conceptualization of constancy in human nature would probably fall away.

Although commercial society had started to take shape, over the previous 100 years or so, the institutional and policy requirements were not fully understood. However, again Hume needed a starting point in simpler, less complex society in order to be able to show the full advantages from cooperation in political and economic terms. The 'savage', the solitary worker in an unimproved context, as in the economic passages in the *Treatise* and *ECHU*, the simple society and its indigent nature and comparative lack of subordination are not entirely without interest in the contriving of a developmental story. Hume's more consistent concern for simpler societies, outside of the *History*, and their progress is found mainly in his essays where, again the topics are of significance as story-telling episodes that focus change. Thus there are elements of 'stadial story-telling' in, for example, the essay 'Of Money' when Hume work for subsistence and self-sufficiency as opposed to the more advanced exchange economy in which money exchanges predominates. Indeed Hume's conceptualization of economic life under a monetized economy may have suggested Smith's notion of commercial society as a stage in which every man becomes in 'some measure a merchant' (*WN*. I. iv. 1). It speaks to the unity on Hume's approach to the development of individual essays that key ideas such as the advantage of refinements in taste, individual motivation based on desires and production processes recur in different contexts.

'Of the Populousness of Ancient Nations' is to some extent an exception, in that the developmental issue is central to the analysis rather than merely ancillary. It deals with 'civilized' rather than barbaric society but its theme (economic and social improvement and population growth) is a theme central, as will be shown, to the developmental concerns of 'stadial theory'. Brewer (1995, 623) holds that Hume's 'comments' on growth are 'very thinly' scattered through the *History*. For Hume's conceptualization of progress in general, Hume's essays are a more significant location. 'Of the Populousness of Ancient Nations' will be subject of a separate and section.

The fascination with earlier social formations was not unique to Hume. The issue of feudal society was alive in the environment as the aristocracy and landed gentry held power because of their landed interests. These interests were feudal in origin as were many of the privileges that they claimed. Trade was still restricted, to some extent, by guilds, and apprenticeships, as criticized by Adam Smith, were of long duration. In Scotland there were still striking contrasts between social, economic and political conditions between the Highlands and Lowlands, and in the administration of justice in the two different geographical domains, at least until 1746. The prospect of 'naked' Highlanders was just as strange and threatening, to the Presbyterian lowlanders, as images of 'naked savages' later evoked by Smith's stadial theory. The colonization of North America, for example, had brought Europeans into contact with well-developed hunter-gatherer societies. It seemed to many that these societies and their rules, customs and manners could be used to throw light on the laws, customs and manners of early European societies during and after the fall off Rome. With whole new tracts of unalienated nature now suddenly available, property and property rights were back on the intellectual agenda. Locke tackled this in the late seventeenth century and developed a theory of alienation based upon labour, on productivity and on restraint in the extent of individual acts of alienation.

It is clear from the *Treatise* that Hume is concerned with the nature of justice and with the evolution of property rights and though he toys with, he does not develop a complex four-stage model of development nor does he use such a model systematically to construct arguments in the essays. This is what, it could be argued, Rotwein (1955, xxiv) means by his statement, with respect to the essays, that Hume's 'historical sequences do not appear in a conspicuously systematic form'. Turgot in France and Smith in Britain worked to develop a more formal model of social change based on the idea of sequential stages starting in hunter-gathering and moving to pastoralism, to agriculture and from there (in the case of Smith) to a fourth stage, that of commercial society, a society in which every man becomes to some extent a merchant. Hume works rather, in his essays at least, with a simple agrarian society (subsistence based, though with a marketable surplus) and a model of a developed commercial society (market oriented).

Smith's account is, perforce, much more complex than the simple four-stage model first set out in the *Lectures on Jurisprudence* (*LJ*). Given the long period of time that humans experienced the stage of agriculture, Smith has need of subsidiary theories to support his analysis. Smith published his fully developed account of stadial theory in the *WN* but lectured on stadial development in his *Lectures on Jurisprudence* when he was professor at Glasgow. According to Meek, he may even have held a form of stadial theory very much earlier, perhaps as early as his first public lectures in Edinburgh, given on his return from Oxford. Hume, nonetheless, has an interest in the notion of social change and of political and economic evolution; even if he does not have a clearly defined stadial model, he has, in his general essays, some of the elements that emerge in the work of later theorists in what we call the 'Scottish Historical School'.

Stadial theory in Smith: a brief account

Hume's initial comments on issues related to stadial theory pre-date Smith's published work. Hume's general essays and his 'Of the Populousness of Ancient Nations' undoubtedly had an influence on Smith. It is probably easier to start with Smith, as it is Smith who establishes the fullest set of stages in socioeconomic development and so sets the standard for comparison, before looking more closely at Hume. Smith developed his ideas in the context first of his *LJ* and then in the *WN*. The content in both works is similar but the role is not quite the same. In the *WN*, stadial theory and stadial story-telling share an almost equal part with the notion of specialization and the division of labour. Smith tells us as much in the 'Plan of the Work' (*WN*, [I] 3–5]. Stadial theory appears in just about every chapter and is never far from sight in one form or another. It is integral to his notion of growth. Even Smith's concern for the division of labour has its roots in his concerns for a foundational link between human nature and economic activity. Book One, Chapter two of the WN is probably best read as a sustained episode of stadial story-telling, with strong, though unspoken links to Hume.

But what precisely is Smith's stadial theory? The simple answer is that it is the four-stage model of development announced in *LJ* and developed, though not using the four-stage terminology, in the *WN*. The fuller answer suggests something more complex. In this simple model, which has much in common with Turgot's, there are four stages as has already been mentioned, identified by the predominant means of subsistence; the age of hunter-gatherers; of pastoralism; the age of agriculture and the age of commerce.[1] Smith's innovation was to add commerce as a separate stage. The theory is about social and economic progress and the evolution of property, economic life, law and the development of political society. Smith is also occupied with the emergence, over time, of specialist functions within government: legislature, executive and judicial and with the state's capacity to make war.

It should be obvious, on reflection, that there is a problem with this account of Smith's stadial theory and perhaps with the theory itself. The agricultural stage covers a broad sweep of human history and systems of government and power came and went. Greek city-states gave way to the Roman Empire and this in turn gave way to the Dark Ages and then to feudalism. Commerce had a part to play in classical civilization as it did in medieval Europe. Smith is of course aware of the problem and stadial theory must be thought of as the simple four-stage model and a series of related models that focus on changes between and within stages. Thus the move from hunting to animal rearing, in Smith as it is in Turgot, is based on population pressure and the fact that hunters get to know animals and eventually keep some as pets and this in turn leads to the development of pastoralism. These subsidiary models include the capacity to wage war and the opportunity costs involved when economic structures change. Smith needs to account for the fall of the Roman Empire and for the emergence of feudalism from the allodial governments that came into being after the fall of Rome. It is, however, important, as Hume argues in 'Of the Populousness of Ancient Nations' (see below) not to exaggerate the extent of commerce in the ancient world.

Hume's 'Of Commerce' looks at what happens to the supply of men to the army, and the associated costs, in the move from an agricultural society to a society with more than one significant sector and its implications. Smith is engaged in a similar process, though not necessarily with the same conclusions. He looks at defensive states (city-states with secure walls) and with predatory states and sees that these two types must change as economic conditions change. In the WN he identifies the 'division of labour' (whose origin is found in the natural propensity to truck, barter and exchange) in contemporary warfare as arising from government and not through the market. Smith has an advantage in that he is able to link specialization (the theme of many of his stadial story-telling episodes) of labour to the development of specialist machinery and hence form a basis for the discussion of technical change that goes beyond the general notion of Hume's 'progress in the arts'. Where Hume sees the significance of high culture to progress, Smith just as often sees technical changes as the result of artisans or of a lazy boy. However, Hume's idea is that advancement is an interactive process and that: 'Another advantage of industry and of the refinements in the mechanical arts is, that they commonly produce some refinements in the liberal' and then: 'nor can one be carried to perfection, without being accompanied, in some degree, with the other' (II, Essays II, 270).

Smith in 'Of the Natural Progress of Opulence' (*WN*, III. i) also develops a model that accounts for the origins of towns, their relationship to the countryside under natural conditions, and hence with the emergence of commerce. In both 'Of Commerce' and 'Of the Populousness of Ancient Nations' (see below) Hume treats the beneficial relationship of commerce and agriculture in terms of the availability of new products as incentives to boost agricultural productivity and hence output. The relationship between the agricultural stage and the commercial stage is never quite resolved in Smith in a way that is wholly satisfactory, nor indeed is the relationship between 'civilized society' and 'commerce'. The mechanism that drives change for Smith is the human desire for economic betterment, a motivation examined indirectly in Hume's 'Of Commerce', and the associated desire to preserve gains through savings and investment. Smith sees growth, especially in Britain, as having been consistently experienced for decades. Hume is more concerned with changing intensity of resource utilization, the incentive effect of 'luxury' and the interest of new social agents.

Stadial theory, particularly as it is contextualized in the *WN* is complex. It is the necessary counter-part of the division of labour and this is in turn related to the extent of the market. Society has, given the characteristic drives of people, as identified by Smith, a huge capacity to grow in terms of per capital output and in terms of total output. But this process is neither universal nor inevitable, as it has been interpreted in Marx's more extensive version of stadial theory. There are environmental factors at play that can check progress. Thus Tartar society (held in high esteem by both Hume and Smith, partly for their martial qualities and outdoor life that supported such qualities) in interior locations cannot gain easy access to cheap water transportation, an essential element in the development of commercial society in western Europe, and this limits their potential and actual development. In North America the natural path of development is from coastal locations with good access to the sea and from thence up and along navigable river valleys.

There are in addition to geographical factors also institutional and even accidental factors at play as well as 'police' (policy). Primogeniture in England prevented the dissolution of landed estates and the emergence of a market in land but the dissolution of the monasteries and then the selling of crown land by Elizabeth (she had no direct heirs) more than compensated, as did the policy of encouraging agriculture for the benefit of the 'yeomanry of England', at key stages in the transformation process. The English legislature, since the time of Elizabeth had been, according to Smith, 'particularly attentive to the interests of commerce and manufacturers' (*WN*, III.iv.20). The potential is always there but the realization of the potential is in any given place constrained or promoted by laws, customs and manners as well as by natural resource endowments. Smith is as aware as Hume that particular societies can fall as well as rise or simply stagnate.

Hume's approach: the example of 'Of the Populousness of Ancient Nations'

Hume is *not* usually included as a member of what we call the 'Scottish Historical School' if we take that to mean those involved not only in 'history' (the idea that we can by comparisons between modern-day society and early society chart the gradual transition from the earlier form to the later based on an understanding of human nature, and specified as Smith's method by Dugald Stewart) *and* in the development of the stadial theory (Stewart, [1794] 1980, II. 49). In this sense conjectural history is about possibilities rather than necessarily actualities. As Stewart says 'the real progress is not always the most natural'. This suggests, as Hopfl (1978, 23) states, the possibility of narrative history (concerned with unique events) and conjectural history (concerned with what could be taken as typical) and hence diverging.[2] Smith himself articulates this contrast in terms of the 'Natural Progress of Opulence'. The policy of Europe favoured the growth of towns and mercantile trade, whereas the natural growth path would grow out of agriculture and of a sustained agricultural surplus. Hume knew of the significance of agriculture but does not seem to have made the sort of distinction that is an essential part of Smith's treatment of the age of agriculture and, later, of his evaluation of mercantilist policies.

Hume may have held a classical and hence cyclical approach to human history, at least in his essay 'Of the Populousness of Ancient Nations' but also in relation to what he says elsewhere concerning the development and decay of empires. Cicero, who had a refined theory, as well as Plato and Polybius, all held degenerative theories (Radford, 2001, 33). Humankind is destined, because of human nature, to be drawn into repetitive behaviours and traps. 'If anything' because, as Popkin (1976, 92) has argued with respect to Hume's writing on history, outside, I would add, of the conceptual framework of his thought, that for Hume 'history starts nowhere and goes nowhere'.[3] Venning (1976, 92), with respect to Hume's notion of political development holds that: 'Hume, then, was historically oriented but he held no grand cyclical or developmental theories about man's political fate'. Contrast this with simple summative statements: 'Hume subscribed to the common Enlightenment view that society evolves through four stages ...' (Wennerlind, 2008, 106). Brewer is clear that Hume's account of 'growth' and holds that Hume 'seems not to have thought of growth as normal or inevitable in quite the same way Smith did, and his account of economic development was very different from Smith' (Brewer, 1995, 610). It would seem that there is room for further discussion of Hume's notion of progress. It was Skinner's view in 1993 that 'Of the Populousness of Ancient Nations' has 'scarcely received the attention that it deserves' (Skinner, 1993, 235). Amoh's work in 2004 has put this right to some extent but the essay still has interesting insights to yield up.

Hume's opening lines in 'Of the Populousness of Ancient Nations', a startling exordium, announce his views with clarity: 'There is very little ground, either from reason or from observation, to conclude the world eternal or incorruptible' (II, XI, 377). By this he means not only society but the material world itself.[4] However, he did not conclude that his society was in decline when compared to the classical world. Over the time period concerned, he does not accept any variation in human nature and the notion of 'the imaginary youth and vigour of the world' and hence is physical implication of sexual and reproductive robustness, in classical times, is rejected as having no useful explanatory power. This is a criticism of Augustine's notion of historical development as a steadily declining sequence of youth, maturity and old age (see Nisbet, 1980, 65). There is, for Hume, in all people, 'a desire and power of generation, more active than is ever universally exerted' because of constraints which wise government should 'observe and remove'.

In Mossner's words, Hume felt that 'the idea of necessary progress is a myth just as untenable as the idea of necessary decline' (Mossner, 1949, 142). Hume knew his classical sources and of Polybius' judgment on the possible fate of Rome, though he did not share Polybius' views on luxury (for Polybius, see Radford, 2001, 11). This balance should not mean that we close our eyes to the fact that Hume was theoretically aware, in the *Treatise*, of the difference between the indigent nature of savage society ('universal poverty') and no property and hence no need for justice and its natural opposite, a golden age of 'universal abundance' where scarcity is abolished and hence there is also no need for justice, in his sense. This is an institutionalist explanation rather than a 'natural right' explanation. Hume also felt that progress in the arts in any society cannot be sustained forever – the historical experience – and hence after a period decline was inevitable in any given place (II, Essays XI, 37). Hume did not believe in any simple, pre-ordained, unidirectional notion of progress. Hume clearly held that progress was possible but he did not hold that it was necessarily sustained and general. It was potentially capable of being investigated empirically. It is not surprising that Turgot – a thinker with whom both Hume and Smith had ideas in common, including the notion of *douce* commerce – is given more attention than Hume in the context of general discussions about progress or with respect to the narrower notion of economic growth. It would be a mistake however to leave Hume out of any discussion in which advances in the industrial arts, law and institutional arrangements, civic administration and the level of security in human affairs are concerned.

Hume's method in the essay, as well as in his political Essays more generally, is similar to that which has come to be associated with fellow Scots and was influential upon the development of their work. Indeed without Hume's essay, it would have been hard, in the absence of statistical evidence to sustain an argument of developmental progress which must imply sustained increases in population. Even if the outcome of the population debate was not conclusive, Hume's essay remained influential.

Hume starts with a challenge to existing ideas: 'But is it certain that antiquity was so much more populous, as is pretended?' (II, Essay XI, 380). His targets here are various: Vossius, Montesquieu (as acknowledged by Miller) and Robert Wallace, an Edinburgh minister. Wallace had already presented his views earlier to the Philosophical Society of Edinburgh, and whose work Hume had seen in draft in 1751 (Amoh, 2003, 69). Wallace was not alone in holding to the notion of population decline in the modern era. Brewer (1995, 613) talks of Cantillon holding that the population of Italy had declined significantly from what it was in classical times and of Quesnay's views on the decline of the French population. Unlike Hume, Wallace is prepared to make a number of references to 'the sacred records' (Wallace, [1753] 1809; Amoh, 2003, 72). Hume's essay since it is arguing against a set of propositions must perforce look at similar classical sources of evidence from the ancient world. He indirectly acknowledges this later in the argument. When evaluating claims for the size of the Athenian population he states: 'this number is much insisted on by those whose opinion I call into question, and it is esteemed a fundamental fact to their purpose' (II, Essays XI, 427).

Quickly Hume sets out his method: he will deal with '*causes*' and with '*facts*'. His causal analysis is, as Hume says, intermingled with 'facts' but it is clear that the method is that as set out in his logic (*T*, 1.3.15.1–1.3.5.11) and both the causal analysis and the factual claims are subject to scrutiny. Hume is concerned, if I can borrow a phrase from Pompa (1990, 3), writing on features of historical knowledge, with 'valid argument based upon a body of relevant evidence'. Hume, in answering his questions is demonstrating a method of finding a useful way of gaining '*evidential* access to the past' (Pompa, 1990, 3) as well as presenting an alternative idea.[5] The work in this respect was to become significant for individuals in what is called the 'Scottish Historical School'. Hume took the study of history seriously and argued that its utility was that of preventing people from being 'for ever children in understanding' (Essays withdrawn, VI, 566).

Characteristically, as in the *Treatise*, he sets out two clarify in a 'pair' of questions (not framed as such) concerning his topics and objective the answering of which will fulfil the causal and factual ambitions of the essay:

> We shall, *first*, consider whether it be probable, from what we know of the situation of society in both periods, that antiquity must have been more populous; *secondly*, whether in reality it was so. If I can make it appear, that the conclusion is not so certain as is pretended, in favour of antiquity, it is all I aspire to do.
>
> (II, Essay XI, 381)

Hume, accepting the unreliability of the evidence and the need for a carefully constructed basis for comparisons, is content, in his objective, to cast doubt on an existing hypothesis. In other words, Hume is observing the idea that the knowledge base, the facts of the matter, is limited. He proceeds by further division of the topic into comparative exercises in 'the *domestic* and *political* situation of these two periods' (ancient and modern), a method of investigation that taken together with the paired questions, is reminiscent of the *Treatise*. This clarity of questioning, accompanied by clarity of structure together with care in the execution, provides the essay with significant rhetorical power and authority. It is important to note that he maintains from the *Treatise* the notion of the enduring significance of the biological and emotional attributes of humans and hence is happy to posit the capacity, when resources are available, and in line with Wallace, for humans to 'more than double every generation' (II, Essay XI, 381).

Hume rejects any variations in underlying (elemental) human nature (II, Essay XI, 378). He finds large empires to be unstable and modern ones to be short-lived. He is interested in institutional arrangements, including institutions that impact on labour and population (slavery on the one hand and widespread monasticism, always a favourite target, on the other). He contrasts the '*domestic* oeconomy' of the ancients (an economy in which slavery, i.e. human beings as property, rather than free labour was predominant) with that of the moderns. He links the question of increased population to 'virtue' and wise institutions (hence, when taken together, 'happiness') and hence his concern for the political dimensions. He did not make the distinction between 'happiness' and being worthy of 'happiness', later made by Kant. He evaluates, in this, and other essays, institutions, their rules and associated behaviours. In this both he and Wallace share the same focus of interest though they differ with respect to the evaluation of modern civilization (Amoh, 2004, 70). In this sense the domestic context (in essence, lots of healthy children) was key to the notion of happiness. Smith took population increases to be an indication of prosperity and well-being (*WN*, I, viii. 23). Robertson later affirmed: 'the private and domestic situation of mankind is the chief circumstance which forms their character and becomes the great source of their happiness and misery' (quoted in Hopfl, 1978, 36). Taking different geographical circumstances into account,

Hume nevertheless holds generally that 'it seems natural to expect, that, wherever there are most happiness and virtue, and the wisest institutions, there will also be most people' (II, Essay XI, 382).

He tests the initial evidence. He rejects the first appearance of things (also a hallmark of Smith's approach often contrived by undercutting initial statements[6]) and reflects more deeply on the condition of slaves: 'But if we enter more deeply into the subject, we shall perhaps find reason to retract our hasty determinations' (II, Essay XI, 387) and uses present evidence ('To rear a child in London') to consider past problems. His method is comparative and forensic and the writing is carefully signalled and structured around the key questions he holds relevant to his investigation.

Slavery and its contrast: Hume also uses contemporary observation and notions of cause and effect to reflect upon classical forms of slavery (all checks were on the behaviour of the social 'inferior'), as compared with the servant–master relationship in the contemporary world (the checks are 'mutual', because of the implied existence of a market for labour, 'suitable to the inviolable and eternal laws of reason and equity'). Hume's main purpose with respect to slavery is not primarily that of outright condemnation and indignation but is rather 'to consider the influence of slavery on the populousness of a state' (II, Essay XI, 386). The case against slavery in Hume, more generally, is a case built, as it is in Smith, on both morality and upon alternative, and more productive, economic possibilities after the ideas of John Locke. He finds slavery, after along investigation, to have a negative impact on population and indeed on 'manners' and hence to be unlikely to promote widespread 'happiness'.

In his opening moves he makes a claim, based upon modern-day observation, that is then in the second sentence justified in terms of behaviour of those in authority under the current-day observable circumstances of slavery. The idea is to take this current-day reaction and project it backwards in time:

> The remains which are found of domestic slavery, in the AMERICAN colonies, and among some EUROPEAN nations, would never surely create a desire of rendering it more universal. The little humanity, commonly observed in persons, accustomed, from their infancy, to exercise so great an authority over their fellow-creatures, and to trample upon human nature, were sufficient alone to disgust us with that unbounded dominion.
>
> (II, Essay XI, 383–384)

Here, again, is the drawing of an analogy between past and present.

The factual evidence presented is drawn from the best available Roman classical sources and the experience being called upon is primary, an edict of Claudius and the self-confessed behaviour of Cato, who sold his 'superannuated slaves for any price, rather than maintain what he esteemed a useless burden' (II, Essay, XI, 384), and numerous other Latin, and some Greek, authors.[7] To initiate the investigation of cause, he states in an apparently approving manner the paternalistic apology of slavery, an aspect found in Wallace, and of its alleged benign effect of population growth. This is the counter-case to his earlier statement about 'manners'. The evaluation of counter-cases is part of his method as articulated in the *Treatise*. No proposition is to be accepted at face value. In the contemporary world, 'masters discourage the marrying of their male servants' (again the resort to analogy) but slaves are the property of a master then such a one 'encourages' it would seem 'their propagation as much as that of his cattle'. Hume is intent on painting a clear picture: 'The opulent are, by this policy, interested in the being at least, though not in the well-being of the poor'.

Here is the appearance of things: great care, in this argument, is extended to slaves and their reproduction and maintenance as it would be extended to animals. This analogy is 'shocking' but Hume insists of carrying through the analysis using contemporary evidence. Hume's views on analogy in the *Treatise* are that the degree of assent to them is likely to be less than to a more direct and habitually established experience (*T*, 1.3.12.25).[8] This simply implies caution. 'Cattle' are not 'people' and slaves, while certainly property, are not cattle either. Nonetheless the analogy, cattle are to London as slaves are to Rome, can be explored. The connecting principles are about market value and relative costs and benefits in production. Modern conditions give rise to inferences that are then cast backwards in time.

Before the exploration of this analogy develops it is necessary to pause and consider Hume's approach. There is, as Pompa (1990, 50) has shown, a circularity involved in using the science of human nature to explore history in order to 'discover the constant and universal principles of human nature' (*ECHU*, 8.1.7). Hume, despite his understanding that the course of nature may change, seems, according to Pompa, determined to hold to unchanging human nature. However, Pompa in this account overstates his case. It would be a very strange sort of historian, or social scientist, for Hume's social interests are merged together, who did not express a willingness to consider human nature, as Pompa concedes. Hume, in practice, is trying to avoid *a priori* principles by grounding the initial considerations for an investigation in a knowledge of instinctive human nature. Pompa's does not think Hume achieves this. Pompa's point more generally is that Hume's version of the 'science of man', and his justification of his approach to history as set out in the *ECHU*, where Hume's views in this respect are modified slightly from those of the *Treatise*, has human nature stand outside history. Schumpeter did not make this error and is clear that Hume 'insisted' on the 'relativity to time and place of all policies', and that he avoided as a consequence the rigidities of classical school thinking (Schumpeter, 1954, 293–294).

Those who disagree with Pompa argue that Hume's notion of human nature is abstract or instinctive and that he intends history, but we should add also future and as yet unforeseen changes in the course of human social evolution, to clothe it in significant terms.[9] Recall that Hume, in the context of applying his science, rejects the social contract theory partly because of its ahistorical nature.

Hume's idea is that humans in the everyday business of life make connections and adjust them in the light of experience. As the everyday business of life changes, so do 'customs and manners'. Hume says that 'would you know the sentiments, inclinations, and course of life of the Greeks and Romans? Study well the temper and actions of the French and English: you cannot be much mistaken in transferring to the former most of the observations which you have made with regard to the latter' (*ECHU*, 8.1.7).[10] He cannot mean substitute a study of the French and English for a historical study of the Greeks and Romans. This would be nonsense. He must mean that if you are going to study rivalry in the classical world between civilizations, be informed in framing your questions by knowledge of rivalry between the French and the English. This is recognition of a kind of resemblance, an argument by analogy. In the 'Balance of Power' Hume reverses the notion and argues, normatively, that the English, in the pursuit of their quarrels with the French, have been worse than the Greeks in the pursuit of their quarrels with their enemies. This search for knowledge is by implication potentially helpful in the interpretation of motives or at least in the formation of useful analogies (*ECHU*, 9.1 and 9.5, n. 20), a means towards framing causal statements and establishing inferences and of expanding the range of relevant experiences. The notion of 'inclinations' (inclinations lead to actions) and 'course of life' (as in giving rise to normal or expected connections) suggest as much. Such questions do not then arise *a priori* but are based on observation in comparative contexts and the comparisons can be justified (see *T*, 1.1.5.3–10). Hume recognizes, implicitly, in his hyperbole – a device that Hume resorts to for effect and one that any reader needs to interpret rather than swallow whole – that humans are meshed in culture ('beliefs', customs and manners), an inevitable outcome of human nature itself.[11]

In the example here the analogy and its tentative conclusions or inferences is examining behaviour on the notion that economic constraints and motivations are more or less the same over time. Hume's inference in principle at any rate can be tested against the available facts. He concedes this strongly in the essay. Hume knows that analogies can be dreamed up in the imagination and that there is a need to try and engage with the facts. Such facts are not directly available and sources need to be interpreted. But the analogy is based on regularities and expected regularities ('uniformity in human action'). There are (implicitly and explicitly in the *ECHU* and in 'Of the Populousness of Ancient Nations') markets; there are prices; supplies and demands; incentives and disincentives: in principle, these can be pointed to or, if there is no direct evidence, behaviours inferred. It is such markets and their expected regularities that make the analogy operative. Cattle are not reared near London where everything is expensive. They are reared and bought from afar (Scotland and Ireland in his day).

So by implication, cattle are to London as slaves are to Rome. Hume then makes the same analysis of the raising of children in London (also an expensive business) and draws the implications for the breeding of slaves: in populous and hence expensive areas, the rich 'would discourage the pregnancy of the females, and either prevent or destroy the birth' (Hume, Essays, XI, 388). Using modern-day analogies, Hume throws strong doubt on the superficial paternalistic argument. It ignores costs and concentrates only on (what he would see as distant and uncertain) benefits. He could have added that humankind prefers that which is close in the future to that which is further away in the future. He had already established this aspect of time preference in the *Treatise*. The time periods and the long dependency of offspring would seem to make breeding a risky activity. Slave prices were also variable: low, as Wallace argues, after a major military campaign and the market had unforeseen risks.

Slave breeding in the American South only became a profitable activity with the outlawing of the international slave trade, and hence the reduction of supply that this entailed after 1807, and the huge increase in demand as a result of changed technology. Hume's economic prediction (his economic model built by analogy from empirical data in the mid-eighteenth century) that slaves would only be bred in substantially cheaper locations can be, and has been, experienced and empirically tested with respect to the American South.

London needs an inflow of population to make up for the low birth rate and high death rate (he does not directly say this). The evidence from 'ancient authors' was that of a perpetual demand for slaves in Rome and Italy more generally. He follows the topic through citing original sources and linking to at least one robust modern example: 'CONSTANTINOPLE, at present, requires the same recruits of slaves from all of the provinces, that ROME did of old; and these provinces are of consequence far from being populous' (II, Essay XI, 397–398). The move here is, once more, from the present to the past.

Hume cannot resist taking a swipe at 'modern convents' and 'monastic vows' but despite his prejudicial, but expected, statements on their usefulness ('popish institutions, … nurseries of superstition, burthensome to the public, and oppressive to the poor prisoners') is prepared to allow that they may be less harmful a device for population control than infant exposure.

Political contrasts: This is by far the longest section of the essay and, as with the account on domestic economy, the textual method used here will be summarization. His approach, in forensic terms is characteristically clear: 'we shall now examine the political customs and institutions of both ages. And weight their influence in retarding or forwarding the propagation of mankind' (II, Essay XI, 400). This is, of course, as much Ciceronian as it is the outcome of the 'science of human nature'. The advantage of the

Ciceronian approach is that the intended audience did not need to struggle towards the more complex schema required for reading the *Treatise*. Argument by example is less demanding than a complete process of induction. Hume maintains the same attitude as motivates his original 'rhetorical turn': There are lots of problems that flow from examining scattered evidence: 'what can we do but amuse ourselves by talking *pro* and *con*, on an interesting subject, and thereby correcting all hasty and violent determinations?' In talking in this manner, Hume, like, turns to history for 'an empirical test for ... ethical claims' (Colish, 1985, 73). Instruction and amusement, and perhaps the cultivation of an open frame of mind, also essential to the development of polite conversation, remain his literary objectives, as it does for Wallace. Hume is not idiosyncratic in this respect but acting within an established set of cultural expectations and even within the legacy of Cicero. Philosophical works, even if instructive, need not be dull.

Bloody and perpetual war marks the ancient world. Hume argues that it was only the prospect of prisoners and slaves that moderated the zeal for killing. Life and property were uncertain. Civil life too was riven with strife and butchery. City-states, Hume argues, were arenas of political and blood revenge and the rich were subject to murder and 'forfeiture' (II, Essays XI, 411). Jealousy was everywhere.[12] Factional triumphs were always taken to extremes of revenge. By extension, Hume argues that the customs of less refined states such as Gaul must have been as bad as or, more likely, worse than in Greece or Italy. Hume argues that: 'In those days there was no medium between a severe, jealous Aristocracy, ruling over discontented subjects; and a turbulent, factious, tyrannical Democracy' (II, Essays XI, 416). His world has the advantage of stability even if it has increased inequality and, apart from outbreaks of religious violence, a constrained even if still robust factionalism. The only potential advantage that the ancient world had was its equality.

Hume, in his third comparison, looks at commerce: 'trade, manufactures, industry, were nowhere, in former ages, so flourishing as they are at present in EUROPE' (II, Essays XI, 416). Hume is making an analysis of the 'police' (policy) of the city-states and drawing out implications. Commercially, the ancient world was not as well developed, in Hume's eyes, as it would seem. Hume presses into the account an examination of the high rates of interest consistently reported upon. He argues that: 'great interest of money, and great profits from trade, are an infallible indication, that industry and commerce are but in their infancy' (II, Essays XI, 417). He explores this notion more fully in the exordium to 'Of Interest': 'Nothing is esteemed a more certain sign of the flourishing condition of any nation than the lowness of interest: And with reason; though I believe the cause is somewhat different from what is commonly apprehended' (II, Essay IV, 295). Such limited exchange that did take place is, according to Hume, largely in natural rather than manufactured commodities 'for which different soils and climates are suited'.

Citing examples from both the ancient and the modern world, Hume accepts the productivity of ancient agriculture and its capacity to support 'multitudes' even where industry is deficient. But Hume pushes the reasoning and asks if it is reasonable to suppose no further developments:

> The most natural way, surely of encouraging husbandry, is, first, to excite other kinds of industry, and thereby afford the labourer a ready market for his commodities, and a return of such goods as may contribute to his pleasure and enjoyment. This method is infallible and universal; and as it prevails more in modern government than in ancient, it affords a presumption of the superior populousness of the former.
>
> (II, Essays XI, 420)

This is a productivity-stimulating argument already familiar from 'Of Commerce'. It is also further testimony that in all aspects of his social thought, Hume is concerned with the nature of economic change and the mechanisms for progress. For Xenophon (*Oeconomicus*) the only significant input into agriculture was labour and while labour remains significant in Hume's world, other inputs were also important including (though these are not specified) extensive manuring of the fields, knowledge of draining, better implements and so on. This increased productivity is general and a result of a whole range of improvements in the arts.

Hume's conclusion from his causal analysis that 'it seems impossible to assign any just reason, why the world should have been more populous in ancient than in modern times' (II, Essay XI, 420).

Factual analysis: He then deals with the factual analysis rather than with his 'conjectures'. But the facts are uncertain. It is difficult enough to know the population of modern states so the population ancient states must also be uncertain. There is no 'large enough view for comparison'. He argues that it is 'a usual fallacy, to consider all the ages of antiquity as one period, and to compute the numbers contained in the great cities mentioned by ancient authors, as if these cities had all been contemporary' (II, Essays XI, 426).

Hume has no option, in addition to pointing out inconsistencies, but to evaluate the evidence, and those supplying it, using the same kind of logic that he has used with the causal analysis. Huge armies require subsistence especially where mercenaries are involved: 'The United Provinces never were masters of such a force by sea and land, as that which is said to belong to DIONYSIUS; yet they posses as large a territory, perfectly well cultivated, and have much more resources from their commerce and industry' (II, Essay, XI, 426). Later, Smith would point out that the technology of warfare changes as a result of technological change and of government's role in the development of specialist armies. Agrigentum 'when it was destroyed by the Carthaginians' is unlikely to have the numbers claimed by 'DIODORUS SICULUS' because it merely cultivated, however industriously, 'neighbouring fields, not exceeding a small ENGLISH county'

(II, Essay XI, 423). Hume is firm on the point of the agricultural basis of society and its economic consequences: 'In a state where agriculture alone flourishes, there may be many inhabitants; and if these be all armed and disciplined, a great force may be called out on occasion: But great bodies of mercenary troops can never be maintained, without either great trade and numerous manufactures, or extensive dominions' (II, Essays XI, 426).[13]

He also questions motives, in the case of Polybius and Rome between the Punic Wars: 'But might not the numbers be magnified, in order to encourage the people?' There is a need to be critical of the motivation behind the written sources.

From this general review, Hume moves to a consideration of the population of given cities in the ancient world. His review is thorough and his argument against the reported size of the Athenian population is set out in ten points and then extended to other cities in Greece. He then focuses his attention on Italy and Rome and thereafter on Gaul, Germany and so on. But his overall contention is the same: 'We shall find, upon the whole, a great difficulty, in fixing any opinion on that head; and no reason to support those exaggerated calculations, so much insisted upon by modern writers' (II, Essays, XI, 437). His evaluation continues to be interwoven with comparative modern examples and a search for some meaningful basis for making the comparisons given the different times and locations for which evidence of sorts are available. He alights on this nicely when he unties the modern and ancient world, as far as population goes in a wonderfully insightful paragraph that gives, in the manner of the *Treatise*, an experimental educational activity to the reader:

> Chuse DOVER or CALAIS for a center: Draw a circle of two hundred miles radius: You comprehend LONDON, PARIS, the Netherlands, the UNITED PROVINCES, and some of the best cultivated parts of FRANCE and ENGLAND. It may safely, I think, be affirmed, that no spot of ground can be found, in antiquity, of equal extent, which contained near so many great and populous cities, and was so stocked with riches and inhabitants. To balance, in both periods, the states, which possessed most art, knowledge, civility, and the best police, seems the truest method of comparison.
>
> (II, Essay XI, 448)

This is a devastating analogy and cuts through all the confusion inherent in the lack of a consistent time-period for making a rigorous set of comparisons, a significant flaw in Wallace's work. This did not however deter Wallace, whose published work niggled away at numerous details of Hume's essay. Hume and Wallace share the assumption of the natural capacity, and of possible modifications of that capacity due to circumstances, to reproduce though strictly speaking, Wallace probably got there first.[14] Uncharacteristically, Hume responded to some of Wallace's critical comments but none of the very minor changes altered the tenor of Hume's argument (Amoh, 2004, 82).

The essay is complex and contains yet more extensions to the arguments that need not detain us. The tenor is of course that the economic circumstances of the modern world, a predisposition to improved agriculture and to trade, including long-distance trade, a turning away from slavery towards free labour, political stability and the limitations of factionalism, imply that there are more people in the modern worlds than there ever was in the ancient world. His method of analysis is both historical and conjectural and his conjectures governed by his determination to trace out casual linkages and inferences in the general manner set out in the *Treatise*. It is a balanced exercise in comparison and a vindication of his philosophical desire for clarity, for systematic evaluation and for no question to be taken on trust. Hume's use of formal argument by analogy (in the case of slavery), given the conscious effort to clarify contexts, specify relationships and search for supporting evidence, is another kind of model-building that grows out of his efforts in the *Treatise* and based on his belief in the comparative method.

The influence of the essay

The essay is quoted for example in Kames' *Sketches of the history of man* and in Millar's *Origins of the Distinction of Ranks* and used by Robertson in the development of their approaches to historical experience and stadial notions. It was the subject of a lengthy response in an appendix by Wallace, who had already argued the opposite case before the Philosophical Society of Edinburgh published his original dissertation very quickly after the essay itself in 1753. Whereas the members of what we know at the Scottish Historical School benefited from Hume's methodology, Wallace, though also of an empirical turn of mind, tends to ignore it and concentrates on challenging details. Wallace, culturally in tune with ideas of the day, reflects on population progress in stadial terms (Wallace, [1753] (1809) 15). It was especially significant for Smith and some of the insights in his stadial story-telling are derived in part, though not in whole, from Hume. It also deals with subsidiary issues relevant the development of Smith's stadial theory, for example the political institutions supportive of Holland's modern success or warfare in the classical world.[15] None of this is to suggest that Smith did not draw independently from sources also used by Hume.

Why was the essay so influential? It deals with a significant cultural and practical question: the comparative size of ancient and modern populations. Success with respect to growth in population size was taken as a measure of economic success (and, taking into account the contrast between slavery and free labour, of moral virtue) as well as entailing implications for political structures and organization in 'small states' and 'small commonwealths'

(Essay, XI, 401). The scale of society and its implications for political structures and institutions are essential elements of Smith's stadial theory and this could have hardly been pursued without the insight that modern populations were in fact bigger than those of the ancient world. The notion of progress would also have been in difficulty if it was not accompanied by the development of virtuous institutions, hence Hume's stress on both virtue and happiness.

In the essay on population, Hume is using his well-established method of contrast and is in fact comparing one urban civilization with another. Otherwise his method is not dissimilar to that of Smith with respect to past/present conditions.[16] He uses observation (then and now), comparison and analogy, logic, cause and effect and reflection. Balancing of evidence (assessing, evaluating) is central to Hume's approach both in the essay and in other of his works. Adam Smith can be seen at work in similar ways and it was Smith's task to construct a coherent and integrated account of human socioeconomic development. Hume's technique and results are in evidence in a number of Smith's stadial story-telling episodes. In the *WN*, for example, Smith's discussion of historical improvements in the arts of cultivation in Lower Egypt, as the result of river navigation, in the past 'nearly in the same manner as the Rhine and Maese do in Holland at present' (*WN*, I.iii.6) and the extension of the argument to 'Bengal' and 'the Ganges', shows the method in operation.[17]

Smith, as did Hume, stressed constancy in human nature: 'In every age and country of the world men must have attended to the characters, designs, and actions of one another, and many reputable rules and maxims for the conduct of human life, must have been laid down and approved of by common consent' (*WN*, V.i.f. 25). By calling upon universal elements of human nature and the notion of the undifferentiated life of the savage (*WN*, V.i.f.51), Smith's idea is that the 'rude stages' of society, and the search for subsistence, would be very similar in different human societies. Both recognized that culture was deep and in some instances enduring, as in the example of primogeniture. Smith is also keenly aware of the human capacity to multiply 'in proportion to their means of subsistence' (*WN*, I.xi.a–b. 227). This capacity is both a measure of success and source of further economic changes.

Did Hume have a developed stadial theory?

Answering the question has a problematic element for its answer depends upon what holding a stadial theory is taken to mean. It is hard to answer the question without having Smith's 'four stages model' in mind.

Hume's essay on population is constructed as a set of comparisons between one type of society and another but a complete set of stadial elements is lacking in the essay and in the *Treatise* and *Enquiries*. In Book three of the *Treatise* Hume makes a relatively extensive discussion of the laws of property and the development of human conventions. His concern is with the development of a system of ethics rather than the precise institutional forms in which property is held and within which the details of property relations emerge. Smith's four-stage theory emerges in just such a context. There is no discussion of stages with respect to the development of justice and hence of property. His concerns are not historical and descriptive but primarily conceptual. He acknowledges 'the variety of municipal law' but feels that 'their chief outlines pretty regularly concur' but hardly dwells on the matter (*ECPM*, 3.2. 45). His interests are general rather than particular, in maxims rather than details. This is evidenced in his conclusions in the *Treatise*: 'We have now run over the three fundamental laws of nature, that of stability of possession, of its transference by consent, and of the performance of promises' (*T*, 3.2.6.1). The form of property (instruments, cattle or sheep, land, housing) and the rules of inheritance under different social conditions – the interests of 'a hundred volumes of laws, and a thousand volumes of commentators' – do not much concern Hume within the *Treatise* or the *Enquiries*.

The savage origin of society is acknowledged but there is no historical conceptualization of the process of the emergence of property. Hume acknowledges clearly in the *ECPM* that institutional arrangements arise out of 'necessities of human society' and hence implicitly acknowledges, through comparative analysis, difference in societies:

> All birds of the same species in every age and country, build their nests alike: In this we see the force of instinct. Men, in different times and places, frame their houses differently: Here we perceive the influence of reason and custom. A like inference may be drawn from comparing the instinct of generation and the institutions of property.
>
> (*ECPM*, 3.2.44)

There is nothing exactly similar to Smith's detailed interest in the details of jurisprudence (Roman law, feudal law and so on) as found in Smith's *Lectures on Jurisprudence,* where he articulates the four-stage theory. In Hume, the fine details of the law of property are developed by 'analogy' and in the 'imagination' without any significant historical exemplification, real or imagined. There are no students for whom the heuristic, and pre-organizing, device of a four-stage model, such as Smith uses in *LJ*(A) is useful.

There are, however, fragments (this word implies, unfortunately, a pre-ordered unity that has somehow been smashed) of stadial thinking in the *Treatise* and the *Enquiries*, where social development is the focus. In providing exemplification, Hume calls on material as he sees fit, including life in simpler societies. In the *Treatise* he is concerned with the evolution of authority and allegiance with respect to sovereignty and class upon a variety of examples, including Salic law. However, a key concern is to establish that, with respect to legitimacy, history 'teaches us to regard the controversies in politics as incapable of any decision in most cases, and as entirely subordinate to the interests of peace and liberty' (*T*, 3.2.10.15). In the *ECPM*, he draws attention to the condition of women in 'many nations' where they are 'reduced to like slavery, and are rendered incapable of all property'. Women can with skill 'break the confederacy' against them as a result of their nature, 'and share with the other sex in all the rights and privileges of society' (*ECPM*, 3.2.19). This is merely stated as a fact. There is no sustained development of such transformational processes within a four-stage model nor is the issue of slavery (women or otherwise) identified as a stage as it was to be in Marx and Veblen. Veblen (1898) makes a special study of women's status in barbarian society. In the same section, though, Hume clearly affirms his belief in the 'natural progress of human sentiments', themes articulated in his political and economic essays but again at a general level.

Hume is concerned with moral, social, political and economic progress in his essays as has been amply evidenced in the previous two chapters. Commercial society emerges from earlier social formations. Social stratification becomes more complex and the frugal and industrious merchant class becomes a significant force in the economic animation of society. His concerns go beyond that of economic growth theory in that in his political and economic essays he sees a close relationship between economic and political development (McArthur, 2007, 35). That there are fragments or episode tinged with stadial thinking is inevitable given his empirical interests and method of comparison, such as Hume uses in the opening moves in his *History* when writing about the Britons. But in the case of the Britons, these are matters of fact, even if somewhat stylized, rather than episodes in a theoretical analysis.

In the *Treatise*, when dealing with the concept of allegiance, Hume invokes the North American '*Indian*'. This is an example of the presumed equality of life in simpler societies and of the lesser levels of temptation. There is no systematic development of links between the establishment of law and the detailed evolution of government, the distinctions of property law and the development of the economic base of given types of societies. Here is part of his discussion, of the invention of government:

> But still this weakness is less conspicuous, where the possessions, and the pleasures of life are few, and of little value, as they always are in the infancy of society. An *Indian* is but little tempted to dispossess another of his hut, or to steal his bow, as being already provided of the same advantages; and as to any superior fortune, which may attend one above another in hunting and fishing, 'tis only casual and temporary, and will have but small tendency to disturb society.
>
> (*T*, 3.2.8.1)

In looking at the origins of government, Hume resorts again to *American* tribes. He also associates the development of warfare with the development of government and the development of cities from the development of military camps (*T*, 3.2.8.2). This latter aspect emerges from his historical investigations. Elements of this turn up in Smith's account.

Hume's account of progress is as has been evidenced in the chapters on his political and social essays emphasizes the passions, human desires and increased incentives to produce within a society structured around the interest of particular classes. His stadial notions are more to the fore in his political and economic essays than in the more philosophical writing. It is in his 'Of the Rise and Progress of the Arts and Sciences'[18] that Hume explores the problems of the 'barbarous monarch'. Such a one is briefly mentioned in 'Of the Origin of Government', a tract that is in essence a summative version of his views on social formation as first set out in the *Treatise*. These considered are akin to Smith's exploration of the details of the development and progression of specialist functions of government though in a very loose way. Hume does not abandon his characteristic method. Hume prefers to be historical rather than conjectural and when he is conjectural prefers to be cautious and general. He advises caution, an already established hallmark of his approach to social analyses: '... there is no subject, in which we must proceed with more caution, than in tracing the history of the arts and sciences; least we assign causes which never existed, and reduce what is merely contingent to stable and universal principles' (I, Essay XIV, 113). Hume's empiricism, and his caution in the formulation of maxims about human behaviour and conditions, takes precedence over the formulation of social science rules in the most evolutionary of his essays. And the outcome of the essay is that 'the arts and sciences' regularly require 'fresh soil' in new lands.

Although details of the socioeconomic analysis pursued by Smith and Hume differ, Smith paralleled some of Hume's thinking into the extended version of stadial thinking developed in the *WN*. Hume, though interested in the progression to commercial society, had no sustained and integrated stadial account in either his philosophical works or in his essays. He does not share fully Smith's fascination with the details of the life of the Tartars. Besides which Hume's concerns are with the contrasts between instinctual human nature and human artifice and with human kind in general. Details, in his major philosophical writing, other than on religion, including the detailed articulation of a fully developed stadial model, are not usually his concern, maxims are, as is maintaining the vitality of developing commercial society by installing the 'arts and sciences' (Davie, 1981, 15). Comparative analysis and narrative history are significant for his reasoning about society and hence the presence of comparative instances, some of which sustained. 'Of the Populousness of Ancient Nations', essentially a comparison of two civilized cultures each exhibiting high levels of urban development, but there is no consistently articulated and integrated four-stage model. But the possibility of developing such a model is certainly suggested by sustained episodes in his work.

Outcome

Hume's 'Of the Populousness of Ancient Nations' was not only popular, in that it was widely read, but it was immediately influential. It had an impact that was felt in terms both of its method and of its content on a number of participants in the 'Scottish Historical School'. While Smith seems to have ignored Hume's discussion of money and interest, there is no doubt that ideas that Hume articulated in his essays make their way into the formulation of incidents in Smith's extended version of stadial theory as developed in the *WN*.

What has not been explored here is the relationship between the model of writing in Hume's essays in terms of their structure, and accessibility may have had some impact on Smith's writing. In the opening chapters, the *WN* exhibit the same concern for an attractive and mildly challenging exordium as an opening move, the same commitment to evidence and evaluation and the same rousing peroration. Smith's opening moves in the *WN* are informed by a sense of audience in a market place already established by Hume. The first three chapters of the *WN* could be seen as having been written in the essay format supported by argument by example. Smith had already demonstrated a fine turn of phrase in *TMS*, and a capacity to respond to his students in the *LJ*. Direct Humean philosophical influence is clearly felt in Book one, Chapter two (Henderson, 2004) as are common examples though Smith does not swallow Hume whole. Smith must have looked at the commercial success of the Hume's essays and pondered. The opening chapters of the *WN* are acts of rhetoric, rather than simply mere acts of science, intent upon quickly shaping the audience in conformity to Smith's intentions.

Hume's essays, his concern for causality, for evidence and counter-evidence and rigorous evaluation, could not have been written, despite their Ciceronian shape, without Hume's work on the content of the science of human nature. It is the pious hope of those who write on the history of economic thought that the intended reader will be inspired to read the original works. This is a hope that must often go unfulfilled. But if any actual reader has the characteristics of the intended reader, i.e. new to Hume, and wishes to read something in order to experience, without too much difficulty, Hume's mind at work, then 'Of the Populousness of Ancient Nations' makes an interesting choice. It pushes the philosophically informed essay format to its limits while remaining accessible, lively, instructive and, as Hume hoped, entertaining. It illustrates Hume's concerns for economic and political analysis and his commitment to a clarification of questions, to rigorous investigation of evidence and to the establishment of causal connections. It is an exemplification of Hume's philosophical and social analysis in action. Its format, structure and rigour challenge Kruse's sometime influential, overgeneralization (applied albeit to the essays of the *Enquiries*) that the essay format requires the sacrifice 'of all systematic arrangement' (Kruse, 1939, 34). It is an excellent example of how Hume combines relative (for the essay is demanding) accessibility with, in the broadest sense, philosophical insight. It provides, along with his monetary essays, the fullest justification for the anticipated utility of his rhetorical turn.

Notes

1 David Hume

1 Kruse feels essentially, even if he does not say it directly, that Hume fell victim, as a result of the public's apparent reject of the *Treatise*, to a fault identified in Hume's discussion of 'Of the Love of Fame' in the *Treatise*: 'Proud men are most shock'd with contempt, tho' they do not readily assent to it; but it is because of the opposition betwixt the passion, which is natural to them, and that receive'd by sympathy' (*Treatise*, 2.1.1.11.19). Kruse argues that Hume's psychological make-up turned the 'fiasco of the Treatise' into the 'supreme event of his manhood' (Kruse, 1939, 8). It does not occur to him that Hume needed an income and to find an income he needed to find or create an audience. As we shall see Hume does not feel that he experienced much in the way of calamities.

2 In the *Abstract* he opens with: 'This book seems to be wrote with the same plan with several other works that have had a great vogue of late years in *England*'. This is not an isolated thought but used to develop the first two paragraphs (T, Abstract, 1).

3 Finlay argues that Hume's period in France during the writing of the *Treatise* gave him ample opportunity to contrast English and French manners and hence assisted him in the development of his concept of human nature (Finlay, 2007, 19). The 'personal' in this sense is omnipresent.

4 Macaulay in a footnote on the same page refers states: 'See a very remarkable note in Hume's History of England, Appendix III'. Macaulay is referring to footnote 'c 'in Appendix III and to Hume's view that the huge expansion in the public debt is 'the direct road to national ruin' and that the outcome of such an expansion is the loss of 'title to compassion, in the numberless calamities that are waiting for us'. Macaulay is not impressed by Hume's judgment on the economic consequences of such a rapid expansion of debt in Hume's lifetime. Macaulay has the benefit of hindsight. Macaulay tends to see this view as a general prejudice only avoided by Edmund Burke.

2 Textual thinking

1 This is a convention that is not fixed. Some histories start with the development of marginal analysis.

2 This problem is one that all attempts at setting out the intellectual history of economics must face. Spiegel (1971) in searching for a way of integrating 'periods' in the development of economics thinking poses the question: *'How did a writer or his* school propose to cope with the fundamental economic problem of scarcity?' This is both a means of summarization and of integration.

Galbraith, however, complains in the opening chapter of his history that 'even the best scholars' in attempting to avoid professional criticism, in composing their histories, 'spread themselves widely over the important and also the expendable' (Galbraith, 1989, 1). This is a complaint about a perceived refusal to select! Perhaps the ambitions of Ekelund and Hébert should be mentioned by way of contrast, 'this book offers an in-depth survey of the complete range of economic ideas from ancient times to the present' (1997, xv). It should come as no surprise that Hume as a monetary theorist makes a brief appearance in this vast survey. In Galbraith's text he is mentioned only in passing as a source of some of Smith's ideas. Guy Routh, interested in unorthodox economics, sets out his criteria for selection clearly: 'first the writer should be an economist ... and second, his criticisms should go to the root of orthodox thought' (Routh, 1989, 1–2). Hume is criticized for his commercial optimism. Point of view is clearly important for representation.

3 Reading Hume's *Treatise* through the *Abstract*

1 Of course, references to 'Tryane of thoughts' (Hobbes) and chains of propositions can be found in both Hobbes and Descartes (Danford, 1990, 43 and 44).
2 And it appears in other areas too; 'There remain, therefore, algebra and arithmetic as the only sciences, in which we can carry on a chain of reasoning to any degree of intricacy, and yet preserve a perfect exactness and certainty' (*T*, 1.3.1.5)
3 Hume praised Newton in the highest terms in his *History of England*.
4 Cicero's philosophical and oratorical skills were held in high esteem prior to and during the eighteenth century. He was also seen in the eighteenth century as a model statesmen who sacrificed popularity for virtue (Richard, 2003, 187). Hume was influenced by Cicero's humanistic thinking and by Cicero's desire to link philosophy and rhetoric.
5 In a footnote to the Introduction to the *Cambridge Companion to Hume*, Norton writes: 'As it is now clear that Hume is the author of the Abstract, this short work can be enthusiastically recommended to those who wish to consider Hume's own account of the chief argument of the *Treatise*' (Norton, 1993, 31). Box calls it an 'advertisement as well as an aid to study' (Box, 1990, 61).
6 The review displeased Hume. Greig, writing in 1934, takes a more balanced view of the review than most, including Hume himself: 'A long, critical, sometimes sarcastic, but often pertinent review of the *Treatise* appeared in the November and December numbers of the *History of the Works of the Learned*. The reviewer, whoever he may have been, spoke of the book as juvenile, and inadequate to its 'vast' and 'noble' subject – which is precisely how Hume himself came to speak of it in later life. He summarized the argument, not at all unfairly...' (Greig, 1934, 106).
7 Taking the *Treatise* as a whole, the other significant development from the point of view of social analysis must be the notion of justice as an artificial virtue and the analysis behind that view (see Baier, 1988, 757–778).
8 Keynes and Sraffa hold that Hume's criticism of Locke is 'not to be found in the *Treatise* or its Appendix'. Hume mentions 'innate ideas' in various places in the *Treatise*, e.g. *T*, 1.3.14.4; *T*, 1.3.14.10).
9 This is not the final statement of the 'chain of reasoning' and in a later chapter dealing with the *Enquiries* we will look at the footnote on Section IX, 84).
10 This is a significant claim and one that suggests to Penelhum the 'lingering strength' of Hume's Newtonianism (Penelhum, 1993, 121).

4 The *Treatise*

1 Hume later used differences within nature, in 'Of the Jealousy of Trade', to argue for trade.

2 There was a fascination about 'savage' society among the writers of the Scottish Enlightenment and about the contrasts between 'rude' and 'commercial' society. Moloney (2005, 237) suggests that a significant feature of the Scottish Enlightenment was the notion 'that sexual desire *did* have a history'. Hume's relationship to stadial theory is discussed in detail in Chapter 8.

3 This is an instance of a general characteristic of Hume's thought with respect to nature and human nature. Hume's 'naturalism' according to Whelan, "involves a tendency to regard human nature so delineated as part of nature in a broader sense, in which all normal organisms are understood as being well suited, in their capacities, to their environments and coexistent in a general system of fundamental harmony'. (Whelan, 1985, 68). This may well be a 'half-hearted' remnant of the 'theistic view of Nature' that Kemp Smith ([1941] (1964) 564) criticizes.

4 Hume makes various references to the 'savage' condition (in the *Treatise* and in the essays) both in setting out his ideas of progress and for the purposes of comparison between the savage stage and the civilized state. He does not articulate, as does Smith in the *Lectures on Jurisprudence* and in the *WN*, a four-stage model (now known as 'stadial theory') of human socioeconomic progress, linking laws, customs and manners to the material basis for subsistence. See Chapter 8.

5 Hume was of course drawing not only upon observation and reflection but also he was drawing on earlier ideas. Here is a passage from Samuel Pufendorf that is suggestive of at least a possible input into Hume's thinking in the passages surveyed in this section:

> ... man is indeed an animal most bent upon self-preservation, helpless in himself, unable to save himself without the aid of his fellows, highly adapted to promoting mutual interests; but on the other hand no less malicious, insolent and easily provoked, also as able as he is prone to inflict injury upon another. Whence it follows that, in order to be safe, he must be sociable, that is must be united with men like himself, and so conduct himself toward them that they may have no good cause to injure him, but rather may be ready to maintain and promote his interests'.
>
> (Pufendorf, quoted in Stewart, 1992, 134)

6 Readers may consult the *Treatise* and pursue the comparisons between the earlier and later passages on 'that natural appetite between the sexes'.

7 There is a link between 'possessions' or goods and the passions of pride and humility. The comparison here is not between individuals and their attributes but between individuals and their possessions (see Stewart, 1992, 112). Pride is involved in the display of possessions as in Smith's *TMS*.

8 Kemp Smith's analysis of the difficulties encountered with Hume's use of the term 'fiction'. Hume's is more concerned with the sense of 'illusion' than the way in which the term is used in these passages (Kemp Smith, [1941] (1964) 137). Passmore (1952, 43) also makes reference to the meaning to be given to 'fictions' in the *Treatise*. In the text here, 'fiction' holds its everyday meaning ('story-telling').

9 Hume does not think that 'labour' as in any way a unique source of property (see Miller, 1981, 69). Of course conquest, possession, inheritance gain by sale.

10 We need to be clear that Hume does accept the power of 'benevolence'. He is confident that we rarely meet 'with anyone, who loves any single person better than himself'. He is also confident that it is 'rare to meet with one, in whom all

the kind affections, taken together, do not over-balance all the selfish' (*T*, 3.2.2.5; see Chapter 5)

11 It is interesting that Hutcheson uses a Newtonian metaphor, that of gravity, for the relationship between 'benevolence' and 'social distance' (Stewart, 1992, 88).

12 There are a number of artificial virtues including good manners. Smith incorporates issues of 'customs and manners' into the *Wealth of Nations* including outmoded behaviors such as those associated with primogeniture (Henderson, 2006, 134).

13 John Ruskin in the middle of the nineteenth century tried to set out, in the face of laissez-faire, an economic role for active government based around Prudence.

14 This acceptability is located in a sense of 'interest' and not on 'promise'. I wonder if Wennerlind does not, in the light of this passage, overstate his case that Hume in talking about 'promises' is talking about 'money' (Wennerlind, 2008, 106; see Chapter 7).

15 At the grand Methodological level, Passmore compares Hume's 'rules for judging of causes and effects' with Mill's 'canons of induction' (Passmore, 1952, 52).

16 Hume thought that overall, benevolence outweighed selfishness in most individuals (see Note 8). His point was not a lack of, or a denial of, benevolence but rather a lack of sustained general benevolence in the context of complex societies.

17 Ayer in considering Hume's view of justice comments, with respect to equality of distribution: 'this is, however, a defect that is easily remedied since the conventions can always be adjusted to suit any ranking that the members of society can be induced to accept' (Ayer, 2000, 112).

5 Hume's social and moral economy

1 At *ECHU*, Section VIII, part I, 65 there is a further reflection on the nature of experience, and the uniformity in human actions, as it applies to agricultural production: 'Why is the aged husbandman more skilful in his calling than the young beginner but because there is a certain uniformity in the operation of the sun, rain and earth towards the production of vegetables; and experience teaches the old practitioner the rules by which this operation is governed and directed?' It is the uniformity of human actions in general (there are always individual exceptions) that makes anticipation possible.

2 Hume thought of Book III as being 'in some measure independent of the other two' and hence not requiting the reader to 'enter all of the abstract reasonings contain'd in them' (*T*, Advertisement, Book III) though he does make use of the technical apparatus first developed in Book I.

3 His concerns with reviewing 'Personal Merit' in the *ECPM* are in keeping with the 'survey of character' in Book III (*T*, 3.1.2.2).

4 This can be seen is in the final passage of the main text of *ECPM* and expressed in language and in sentiments that are very close in sentiment to similar passages in Smith's *Theory of Moral Sentiments*:

> But were they ever so secret and successful, the honest man, if he has any tincture of philosophy, or even common observation and reflection, will discover that they themselves are, in the end, the greatest dupes, and have sacrificed the invaluable enjoyment of a character, with themselves at least, for the acquisition of worthless toys and gewgaw. How little is requisite to supply the necessities of nature? And in a view to pleasure, what comparison between the unbought satisfaction of conversation, society, study, even health and the common beauties of nature, but above all the peaceful reflection on one's own conduct; what comparison, I say, between these and the feverish, empty

amusements of luxury and expense? These natural pleasures, indeed, are really without price; both because they are below all price in their attainment; and above it in their enjoyment.

(*ECPM*, 233)

Smith takes this view of the duped nature (or situational irony) of the aspirations for economic self-improvement and turns it into a robust satire.

5 Where, according to Hume, is this combination of 'happiness' and 'honour' most likely to be found? 'I should now return form this Digression, and show, that the middle Station of life is more favourable to Happiness, as well as to Virtue and Wisdom: But as the Arguments, that prove this, seem pretty obvious, I shall here forbear insisting on them' (Hume, 'Of the Middle Station of Life' [1742], 551).

6 Smith also makes use of the term 'utility' particularly in the *Theory of Moral Sentiments*. His sense, like that of Hume, is that of 'aptness', a contribution towards functional efficiency. The admiration for utility can degenerate into a search for 'trinkets of frivolous utility' (*TMS*). This sense of utility, related to functional efficiency carries something of Hume's usage as well. The 'utility' of gold, when it is discussed in such terms in the *Wealth of Nations*, WN I.XI.C.31) distinguishes the aesthetics (the subjective beauty of gold) from its 'utility' (its objective list of useful attributes). I am grateful to Luís Carvalho for this reference.

7 Schatz (1902) refers to Hume's exploration of 'neo-communist' thinking. It is important to state that Hume does not dismiss equal proportion of the 'presents' of nature completely out of hand. His depiction of the possibility of equality is to be found at *ECPH 155*. His understanding of the moral choices and of the utility of goods to different classes of people is economically precise and worthy of reflection: 'It must also be confessed, that, wherever we depart from this equality, we rob the poor of more satisfaction than we add to the rich, and that the slight gratification of a frivolous vanity, in one individual, frequently costs more than bread to many families, and even provinces'. In what continues, Hume states that 'the rule of equality, as it would be highly useful, is not altogether impracticable; but has taken place, at least in an imperfect degree, in some republics; particularly that of Sparta; where it was attended, it is said, with the most beneficial consequences. When Hume considers the case in general he shifts to a consideration of '*perfect* equality' and traces out the impact on the poor. He also considers that enforcing such a society would lead to a decrease in liberty (and stability) and the imposition of tyranny. In other words, Hume is not indifferent to the lot of the poor. He sees society as having, just as individuals have, more than *one* desirable end.

8 Though again Hume in the *Treatise* holds that in any given individual, benevolence outweighs self-interest (most expenditures of a head of household are made on behalf of others). It is the extent of benevolence (it is socially restricted in its scope) that is in question.

9 Hume's view of this balanced way is stated again in 'Of Refinement in the Arts', where he holds that 'The bounds between the virtue and the vice cannot here be exactly fixed, more than in other moral subjects' (Hume, [1752]: in Miller 1987, 268). Hume explores various contexts where balance is lacking. He refers indirectly to Mandeville's views and those of religious enthusiasts. Hume sets out to 'correct both these extremes' in order to make an evaluation of the effects of 'refinement' on '*private* and on *public* life'. His concern for balance when it comes to making judgments about 'luxury' is found also in the preceding essay 'Of Commerce' in which he says: 'There may be some circumstances, where the commerce and riches and luxury of individuals, instead of adding strength to the public, will serve only to thin its armies, and diminish its authority among

the neighbouring nations' (Hume, [1752]: in Miller 1987, 255). This is a quest for balance in making judgments or generalizations about 'luxury'.

10 Hume maintains this sense of balance with respect to the development of his economic thinking: 'Human happiness, according to the most received notions, seems to consist in three ingredients; action, pleasure, and indolence: And though these ingredients ought to be mixed in different proportions, according to the particular disposition of the person; yet not one ingredient can be entirely wanting, without destroying, in some measure, the relish of the whole composition' (Hume, Of Refinement in the Arts, [1752]: in Miller 1987, 270). Hume is scathing about the lack of balance exhibited in the life of the miser. In 'Of Avarice' he comments as follows: 'There is only one vice, which may be found in life with as strong features, and as high a colouring as needs be employed by any satirist or comic poet; and that is AVARICE. Every day we meet men of immense fortunes, without heirs, and on the very brink of the grave, who refuse themselves the most common necessaries of life and go on heaping possessions on possessions, under all the real pressure of the severest poverty' (Hume, 'Of Avarice' [1741]: in Miller 1987, 570).

11 Smith followed Hume in placing a high value on 'Friendship' and holding that it is found it its best developed form in the 'middle Station of Life': 'But there is another Virtue, that seems principally to ly among Equals, and is for that reason, chiefly calculated for the middle Station of Life. This Virtue is FRIENDSHIP' (Hume, [1742]: in Miller 1987, 547). It is to this middle station that 'all discourses of Morality ought principally to be address'd'.

6 Hume's Essays

1 He may have felt that Cicero was an example of the 'easy and obvious' philosophy but this did not prevent Hume from making use of 'devices of Ciceronian rhetoric' (Desjardin, 1967, 237).

2 For a different view see Finlay, 2007, 52–58.

3 This cultural context of 'polite society' and its concerns is reviewed in Finlay's (2007, 12–43) 'Hume's Social Contexts'.

4 'What an insipid comedy should we make of the chit-chat of the tea-table, copied faithfully and at full length?' (I, Essay XX, 191–192).

5 Cicero also holds that the rhetorician is akin to the poet (*De Oratore*, 128, 158).

6 For an account of 'conversazione' see Miller (2006, 12).

7 If Lovell Edgeworth thought that it was appropriate to present his daughter Maria Edgeworth with a copy of the *WN* when she left school, Hume is somehow responsible!

8 He himself had undertaken a juvenile exercise in producing such a work.

9 What Hume means by 'entertainment' is fairly clear: 'The perusal of history seems a calm entertainment; but would be no entertainment at all, did not our hearts beat with correspondent movements to those which are described by the historian' (*ECPM*, 5.2.32). Sentiment is essential. The current vogue in the UK for narrative history would have satisfied Hume.

10 Possible contrasts in culture crop up in a number of places. Here is a short passage from Hume's 'A Dialogue', a short tract concerned with just such an issue: 'What wide difference, therefore, in the sentiments of morals, must be found between civilized nations and Barbarians, or between nations whose characteristics have little in common? How shall we pretend to fix a standard for judgments of this nature?'. Hume responds to this question in terms of the 'first principles, which each nation establishes, of blame and censure' (Hume, Dialogue, 333).

11 'When he maintained that industry promotes the cultivation of the mind, the enlightenment of reason, the moderation of passion, and the development of frugality' in the Stoic, 'Hume confirmed the historical experience of his class, and generalized that experience into an articulated view of social life' (Hundert, 1974, 140).

12 The first three or so chapters of Adam Smith's *WN* open with interesting propositions – propositions rather than questions but the rhetorical function is the same – which are then 'scientifically' investigated in terms that are not dissimilar to Hume's textual method in this essay (see Henderson, 1966).

13 Hume returns to the subject of Poland in 'Of Refinement in the Arts' and makes the following barbed comment: 'POLAND seems the most defective in the arts of war as well as peace; yet it is there that venality and corruption do most prevail. The nobles seem to have preserved their crown elective for no other purpose, than regularly sell it to the highest bidder. This is almost the only species of commerce, with which the people are acquainted' (II, Essay II, 276).

14 Including rules for passing on a highway ('Of Parties in General', I, Essay VII, 60).

15 Brewer puts Cantillon's interests thus: 'He did, however, assume that state power was a relevant aim for policy makers and that it could be increased by an increase in population (and hence in potential military manpower) or in potential tax revenues measured in internationally acceptable money (to be used to hire mercenaries, pay bribes, and the like)' (Brewer, 2001, xxiii).

16 The last paragraph of 'Of Money' states: 'In the following Essay we shall see an instance of a like fallacy, as that above mentioned ...'(II, Essay III, 294). In opening sentence of 'Of the Jealousy of Trade' states; 'Having endeavoured to remove one species of ill-founded jealousy, which is prevalent among commercial nations, it may not be amiss to mention another, which seems equally groundless' (II, Hume, Essay VI, 327).

17 Edward Misselden, quoted in Grampp, 195, 469, states: 'And what has more relation to matters of state, than Commerce of merchants? For when trade flourishes, the King's revenue is augmented, lands and rents improved, navigation is increased, the poor employed. But if trade decay, all these decline with it' (1622).

18 Hume, as someone who was concerned with commercially based liberal society, had no love of Sparta and its single-minded military preoccupations. There are states in the modern world with fixed ideas of a military bent, such as Israel or better still North Korea. Hume in the *ECHU*, admits that there are 'exceptions to all the measures of conduct which have ever been established for the government of men' (*ECHU*, 8.1.12.). Rousseau was interested in and impressed by participatory democracies, including Sparta, and also acknowledges that this type of government is unlikely to be achievable in the world of his day.

19 It is Smith's innovation to link 'improvement in the arts' to improvements in technology brought about by the division of labour. Specialist labour required specialist equipment and hence technological change.

20 Hume's curious exit point in the essay is in keeping with the mercantilist notion that diligence is promoted by the difficult conditions under which people lived (see Grampp, 1952, 484 for mercantilist thinking on that point). The tropics were easy hence the relative differences in perceived economic activity.

7 Hume and economic knowledge

1 Emerson (2008, 10) goes on to argue that this tendency towards historical examples 'facilitated understanding of his work abroad'. There is undoubtedly a

marketing element in Hume's approach but it is also linked to his notion of the 'science of man' and its universal aspect as well as to his search for general maxims.

2 Although this present work is an 'internal' study of Hume's writing, it is appropriate to look at outside influences from time to time.

3 Another possible link between Hume and Cantillon is that Cantillon had also read Cicero (Higgs, [1892], 1991 2).

4 Private correspondence from Mark Thornton on the 29 September 2009 states that 'Hayek also insisted that there was a connection but didn't call it plagiarism. Blaug said his call was a mistake when I asked him about it'.

8 Stadial notions and Hume's influence

1 Cantillon has several pages in his Essay, thought to have been written sometime in the 1730s (Brewer, 2001, ix) on the origins of 'Human Societies' and on the development of land, property, villages, towns and cities, and Cantillon is clear that land ownership always implies law 'to settle Ownership in order to establish a Society, whether the law rested upon force or upon Policy'. The comments have stadial elements (Cantillon, [1755]: in Brewer 2001, 5–11).

2 There are alternative names for the enterprise: 'theoretical' or 'natural' history' or 'scientific' or 'philosophical' history' (Skinner, 1967, 33).

3 Even this needs to be treated with care. Hume's 'Of Commerce' makes an argument about the progress of state power in relation to the development of 'luxury' that also influenced Adam Smith's stadial theory. It is a short step from Hume's views to the possibility of a theory of sustained economic progress. Hume treats of economic progress but does not accept that any state of society is necessarily a final state.

4 See also Essay VII 'Whether the British government inclines more to absolute monarchy or to a republic': 'It is well known, that every government must come to a period, and that death is unavoidable to the political as well as to the animal body' (I, Essay VII, 52).

5 Pompa is talking in general and philosophical terms about the purposes of history rather than at this point about Hume.

6 This undercutting is found in many parts of the WN. Animal nature is used, for example in WN I.ii 2, to undercut the human nature of the beggar who fawns like an animal on the rich and the beggar's behaviour is then undercut: 'Nobody but a beggar chuses to depend chiefly on the benevolence of his fellow citizens. Even a beggar does not depend upon it entirely'. Smith later argues that the beggar's wants 'are supplied in the same manner as those of other people, by treaty, by barter and by purchase'.

7 Cato, according to Wallace, is 'said to have bought a great many slaves; for he bought them at the sales of prisoners of war, when they would certainly be cheapest ...' (Wallace, [1753], (1809), 182]. Wallace disputes the idea that he did not allow his slaves to breed.

8 Analogy is fundamental to Hume's notion of causality, or at least 'a species of Analogy'. Our experience of past events is that similar effects give rise to similar causes. If we expect the habitual causal event in the future then we by analogy expect the effect. In historical analysis the present can be used to make casual links when considering similar circumstances in the past. Later, in a footnote to subsection 84 he argues: 'When we reason by analogies, the man who has the greater experience or the greater promptitude of suggesting analogies, will be the better reasoner'. Experience can be expanded by reading the right kind of books.

9 See the passage in 'On Civil Liberty' that deals with future possibilities (*Essays* I, XII, 87): 'we have not as yet had experience of three thousand years; so that

not only the art of reasoning is still imperfect in this science, as in all others, but we even want sufficient materials upon which we can reason. It is not fully known, what degree of virtue and vice human nature is susceptible of ...'

10 Hume is sensitive to differences.

11 See the passage in *ECHU* in which he talks of custom: 'We learn thence the great force of custom and education, which mould the human mind from its infancy and form it into a fixed and established character' (*ECHU* 8.1.11).

12 Cicero is very clear on jealousy and on its economic and wealth related dimension: 'since most people are jealous, and this feeling is remarkably general and widespread, while jealousy is attracted by surprisingly brilliant prosperity'. Cicero is talking about rhetorical moves to quench the passion and does so by suggesting that 'what is supposed to be outstanding prosperity shall be seen to be thoroughly blended with labour and sorrow' (*De Oratore*, II. Lii, 210). 'Of the Jealousies of Trade', a very complex piece and interestingly analysed by Mankin (2005), in a very general sense has some relationship with the Ciceronian approach. Mankin does not, however, mention Cicero, though he mentions Hume's reworked knowledge of Latin and Greek, in his analysis of the significance of 'jealousy'.

13 Consider this from the *ECHU*: 'And if we would explode any forgery in history, we cannot make use of a more convincing argument, than to prove, that the actions ascribed to any person are directly contrary to the course of nature....' (*ECHU*, 8.1.8). Hume is talking about human actions and human nature but the general argument in 'Of the Populousness of Ancient Nations' here is along similar lines.

14 O'Brien puts it like this: 'Hume, with regard to his writings on population, was not without his critics in Scotland of his time. Yet one of the most important of these critics, Wallace, was in agreement with Hume on this fundamental view of the population mechanism' (O'Brien, 2004, 67). Wallace amended his thesis in the body of his Dissertation as published which contains his view of the nature of the dynamics. Hume may have seen this is version in 1751, prior to publication though the evidence is unclear (Amoh, 2004, 83 f3). Hume draws upon Wallace or at least holds ideas very similar to Wallace, with respect to the positive effect of equality in land holdings on population in city-states.

15 Hume is clear in 'Of Commerce' that 'As the ambition of the sovereign must entrench on the luxury of individuals; so the luxury of individuals must diminish the force and check the ambition of the sovereign' citing Sparta as an example of a state lacking luxury but supporting powerful forces (II, Essay 1, 1752, 257).

16 He was aware of its possibility: 'As soon as men quit their savage state, where they live chiefly by hunting and fishing, they must fall into these two classes [*husbandmen*; *manufacturers*]; though the arts of agriculture employ at first the most numerous parts of the society' (Hume, Essay 1, 1752, 256). Also by positing both a 'barbarous monarch' and the concept of a 'civilized monarchy' Hume is too good a theorist not to speculate on how you go from one to the other (See McArthur, 2007, 69).

17 The comparative ease and cheapness of water carriage is, as will be shown, important for Smith's geographical analysis of prospects for sustained economic development.

18 The essay's exordium is interesting as it restates Hume's approach to causality: 'Nothing requires greater nicety, in our enquiries concerning human affairs, than to distinguish exactly what is owing to chance, and what proceeds from causes...' (Essay XIV, 111). His subject is the 'the domestic and gradual revolutions of a state' (Essay XIV, 112).

Bibliography

Alanen, L. (2006) 'The Powers and Mechanisms of the Passions' in S. Traiger (ed.) *The Blackwell Guide to Hume's Treatise*. Oxford: Blackwell pp. 179–198.

Amoh, Y. (2003) 'The Ancient-Modern Controversy in the Scottish Enlightenment' in T. Sakamoto and H. Tanaka (eds) *The Rise of Political Economy in the Scottish Enlightenment*. London: Routledge pp. 6–85.

Appleby, J. (2006) 'Money, money, money'. *Common-place* vol. 6, no. 3. www.common-place.org (accessed 6 October 2009).

Ayer, A. J. (1980) *Hume: A very short introduction*. Oxford: Oxford University Press.

Ayer, A. J. (2000) *Hume: A very short introduction*. Oxford: Oxford University Press.

Backhouse, R. E. (2002) *The Ordinary Business of Life: A history of economic thought from the ancient world to the twenty-first century*. Princeton: Princeton University Press.

Baier, A. (1988) 'Hume's account of social artifice – its origins and originality'. *Ethics* vol. 98, no. 4 pp. 757–778.

Baier, A. (1991) *A Progress of Sentiments*. Cambridge, MA: Harvard University Press.

Baillie, J. (2000) *Hume on Morality*. London: Routledge.

Battersby, C. (1976) 'Sketicism and Cicero' in D. F. Norton, N. Capaldi and L. Wade (eds) *Robison McGill Hume Studies*. San Diego: Austin Hill Press pp. 239–252.

Bazerman, C. (1988) *Shaping Written Knowledge: The genre and activity of the experimental article in science*. Madison, WI: University of Wisconsin press.

Beauchamp, T. L. (1998) (ed.) *David Hume An Enquiry concerning the Principles of Morals*. The Clarendon Edition of the Works of David Hume. Oxford: Clarendon Press.

Beauchamp, T. L. (1999) (ed.) *David Hume An Enquiry Concerning Human Understanding*. Oxford Philosophical Texts Oxford: Oxford University Press.

Bell, J. F. (1953) *A History of Economic Thought*. New York, NY: Roland Press Company.

Berry, C. J. (1986) *Human Nature*. Atlantic Highlands, NJ: Humanities Press International.

Berry, C. J. (2008) 'Hume and Superfluous Value (Or the Problem with Epictetus' Slippers)' in C. Wennerlind and M. Schabas (eds) *David Hume's Political Economy*. London: Routledge pp. 49–64.

Blackburn, S. (2008) *How to Read Hume*. Croydon: Granta.

Blair, H. [1783] (2005) *Lectures on Rhetoric and Belles Lettres* edited by L. Ferreira-Buckley and S. M. Halloran. Carbondale, IL: Southern Illinois University Press.

Blaug, M. (1991) *Richard Cantillon (1680–1734) and Jacques Turgot (1727–1781)*. Brookfleid, VT: Edward Elgar.

Box, M. A. (1990) *The Suasive Art of David Hume*. Princeton, NJ: Princeton University Press.

Brewer, A. (1995) 'The concept of growth in Eighteenth-Century Economics'. *History of Political Economy* vol. 27, no. 4 pp. 609–638.

Brewer, A. (2001) (ed.) *Richard Cantillon, Essay on the Nature of Commerce in General* translated by Henry Higgs [1931].

Broadie, A. (2000) *Why Scottish Philosophy Matters*. Edinburgh: Saltire Society.

Brunius, T. (1952) *David Hume on Criticism*. Stockholm: Almquist and Wiksell.

Buckle, S. (1991) *Natural law and the Theory of Property: Grotius to Hume*. Oxford: Clarendon Press.

Buckle, S. (2001) *Hume's Enlightenment Tract: The unity and purpose of An Enquiry Concerning Human Understanding*. Oxford: Clarendon Press.

Burke, K. (1945) *A Grammar of Motives*. New York, NY: Prentice-Hall.

Burke, K. (1969) *A Rhetoric of Motives*. Berkeley, CA: University of California Press.

Caffentziz, C. G. (2008) 'Fiction or Counterfeit? David Hume's Interpretations of Paper and Metallic Money' in C. Wennerlind and M. Schabas (eds) *David Hume's Political Economy*. London: Routledge pp. 146–167.

Calderwood, H. [1898] (1989) *David Hume*. Bristol: Thoemmes.

Catlin, W. B. (1962) *The Progress of Economics, A History of Economic Thought*. New York, NY: Bookman Associates.

Checkland, S. G. (1956) 'David Hume. Writings on Economics by Eugene Rotwein'. *The Economic History Review*, New Series vol. 9, no. 2 pp. 386–388.

Christensen, J. (1987) *Practicing Enlightenment: Hume and the formation of a literary career*. Madison, WI: University of Wisconsin Press.

Cicero, Marcus Tullius [ ] *Paradoxa Stoicorum*.

Cicero, Marcus Tullius [55 bce] (2001) *De Oratore* translated by E. W. Sutton and completed by H. Racham Loeb, Classical Library. Cambridge, MA: Harvard University Press.

Cicero, Marcus Tullius [46–43 bce] (2001) *De Officiis* translated by Walter Miller Loeb Classical Library. Cambridge, MA: Harvard University Press.

Cohon, R. (2006) 'Hume's Artificial and Natural Virtues' in S. Traiger (ed.) *The Blackwell Guide to Hume's Treatise*. Oxford: Blackwell pp. 256–275.

Colish, M. L. (1985) *The Stoic Tradition from Antiquity to the Early Middle Ages*, vol. 1. Leiden: E. J. Brill.

Commons, J. C. (1931) 'Institutional Economics'. *American Economic Review* vol. 21, Dec pp. 648–657.

Conniff, J. (1976) 'Hume's Political methodology: A reconsideration of "That Politics May Be Reduced to a Science"'. *Review of Politics* vol. 38, no. 1 pp. 88–108.

Connon, R. W. and Pollard, M. (1977) 'On the Authorship of "Hume's" Abstract'. *The Philosophical Quarterly* vol. 27, no. 106 pp. 60–66.

Copleston, F. (1964) *A History of Philosophy Volume V Modern Philosophy: The British Philosophers Part II Berkley to Hume*. Garden City, NY: Image Books.

Danford, J. W. (1990) *David Hume and the Problem of Reason*. New Haven, CT: Yale University Press.

Davie, G. E. (1981) *The Scottish Enlightenment*. London: The Historical Association.

Deleule, D. (1979) *Hume et la naissance du libéralisme économique*. Paris: Aubier Montaigne.

Desjardin, G. (1967) 'Terms of *De Officiis* in Hume and Kant'. *Journal of the History of Ideas* vol. 28, no. 2 pp. 237–242.

Dow, S. C. (2002) 'Interpretations: The case of David Hume'. *History of Political Economy* vol. 34, no. 2 pp. 399–420.

Emerson, R. L. (1994) 'The 'affair' at Edinburgh and the 'project' at Glasgow: the politics of Hume's attempts to become professor' in M. A. Stewart and J. P. Wright (eds) *Hume and Hume's Connexions*. Pennsylvania: Pennsylvania State University Press pp. 1–22.

Emerson, R. L. (2008) 'The Scottish Contexts for David Hume's Political-economic Thinking' in C. Wennerlind and M. Schabas (eds) *David Hume's Political Economy*. London: Routledge pp. 10–30.

Fieser, J. (1996) 'The Eighteenth-Century Reviews of Hume's Writings'. *Journal of the History of Ideas* vol. 57, no. 4 645–657.

Finlay, Christopher J. (2007) *Hume's Social Philosophy: Human nature and commercial sociability in A Treatise of Human Nature*. London: Routledge.

Fogelin, R. J. (1985) *Hume's skepticism in the Treatise of Human Nature*. London: Routledge.

Frasca-Spada, M. (1998) *Space and the self in Hume's Treatise*. Cambridge: Cambridge University Press.

Galbraith, J. K. (1989) *A History of Economics: the past as the present*. London: Penguin Books.

Gee, J. [1729] (1755) *The Trade and Navigation of Great-Britain Considered*. Glasgow: William Duncan Junior.

Grampp, W. D. (1952) 'The Liberal Elements in English Mercantilism'. *The Quarterly Journal of Economics* vol. 66, no. 4 pp. 465–501.

Gide, C. and Rist, C. (1948) *A History of Economic Doctrines*, second edition translated by R. Richards. London: George G. Harrap.

Ginsberg, R. (ed.) (1987) *The Philosopher as Writer: The eighteenth century*. Selinsgrove, PA: Susquehanna University Press.

Greig, J.Y. T. (1934) *David Hume*. London: Jonathan Cape.

Grose, T. H. (1898) 'History of the Editions' in T. H. Green and T. H. Grose (eds) *David Hume Essays: moral, political and literary*. pp. 15–84.

Hayek, F. A. (1991) *The Trend of Economic Thinking: Essays on Political Economy and economic history*, edited by W. W. Bartlay III and F. Kresge, Collected Works. London: Routledge.

Henderson, W. (2004) 'Appendix 'How does Smith achieve a synthesis in writing? Evidence from his analysis of the propensity to truck, barter and exchange' in W. J. Samuels, W. Henderson, K. D. Johnson and M. Johnson (eds) *Essays in the History of Economics*. London: Routledge pp. 72–89.

Henderson, W. (2006) *Evaluating Adam Smith: Creating the Wealth of Nations*. London: Routledge.

Henderson, W. (2008) 'Charles Ganilh's *An Inquiry into the Various Systems of Political Economy* and Subsequent Writing: English and French contexts'. *Journal of the History of Economic Thought* no. 4 Dec pp. 511–534.

Henderson, W. and Samuels, W. J. (2004) 'The etiology of Adam Smith's division of labor', in W. J. Samuels, W. Henderson, K. D. Johnson and M. Johnson (eds) *Essays on the History of Economics*. London: Routledge pp. 8–71.

Higgs, H. [1886] (2001) 'Life and Work of Richard Cantillon' in A. Brewer (ed.) *Richard Cantillon Essay on the Nature of Commerce in General* translated by H. Higgs [1931]. New Jersey: Transaction Publishers pp. 159–182.

Höpfl, H. M. (1978) 'From Savage to Scotsman: Conjectural history in the Scottish Enlightenment'. *Journal of British Studies* vol. 17, pp. 19–40.

Hundert, E. J. (1974) 'The Achievement Motive in Hume's Political Economy'. *Journal of the History of Ideas* vol. 35, pp. 139–143.

Hundert, E. J. (1994) *The Enlightenment's Fable: Bernard Mandeville and the discovery of society*. Cambridge: Cambridge University Press.

Ingram, J. K. (1910) *A History of Political Economy*. London: Adam and Charles Black.

Ignatieff, M. *Wealth and Virtue: The shaping of Political Economy in the Scottish Enlightenment*. Cambridge: Cambridge University Press pp. 179–202.

Immerwahr, J. (1976) 'A Skeptic's Progress: Hume's Preference for Enquiry 1' in D. F. Norton, N. Capaldi and W. L. Robinson (eds) *McGill Hume Studies*. San Diego, CA: Austin Hill Press pp. 227–238.

Jasinski, J. (2001) *Sourcebook on Rhetoric: Key concepts in contemporary rhetorical studies*. Thousand Oaks, CA: Sage Publications.

Jessop, T. E. [1974] (1990) 'The Misunderstood Hume' in W. B. Todd (ed.) *Hume and the Enlightenment*. Bristol: Thoemmes.

Jessop, T. E. (1966) 'Some Misunderstandings of Hume' in V. C. Chappell (ed.) *Hume: A collection of critical essays*. Doubleday Anchor pp. 35–52.

Jones, P. (1982) *Hume's Sentiments: Their Ciceronian and French Context*. Edinburgh: Edinburgh University Press.

Jones, W. T. (1969) *Hobbes to Hume: A History of Western Philosophy*. Fort Worth, TX: Harcourt Brace Jovanovich College Publishers.

Kemp Smith, N. [1941] (1964) *The Philosophy of David Hume*. London: Macmillan.

Keynes, J. M. and Sraffa, P (1938) Introduction in *An Abstract of a Treatise of Human Nature, 1740. A pamphlet hitherto unknown*, by David Hume. Reprinted Cambridge: Cambridge University Press.

Kruse, F. V. (1939) *Hume's philosophy in his principal work. A treatise of human nature, and in his essays* trans. By P. T. Federspiel. London: Oxford University Press.

Kupyers, M. S. (1966) *Studies in the 18th Century Background of Hume's Empiricism*. New York, NY: Russell and Russell.

Laing, B. M. (1939) 'Reviewed work(s) An Abstract of a Treatise of Human Nature'. *Philosophy*, vol. 35, no. 23 pp. 639–640.

Landau, I. (1992) '*The Suasive Art of David Hume*'. Book Review *CLIO* vol. 22, no. 1 p. 97.

Landreth, H. and Colander, D. C. (1994) *History of Economic Thought*, 3rd edition, Boston, MA: Houghton Mifflin.

Letwin, S. R. (1998) *The Pursuit of Certainty: David Hume, Jeremy Bentham, John Stuart Mill, Beatrice Webb*. Indianapolis, IN: Liberty Fund.

Lucas, F. L. (1959) *The Art of Living: Four Eighteenth Century Minds*. London: Cassell & Company Ltd.

Macaulay, T. B. (1871) *History of England from the Accession of James II*, vol. 4. Philadelphia, PA: J. B. Lippincott & Co.

McArthur, N. (2007) *David Hume's Political Theory: Law, commerce, and the constitution of government*. Toronto: University of Toronto Press.

McCarthy, J. A. (1989) *Crossing Boundaries: A theory and history of essay writing German 1680–1815*. Philadelphia, PA: University of Pennsylvania Press.

Mankin, R. (2005) 'Can Jealousy be reduced to a science? Politics and Economics in Hume's *Essays*'. *Journal of the History of Economic Thought* vol. 27, no. 1 pp. 59–70.

Massie, J. [1750] (1912) *The Natural Rate of Interest*. Baltimore, MD: John Hopkins Press.

Medawar, P. (1984) *Pluto's Republic*. Oxford: Oxford University Press.

Medema, S. and Samuels, W. J. (2003) *The History of Economic Thought: A reader*. London: Routledge.

Meek, R. L. (1971) 'Smith, Turgot and the "Four stages" Theory'. *History of Political Economy* vol. 3, no. 1 pp. 9–27.

Merrill, K. R. (2008) *Historical Dictionary of Hume's Philosophy*. Lanham, MD: The Scarecrow Press.

Merrill, K. R. and Shahan, R. W. (1976) *David Hume: Many-sided genius*. Norman, OK: University of Oklahoma Press.

Miller, D. (1981) *Philosophy and Ideology in Hume's Political Thought*. Oxford: Clarendon Press.

Miller, E. F. (1987) *David Hume Essays, Moral, Political and Literary*. Indianapolis, IN: Liberty Fund.

Miller, S. (2006) *Conversation: A History of a Declining Art*. New Haven, CT: Yale University Press.

Mossner, E. C. (1966) 'Philosophy and Biography: The case of David Hume' in V. C. Chappell (ed.) *Hume: A collection of critical essays*. Anchor Books pp. 6–52.

Mossner, E. C. (1980) *The Life of David Hume*. Oxford: Oxford University Press.

Moloney, P. (2005) 'Savages in the Scottish Enlightenment's History of Desire'. *Journal of the History of Sexuality* vol. 14, no. 3 pp. 237–265.

Murray, T. (ed.) (1841) *Letters of David Hume and Extracts From Letters Referring to Him*. Edinburgh: Adam and Charles Black.

Nakano, T. (2006) '"Let Your Science be Human": Hume's economic methodology'. *Cambridge Journal of Economics* vol. 30, no. 5 pp. 687–700.

Nelson, M. D. (1991) *The Priority of Prudence*. University Park, PA: Pennsylvania State University Press.

Nisbet, R. (1970) *History of the Idea of Progress* New York: Basic books.

Norton, D. F. (1993) 'An Introduction to Hume's Thought' in D. F. Norton (ed.) *The Cambridge Companion to Hume*. Cambridge: Cambridge University Press 1–32.

Norton, D. F. (2000) 'Editor's Introduction' in D. F. Norton and M. J. Norton (eds) *David Hume A Treatise of Human Nature*. Oxford: Oxford University Press pp. 19–199.

Norton, D. F. and Norton, M. J. (2005) (eds) *David Hume A Treatise of Human Nature*. Oxford: Oxford University Press.

Pascal, R. (1938) 'Property and Society: the Scottish Historical School of the Eighteenth Century'. *The Modern* Quarterly March pp. 167–179.

Passmore, J. A. (1952) *Hume's Intentions*. Cambridge: Cambridge University Press.

Penelhum, T. (1993) 'Hume's moral psychology' in D. F. Norton (ed.) *The Cambridge Companion to Hume*. Cambridge: Cambridge University Press pp. 117–221.

Phillipson, N. (1983) 'Adam Smith as civic moralist' in I. Hont and M. Ignatieff (eds) *Wealth and Virtue: The shaping of Political Economy in the Scottish Enlightenment*. Cambridge: Cambridge University Press pp. 179–202.

Pompa, L. (1990) *Human Nature and Historical Knowledge: Hume, Hegel and Vico*. Cambridge: Cambridge University Press.

Popkin, R. H. (1976) 'Hume: Philosophical versus Prophetic Historian' in K. R. Merrill and R. S. Shahan (eds) *David Hume: many sided genius*. Norman, OK: University of Oklahoma Press pp. 83–95.

Potkay, A. (1994) *The Fate of Eloquence in the Age of Hume*. Ithaca, NY: Cornell University Press.

Radford, R. T. (2001) *A Study in the Origins of Republican Philosophy*. Amsterdam: Rodopi.

Radford, R. T. (2002) *Cicero: A study in Republican Philosophy*. Amsterdam: Rodopi.

Richetti, J. J. (1983) *Philosophical Writing Locke, Berkely, Hume*. Cambridge, MA: Harvard University Press.

Robison, W. L. (2006) Hume's other writings' in S. Traiger (ed.) *The Blackwell Guide to Hume's Treatise*. Oxford: Blackwell pp. 25–39.

Rogers, K. (1997) *Self–Interest: An anthology of philosophical perspectives*. London: Routledge.

Roll, E. (1956) *A History of Economic Thought*. Englewood Cliffs, NJ: Prentice-Hall.

Rostow, W. W. (1990) *Theorists of Economic Growth from David Hume to the Present*. Oxford: Oxford University Press.

Rothbard, M. [1982] (1998) *The Ethics of Liberty*. New York, NY: New York University Press.

Rothbard, M. (1995) *Economic thought before Adam Smith: An Austrian perspective on the history of economic thought*, vol.1. Northampton MA: Edward Elgar.

Rotwein, E. (1955) *David Hume: Writings on economics*. Madison, WI: University of Wisconsin Press.

Rotwein, E. (1976) 'David Hume, Philosopher-Economist' in K. R. Merill and R. W. Shahan (eds) *David Hume: Many-sided genius*. Norman, OK: University of Oklahoma Press.

Routh, G. (1989) *The Origin of Economic Ideas*. London: Macmillan.

Schabas, M. (2001) 'David Hume on Experimental Natural Philosophy, Money and Fluids'. *History of Political Economy* vol. 33, no. 3 pp. 412–435.

Schabas, M. (2008) 'Temporal dimensions in Hume's monetary theory' in C. Wennerlind and M. Schabas (eds) *David Hume's Political Economy*. London: Routledge, pp. 127–145.

Schatz, A. [1902] (1972) *L'Oeuvre économic de David Hume*. New York, NY: Burt Franklin.

Schumpeter, J. A. (1954) *History of Economic Analysis*. reprinted 1997. London: Routledge.

Selby-Bigge, L. [1893] (1990) (ed.) *Enquiries Concerning Human Understanding and Concerning the Principles of Morals by David Hume*. Oxford: Clarendon Press.

Shovlin, J. (2008) 'Hume's Political Discourses and the French Luxury Debate' in C. Wennerlind and M. Schabas (eds) *David Hume's Political Economy*. London: Routledge pp. 203–222.

Skinner, A. S. (1993) 'David Hume: Principles of political economy' in D. F. Norton (ed.) *The Cambridge Companion to Hume*. Cambridge: Cambridge University Press pp. 222–254.

Smith, A. [1762–63 unpublished] (1983) *Lectures on Rhetoric and Belles Lettres* J. C. Bryce (ed.) Glasgow Edition of the Works and Correspondence of Adam Smith, Oxford: Oxford University Press.

Smith, A. [1776] (1976) *An Inquiry into the Nature and Causes of the Wealth of Nations*, volumes 1 and 2, R. H. Campbell and A. S. Skinner (eds) The Glasgow Edition of the Works and Correspondence of Adam Smith. Oxford: Clarendon Press.

Soule, E. (2000) 'Hume on Economic Policy and Human Nature'. *Hume Studies* vol. xxvi, no. 1 143–158.

Spann, O. (1930) [1910] *Types of Economic Theory*. London: George Allen and Unwin.

Spiegel, W. H. (1971) *The Growth of Economic Thought*. Durham, NC: Duke University Press.

Stewart, J. B. (1992) *Opinion and Reform in Hume's Political Philosophy*. Princeton, NJ: Princeton University Press.

Stewart, D. [1794] (1980) Account of the Life and Writings of Adam Smith, LL.D. in Adam Smith Essays on Philosophical Subjects, The Glasgow Edition of the Works and Correspondence of Adam Smith, Oxford: Clarendon Press pp. 269–332.

Stewart, M.A. and Wright, J. P. (eds) (1994) *Hume and Hume's Connexions*. University Park, PA: Pennsylvania State University Press.

S.P.L. (1938) 'Reviewed work(s) An Abstract of a Treatise of Human Nature, 1740 A Pamphlet hitherto Unknown, by David Hume by J.M. Keynes; P. Sraffa'. *The Journal of Philosophy* vol. 35, no. 23 pp. 639–640.

Swales, J. M. (1990) *Genre Analysis: English in academic and research settings*. Cambridge: Cambridge University Press.

Thornton, M. (2007) 'Cantillon, Hume, and the Rise of Antimercantilism'. *History of Political Economy* vol. 39, no. 3 pp. 453–480.

Todd, W. B. [1974] (1990) (ed.) *Hume and the Enlightenment*. Bristol: Thoemmes.

Trevor-Roper, H. (1964) 'Review Essay: David Hume. Politico e Storico by Giuseppe Giarizzo'. *History and Theory* vol. 3, no. 3 pp. 381–389.

Turgot, A. R. J. [1750] (2006) *The Life and Writings of Turgot: Comptroller General of France 1774–1776*, edited by W. Walker Stephens Reprint.

Vebeln, T. (1898) 'The Barbarian Status of Women'. *American Journal of Sociology* vol. 4, pp. 503–514.

Velk, T. and Riggs, A. R. (1985) 'David Hume's practical Economics'. *Hume Studies* vol. 11, no. 2 pp. 154–165.

Venning, C. (1976) 'Hume on Property, Commerce, and Empire in the Good society: The role of historical necessity', *Journal of the History of Ideas* vol. 37, pp. 79–92.

Wallace, R. (1753) [1809] *A Dissertation on the Numbers of Mankind in Ancient and Modern Times*. Edinburgh: Archibald Constable and Co.

Wennerlind, C. (2008) 'An Artificial Virtue and the Oil of Commerce: A synthetic View of Hume's theory of Money' in C. Wennerlind and M. Schabas (eds) *David Hume's Political Economy*. London: Routledge pp. 105–126.

Wennerlind, C. and Schabas, M. (eds) (2008) *David Hume's Political Economy*. London: Routledge.

Westerman, P. C. (1994) 'Hume and the natural lawyers: a change of landscape' in M. A. Stewart and J. Wright (eds) *Hume and Hume's Connexions*. University Park, PA: Pennsylvania State University Press pp. 83–104.

Whelan, F. G. (1985) *Order and Artifice in Hume's Political Philosophy*. Princeton, NJ: Princeton University Press.

Index

abstract philosophy 125, 126, 129, 166
Abstract to *Treatise* (Hume, D.) 7, 23,
27, 101, 105, 113, 119, 120, 126;
argument, implications of 37–8,
39–40; benevolence in social and
moral economy 117; cause and
effect, dealing with 46–50, 58–61;
common systems of logic, criticism
of 54; comparison in *Treatise* with
opening moves of 54–6; context
within which *Treatise* was written
52–4; directness in relation to
Treatise 55–6; *Enquiries* and,
relationship between 61–7;
experimental reporting and cause
and effect 46–50; guidance by
summarization 28–30, 31–2; from
Human Understanding to 61–7;
impressions and ideas, distinction
between 56–8; impressions over
ideas, precedence of 57–8; inference
37, 44, 46, 49, 59–61, 66; judgement
of 'the people' in 102; motivation for
writing 66–7; opening moves 52–4;
Preface 8, 17; radical innovation in
Hume's ideas, promotion in 66;
reasoning, chain of 41–6, 47–8,
49–50, 52, 64–5, 66, 71, 77, 80, 82,
87, 93, 103, 105, 112, 116, 117,
130, 140, 193n2, 193n9; relationship
with *Treatise* 31–4, 41–6, 46–50,
50–51, 52–4, 54–6, 56–8, 58–61; as
separate work 50–51; textual method
in 65–6
abstraction, summarization and 28–9
academic life of Hume 5–6
accumulation: economic well-being and
118; of evidence 43; of experience
over time 135; gold as object of 144;

idea of 12, 85, 88; moral limits on
115–16; summarization and 28, 38;
trade development and 153
action and indolence, balance
between 73
Addison, Joseph 17
Advertisement: to Book I of the
Treatise 14–15, 37, 43; to Books I
and II of the *Treatise* 41, 120
agricultural surplus, produce of
industry and 138
Alanen, L. 75
Amoh, Y. 139, 175, 176, 177, 184–5
analogy 178–9; argument by 72, 112,
138, 169, 180, 185; causality,
fundamental to Hume's notion of
199n8; example in Essay XI of 184;
inference and 61; modelling by 166,
181; negative, suppression of 30;
notion of extension by 104–5;
positive, highlighting of 30;
psychology of human motivation and
25; search for 43–4; shaping
comparison through 156–7; use of
20, 60, 103, 126, 131, 142, 144,
164–5, 178–9, 180, 181, 186, 187;
volition and cause and effect 101
Anarcharsis the Scythian 146
Annandale, Marquis of 1
Appendices to *Treatise* 62, 105, 107,
108, 109, 138, 193n8
appetites, satisfaction of 75, 78–9
Appleby, J. 148
Aquinas, St. Thomas 116
argument: by analogy 72, 112, 138,
169, 180, 185; calmness, subversion
of argument through 132; Hume's
adoption of Cicero's manner in 43,
44–5; implications of 37–8, 39–40;

For Product Safety Concerns and Information please contact our EU representative GPSR@taylorandfrancis.com Taylor & Francis Verlag GmbH, Kaufingerstraße 24, 80331 München, Germany

T - #0077 - 230425 - C0 - 234/156/13 - PB - 9780415748315 - Gloss Lamination